W9-AVG-145

TER
& PERFORMING ARTS
CHICAGO PUBLIC LIBRARY
400 SOUTH STATE STREET
CHICAGO, IL 60605

UBIQUITOUS MUSICS

*To Derek, for his excitement and belief in the project,
and to the authors, for their patience and understanding.*

Ubiquitous Musics
The Everyday Sounds That We Don't Always Notice

Edited by

MARTA GARCÍA QUIÑONES
University of Barcelona, Spain

ANAHID KASSABIAN
University of Liverpool, UK

ELENA BOSCHI
Liverpool Hope University, UK

ASHGATE

© Marta García Quiñones, Anahid Kassabian, Elena Boschi and the contributors 2013

All rights reserved. No part of this publication may be reproduced, stored in a retrieval system or transmitted in any form or by any means, electronic, mechanical, photocopying, recording or otherwise without the prior permission of the publisher.

Marta García Quiñones, Anahid Kassabian and Elena Boschi have asserted their right under the Copyright, Designs and Patents Act, 1988, to be identified as the editors of this work.

Published by
Ashgate Publishing Limited
Wey Court East
Union Road
Farnham
Surrey, GU9 7PT
England

Ashgate Publishing Company
110 Cherry Street
Suite 3-1
Burlington, VT 05401-3818
USA

www.ashgate.com

British Library Cataloguing in Publication Data
Ubiquitous musics : the everyday sounds that we don't
always notice. – (Ashgate popular and folk music series)
1. Environmental music. 2. Environmental music – History.
3. Music – Philosophy and aesthetics.
I. Series II. García Quiñones, Marta, editor of
compilation. III. Kassabian, Anahid, editor of compilation.
IV. Boschi, Elena, editor of compilation.
781.5–dc23

The Library of Congress has cataloged the printed edition as follows:
Ubiquitous musics : the everyday sounds that we don't always notice / edited by Marta García Quiñones, Anahid Kassabian, and Elena Boschi.
    pages cm.—(Ashgate popular and folk music series)
Includes bibliographical references and index.
    ISBN 978-1-4094-5133-4 (hardcover)—ISBN 978-1-4094-5134-1 (ebook)—ISBN 978-1-4724-0036-9 (epub) 1. Music—Psychological aspects. 2. Environmental music—Psychological aspects. I. García Quiñones, Marta, editor. II. Kassabian, Anahid, editor. III. Boschi, Elena, editor.
  ML3830.U23 2013
  781'.11—dc23

2012042524

ISBN 9781409451334 (hbk)
ISBN 9781409451341 (ebk – PDF)
ISBN 9781472400369 (ebk – ePUB)

Printed and bound in Great Britain
by MPG PRINTGROUP

Contents

R03243 30624

MUSIC INFORMATION CENTER
VISUAL & PERFORMING ARTS
CHICAGO PUBLIC LIBRARY
400 SOUTH STATE STREET
CHICAGO, IL 60605

List of Figures and Table

Figures

Table

Notes on Contributors

Christina Baade is Associate Professor in Music and Communication Studies at McMaster University in Hamilton, Ontario. She has published work on popular music and jazz broadcasting at the wartime BBC, music and cultural memory and American klezmer, including chapters in *Big Ears: Listening for Gender in Jazz Studies* (Duke University Press, 2008) and *Music, Politics, and Violence* (Wesleyan University Press, 2012), and articles in *Popular Music*, *Journal of Popular Music Studies*, *Journal of the Society for American Music* and *Feminist Media Studies*. Her book, *Victory Through Harmony: The BBC and Popular Music in World War II*, was published by Oxford University Press in 2012.

Elena Boschi is a Postdoctoral Teaching Fellow in Visual Communication at Liverpool Hope University. She completed her PhD on popular songs and cultural identities in contemporary Italian, Spanish and British cinema at the Institute of Popular Music (University of Liverpool) in 2011. She has published on songs in *Radiofreccia* (Luciano Ligabue, 1998), musical simulacra in *Barrio* (Fernando León de Aranoa, 1998) and audiovisual style in the films of Wes Anderson (with Tim McNelis). Elena is also Translations Editor for the journal *Music, Sound, and the Moving Image* and has published a translation of Ennio Morricone's essay 'A Composer Behind the Film Camera'.

Franco Fabbri is a musician and musicologist, and teaches Popular Music and History of Contemporary Music at the University of Turin. His main interests are in the fields of genre theories and music typologies, the impact of media and technology across genres and musical cultures, and the history of popular music. He has served twice as Chairman of the International Association for the Study of Popular Music (IASPM). Fabbri has published on the rapport between music and technology (*Elettronica e musica*, Fabbri Editori, 1984), on the confrontation of musical cultures in contemporary world (*L'ascolto tabù*, Il Saggiatore, 2005) and on the intricate fabric of influences in the history of popular music (*Around the clock*, UTET, 2008). His most read book, *Il suono in cui viviamo* (Il Saggiatore, three editions since 1996) contains articles on diverse subjects including genres, analysis of popular music and aesthetics of sound. He is co-editor (with Goffredo Plastino) of the new book series 'Routledge Global Popular Music'.

Serena Facci teaches Ethnomusicology and Popular Music Studies at the University of Tor Vergata in Rome. Her ethnomusicological researches and publications deal with oral Italian polyphony, the traditional music of Central East

Africa and intercultural perspectives in music education, among other subjects. Since 2005 she has been studying popular music with an ethnomusicological approach, writing, for instance, on the function of songs in ringtones or fitness activity, and on video music in Uganda. Her last book, in collaboration with the historian Paolo Soddu, is *Il Festival di Sanremo: Parole e suoni raccontano la nazione* (Carocci, 2011), on a popular annual song competition that has been running since 1951.

Marta García Quiñones is a PhD candidate at the University of Barcelona where she is preparing a thesis on music listening supervised by Dr Josep Martí (CSIC-IMF, Barcelona). Part of the research was carried out at the School of Music, University of Liverpool, under the guidance of Professor Anahid Kassabian. The thesis explores the centrality of listening to the Western musical experience, and advocates a new understanding of music listening that is able to account for its transformations in the contemporary mediascape. In 2008 she edited the collection *La música que no se escucha: Aproximaciones a la escucha ambiental*, published by l'Orquestra del Caos. She is also a member of the international research network 'Sound in Media Culture: Aspects of a Cultural History of Sound' (2010–2013), funded by the German Research Foundation.

Tony Grajeda is Associate Professor of Cultural Studies in the Department of English, University of Central Florida. He is editor (with Jay Beck) of *Lowering the Boom: Critical Studies in Film Sound* (University of Illinois Press, 2008) and editor (with Timothy Taylor and Mark Katz) of *Music, Sound, and Technology in America: A Documentary History of Early Phonograph, Cinema, and Radio* (Duke University Press, 2012). He was guest co-editor of a special issue on 'The Future of Sound Studies' for *Music, Sound, and the Moving Image* (2008). His work has appeared in *Jump Cut, Film Quarterly, Social Epistemology, Journal of Popular Music Studies, Chain* and *disClosure*, as well as several anthologies, including, *Rethinking Global Security: Media, Popular Culture, and the 'War on Terror'* (Rutgers University Press, 2006). He founded and is former co-chair of the Sound Studies Interest Group of the Society for Cinema and Media Studies.

Anahid Kassabian thinks and writes about: ubiquitous music; music, sound and moving images, especially in digital media (for example, smartphone apps, viral videos, video games); listening; disciplinarity; and feminist, diasporan and postcolonial theories. She is the author of *Ubiquitous Listening: Affect, Attention, and Distributed Subjectivity* (University of California Press, 2013) and *Hearing Film* (Routledge, 2001). Anahid is a past editor of *Stanford Humanities Review* and of *Journal of Popular Music Studies*, as well as a co-founding editor of *Music, Sound and the Moving Image* and a past chair of the International Association for the Study of Popular Music (IASPM). In addition to publishing widely in the areas of film music and ubiquitous musics, she has also written numerous articles, alone and with David Kazanjian, on Armenian diasporan film, and she has curated several Armenian film festivals in San Francisco and New York. She serves on the Board of Directors of Aunt Lute Books, a feminist multicultural publisher, and the Board of Trustees of the Liverpool Arabic Arts Festival, the oldest and largest festival of its kind in the UK.

Lawrence Kramer is Distinguished Professor of English and Music at Fordham University and has been the holder of visiting professorships of music across North America, Europe, and Asia. He is the editor of *19th-Century Music*, a composer whose works have been performed internationally and the author of 12 books, the most recent of which are *Why Classical Music Still Matters* (2007), *Interpreting Music* (2010) and *Expression and Truth: On the Music of Knowledge* (2012), all from the University of California Press. His cantata *Crossing the Water* premiered on the campus of the Santa Fe Opera in 2011, and his song cycle *Another Time*, for voice with violin and cello, premiered in New York City in 2012.

Tim McNelis completed his PhD in Film Music at the University of Liverpool. His research focused on the role that songs and musical performance play in regulating agency and constructing identity in US youth films. Tim has written, with Elena Boschi, an essay on audiovisual style in the films of Wes Anderson that appeared in the *New Review of Film and Television Studies* in 2012. He is also the author of a chapter on the use of anachronistic music in *Dirty Dancing*, published in the collection *The Time of Our Lives: Dirty Dancing and Popular Culture*, edited by Yannis Tzioumakis and Siân Lincoln (Wayne State University Press, 2013).

Amit S. Rai is Senior Lecturer in New Media and Communication in the School of Business and Management at Queen Mary, University of London and Visiting Faculty at the Centre for Media and Cultural Studies, Tata Institute of Social Science, Mumbai. He is the author of *Rule of Sympathy: Race, Sentiment, and Power* (Palgrave, 2002) and *Untimely Bollywood: Globalization and India's New Media Assemblage* (Duke University Press, 2009), a study of new media in India. He has written on Indian masculinity in film, anthropologies of monstrosity, sympathetic discursive relations and the clinamen (swerve) of media ('clinamedia').

Jonathan Sterne teaches in the Department of Art History and Communication Studies and the History and Philosophy of Science Program at McGill University. He is the author of *MP3: The Meaning of a Format* (Duke University Press, 2012), *The Audible Past: Cultural Origins of Sound Reproduction* (Duke University Press, 2003) and numerous articles on media, technologies and the politics of culture. He is also the editor of *The Sound Studies Reader* (Routledge, 2012). You can visit his website at <http://sterneworks.org>.

General Editor's Preface

The upheaval that occurred in musicology during the last two decades of the twentieth century has created a new urgency for the study of popular music alongside the development of new critical and theoretical models. A relativistic outlook has replaced the universal perspective of modernism (the international ambitions of the 12-note style); the grand narrative of the evolution and dissolution of tonality has been challenged, and emphasis has shifted to cultural context, reception and subject position. Together, these have conspired to eat away at the status of canonical composers and categories of high and low in music. A need has arisen, also, to recognize and address the emergence of crossovers, mixed and new genres, to engage in debates concerning the vexed problem of what constitutes authenticity in music and to offer a critique of musical practice as the product of free, individual expression.

Popular musicology is now a vital and exciting area of scholarship, and the *Ashgate Popular and Folk Music Series* presents some of the best research in the field. Authors are concerned with locating musical practices, values and meanings in cultural context, and draw upon methodologies and theories developed in cultural studies, semiotics, poststructuralism, psychology and sociology. The series focuses on popular musics of the twentieth and twenty-first centuries. It is designed to embrace the world's popular musics from Acid Jazz to Zydeco, whether high tech or low tech, commercial or non-commercial, contemporary or traditional.

Professor Derek B. Scott
Professor of Critical Musicology
University of Leeds

Foreword

Derek B. Scott

Anahid Kassabian, Elena Boschi and Marta García Quiñones invited me to write a short Foreword to this book, and I was delighted to accept. I vividly remember hearing Anahid Kassabian speak about 'ubiquitous musics' more than ten years ago and being excited and impressed by her arguments. Like many others who were aware of the research undertaken in this neglected field, I was impatient to see a collection of essays published in one conveniently accessible place. When I received the initial proposal and was asked if I thought it might be suitable for the *Ashgate Popular and Folk Music Series*, I couldn't believe my good fortune. The editors are committed to deepening our understanding of 'ubiquitous musics', and, indeed, the term itself was coined by Kassabian: see her forthcoming book *Ubiquitous Listening: Affect, Attention, and Distributed Subjectivity* (University of California Press). The first step in any investigation, of course, is to name and define the object of study, and that is flagged up in this book's subtitle: *The Everyday Sounds That We Don't Always Notice*. This description implies much more than Muzak or elevator music, and the editors are at pains to explain the breadth with which it may be interpreted. This is the first book-length study to clarify what characterizes ubiquitous musics and to explore the social and cultural meanings of this phenomenon.

In the pages that follow, the reader will find arguments from a multitude of disciplinary perspectives about the music that surrounds us during our everyday activities, but which, in many situations, does not ask for any particular attention on our part. Oddly, although it is not an uncommon experience to find ourselves in such situations, few have thought it to be something worthy of scholarly notice. Those who have been driven to examine musical environments that demand no active listener engagement have come from a diversity of academic backgrounds and have employed a variety of theoretical models. This book recognizes this fact by including contributions that range from cultural sociology and anthropology to musicology and film studies.

The issue for scholars is complex, because today almost any music can be ubiquitous. Music may be carried on an iPod, for example, and played alongside another activity that apparently demands full concentration. Furthermore, any type of music can function as ubiquitous music, although some genres and styles are more likely to be found than others. The research questions that the authors ask are, in these circumstances, not only relevant and interesting, but also, on occasion, provocative. The editors make a strong case for the value of these studies, however elusive this subject matter may appear to be in certain contexts. After all, a great deal of time has been devoted to attentive listening, whereas very little has been given to listening – or simply hearing – as part of a less active or non-engaged consumption of music. Even the work on music and the everyday being produced by those researching the social psychology of music is still in its early stages.

Some of this book's contributors enjoy an international reputation, and it seems unjust to single out essays for special praise in this Foreword, given the wealth of insight found in chapter after chapter. As evidence of the richness of theory and argument on offer, however, I will mention the contributions of Jonathan Sterne and Lawrence Kramer. Sterne's book *The Audible Past* is well known, and I'm sure many of the authors here would acknowledge that it laid something of a foundation for related investigations. Sterne's topic is one that may initially appear stale, because it concerns Muzak. His chapter, however, examines the changes in the use of Muzak (beginning in the 1990s) and its reconceptualization as a 'non-aggressive music' that nevertheless succeeds in driving away teenage gangs and other people viewed as undesirable by some shops and stores. His account of the use of this music in the parking lots of 7-Eleven stores in the US and Canada makes fascinating reading. Without doubt, it is a page-turner, but one that never lacks subtlety in its arguments. Kramer's chapter is a genealogy of ambient music and has all his hallmarks: elegant writing, witty allusions (Penn Station), together with observations that stimulate thought – for example, his reference to the famous covered orchestra pit at Bayreuth and its 'musicalization of space'. This last point relates neatly to the editors' insistence that every physical space is an aural space.

In sum, this book moves ubiquitous musics from the fringes of academia and demonstrates why this is something deserving of attention and further investigation. After reading these essays, key questions about what listening to music means, what our contemporary experiences of listening are, and whether listening necessitates (or should necessitate) attentiveness, rise to the surface once more. It is bound to start a most interesting debate, so thanks are due to Kassabian, Boschi and García Quiñones for getting it going.

Acknowledgements

All three of us would like to thank Derek Scott for thinking that this book is important, Laura Macy, Heidi Bishop, Emma Gallon and Sadie Copley-May at Ashgate for being always ready to answer questions and making the editing process a pleasurable experience, Linda Cayford for her careful copy-editing, and Ross Edwards and Molly Mahon Marler for pitching in at the last minute and helping us with the bibliography and index. I personally also want to thank my co-editors, Marta and Elena, for making this volume possible. Most especially, thanks to all of the contributors for their incredible patience when this project became mired down more than once in the exigencies of my academic and personal life. You are all truly amazing.

Anahid Kassabian

I'd like to thank, in order of appearance, my co-editors Anahid, for giving me the chance to get on board, and Marta, for finally getting us into port, and my co-author Tim, for embarking on the umpteenth adventure, scholarly and otherwise. *Grazie a* Daniela, for her support through the difficult UHT student years.

Elena Boschi

I would like to thank Anahid and Elena for trusting me and allowing me on board this project when it was already afloat – I hope I have been a good sailor. Thanks also to Dr Josep Martí for his useful comments on my essay. Heartfelt thanks are also due to Franco for boosting my confidence, and for chats, walks and much-needed fresh air. Finally, thanks to my family for unfailing moral and material support, especially in the not-so-good times.

Marta García Quiñones

Introduction

A Day in the Life of a
Ubiquitous Musics Listener

Elena Boschi, Anahid Kassabian and Marta García Quiñones

Who listens to ubiquitous musics anyway? However aware of it or not we may be, we inhabitants of urban and suburban areas in much (perhaps most) of the world are the targets of ubiquitous musics on a daily basis. We all breathe music, whether through deep, conscious intakes or through small, unaware movements. For centuries the discourse surrounding music has taken attentive listening for granted, despite the increasing ubiquity of music through the twentieth century up until today. But are we really always listening? However attentive or inattentive our listening might be, the effects that ubiquitous soundtrack is there to produce, what it does to us and what we do with it are all fascinating questions which the authors gathered in this anthology explore. Through different case studies they analyse a range of instances where music resonates in those histories, technologies and spaces we believe we know well. But let's picture – and sound – a day in the life of a ubiquitous musics listener.

What do our lives sound like these days? For a start, the average person may well have ditched the traditional anxiety-inducing alarm clock and perhaps opted for a spaghetti-western-themed polyphonic ringtone to wake up to instead. However, if the sound of the alarm clock on her phone is chosen, much of what she will be hearing throughout the day won't be.

There's more to coffee houses than the expression 'wake up and smell the coffee' suggests. There's a whole aural space constructed to accompany the consumption of a hot drink. The overlapping sounds of the machine, cups and conversations are often blended with the music of the faraway lands where the coffee is grown – or at least countries with which coffee-growing and drinking is associated. Why? Is that extremely problematic marketing genre we call 'world music' meant to play up coffee's exotic origin? What if it evoked images of Third World populations exploited by inequitable First World corporations as well? Our latte might never taste the same again, and perhaps the store manager's musical choices wouldn't be as innocently engaged with as they were intended to be. What if the customer-listeners are not engaged with them at all? Or, is there something in between listening and not listening? Let's suppose that they don't pay attention until the music changes. Is this unawareness turning into awareness?

What about the way our average person listens while doing something else? Once at work, she perhaps needs a little help in keeping going until lunchtime.

If her workplace doesn't come with a pre-packed soundtrack, perhaps she can turn on the radio or choose her own music through the countless listening options a computer connected to the World Wide Web can offer – from iTunes to Spotify, from P2P networks to somebody's SoundCloud profile. Not only are there endless possibilities, but there are also endless questions one can ask about whether, for example, the music she chooses for enhancing concentration works, how the choices Spotify could offer her would influence her performance, cause distraction, transport her elsewhere, and why. Meanwhile, there's music playing while her call is on hold, probably intended to be pleasant, even entertaining or to communicate something about the company she's calling, but does it serve its purpose? Lunchtime arrives. She heads to a noodle bar two blocks down the road, where the inoffensive mix of Chinese remakes of Western hit songs quietly fills the place. Yesterday the Mediterranean cafe where she usually has lunch was playing really loud Middle Eastern pop and she and her colleagues felt as if they were made to finish eating quickly and leave the table for other customers – perhaps the cafe's aim, but did other customers get a similar feeling? Are those customers who are not listening attentively unperturbed by the music? Some might not even realize why they leave rather than linger around.

After work she heads to a department store to find a present for a friend, and there's background music playing. We might assume that it's there exclusively to create atmosphere, but there are several other potential reasons: to aurally cultivate the store's clientele by providing music to match their alleged taste; to connect to their ideal selves, which they can rehearse by singing along; to pace customers' shopping rhythm; to promote certain items; to place employees and customers alike in a comfortable sound belljar in which everybody can relax and spend while someone watches their behaviour and choices, and tunes the musical accompaniment accordingly. But why has she decided to buy two bottles of overpriced Italian designer perfume if all she needed was one gift? Could it be a 'side effect' of Pavarotti's rendition of 'Nessun Dorma' echoing through the store? Later, a carefully constructed mixed tape orchestrates aerobics, and the train station sounds like a concert hall. What if we swapped their respective aural environments? Maybe the gym members would not pay their fee, while the commuters might acquire undesired company and start feeling strangely nervous. But she can drown out the classical music in the train station and let her iPod Shuffle mix the soundtrack for her short journey home. Tonight she's going for a curry and to the movies with some friends. The restaurant will have Indian music playing – quite likely a Bollywood soundtrack and, in any case, not silence – and the film might feature both composed music and popular songs playing on a stereo somewhere in the world the characters inhabit – much like in the world she lives in.

Despite their pervasiveness, the everyday situations just described have so far been largely neglected by music scholars, who – in our opinion – have fallen short of providing the necessary tools to understand what the ubiquity of music implies for the contemporary experience of listening. As others before us have observed,[1] Western classical music has established an aesthetic paradigm whereby musical (master)works and (master) composers[2] occupy the centre of the concert hall, performers are usually judged according to their fidelity to the works, and listeners are expected to be educated enough to appreciate the value and meaning of musical works. Insofar as it is based on that paradigm, the whole enterprise of musicology can be considered a justification of the value of those canonized musical works and of the attentional frame that has been built around them. Within that frame, aesthetic communication is guaranteed by the ability of the listener – obviously, not any listener, but a cultivated one, even an expert – to decode the meaning of the musical work. Although music studies formally abandoned the concert hall as an ideal setting a while ago,[3] the musical contexts in which the aesthetic frame does not apply, and where the listener seems to be more distracted than attentive, have mostly remained below critical radar.

In principle, popular music studies and ethnomusicology are much better equipped than conventional musicology to deal with musical situations that do not necessarily respond to an aesthetic intention, and in fact they have explored a variety of contexts in which listeners are not always meant to be attentive and immobile, or would not even qualify as 'proper listeners' in a conservative musicological sense. Yet, to date, scholars in these areas have shown only a limited interest in the ubiquity of reproduced music. On the one hand, ethnomusicology has given priority of attention to live music from rural non-Western areas and has only in recent decades concerned itself more and more with urban contexts and music recordings or broadcasts.[4] On the other hand, popular music studies, being

---

[1]   See Lydia Goehr, *The Imaginary Museum of Musical Works: An Essay in the Philosophy of Music* (Oxford, 1992); and Christopher Small, *Musicking: The Meanings of Performing and Listening* (Hanover, NH, 1998).

[2]   For a brilliant analysis of the term 'master', see Clyde Taylor, 'The Master Text and the Jeddi Doctrine', *Screen*, 29/4 (1988): pp. 96–105, esp. pp. 97–8.

[3]   See Ola Stockfelt, 'Adequate Modes of Listening', in David Schwarz and Anahid Kassabian (eds), *Keeping Score: Music, Disciplinarity, Culture* (Charlottesville, VA, 1997), pp. 129–46.

[4]   Indeed, some ethnomusicologists have considered the use of recorded music as background, though often within a ritualized framework. See, for instance, Peter Manuel, *Cassette Culture: Popular Music and Technology in North India* (Chicago, IL, and London, 1993); Josep Martí, 'When Music Becomes Noise: Sound and Music Which People in Barcelona Hear but Don't Want to Listen to', *The World of Music*, 39/2 (1997), pp. 9–17; Paul D. Greene, 'Sound Engineering in a Tamil Village: Playing Audio Cassettes as Devotional Performance', *Ethnomusicology*, 43/3 (1999): pp. 459–89; Ernst K.L. Karel, 'Kerala Sound Electricals: Amplified Sound and Cultural Meaning in South India' (PhD dissertation, University of Chicago, 2003), esp. ch. 2; Louise Meintjes, *Sound of Africa! Making Music Zulu in a South African Studio* (Durham, NC, 2003); Charles Hirschkind, *The Ethical Soundscape: Cassette Sermons and Islamic Counterpublics* (New York, 2006), which deals partially with listening to cassette sermons as background; and Serena

historically linked to mass-media audio technologies, have been more receptive to the new listening contexts created by them, and generally to the functions of music in everyday life.[5] Thus, they have encouraged a reconsideration of the actual role of listeners,[6] and in doing so they have provided a theoretical basis for specific studies, historical or otherwise, on particular technologies associated with the ubiquity of music, like audio recording, radio, portable players, music television and so on.[7] However, in some instances our continuous struggle as scholars for

Facci, '"Funziona?" Valori e usi della musica nella contemporaneità', in Serena Facci and Francesco Giannattasio (eds), *Etnomusicologia e musiche contemporanee* (Venice, 2007), <http://www.cini.it/index.php/it/publication/detail/5/id/1020> (accessed 31 May 2012).

[5]   On popular music in everyday life, see Susan D. Crafts, Daniel Cavicchi, Charles Keil and the Music in Daily Life Project, *My Music: Explorations of Music in Daily Life* (Middletown, CT, 1993); Anahid Kassabian, 'Would You Like Some World Music with your Latte? Starbucks, Putumayo, and Distributed Tourism', *Twentieth-Century Music*, 1/2 (2004): pp. 209–23; and Nedim Hassan, '"He'll Have To Go": Popular Music and the Social Performing of Memory', *Journal of the International Association for the Study of Popular Music*, 1/1 (2010), <http://www.iaspmjournal.net> (accessed 31 May 2012).

[6]   Indeed, in many cases the subjects of popular music are not even called 'listeners' but 'audiences', 'consumers' or 'users' – a terminological choice that has important implications in the way in which popular music is studied and in the themes that are addressed. For a critique of the notion of listening from popular music studies, see Keith Negus, *Popular Music in Theory: An Introduction* (Cambridge, 1996), esp. ch. 1; Anahid Kassabian, 'Popular', in Bruce Horner and Thomas Swiss (eds), *Key Terms in Popular Music and Culture* (Oxford, 1999), pp. 113–23; Simon Frith, 'Music and Everyday Life', *Critical Quarterly*, 44/1 (2002): pp. 35–48; Chris Kennett, 'Is Anybody Listening?', in Allan F. Moore (ed.), *Analyzing Popular Music* (Cambridge, 2003), pp. 196–217; Philip Tagg and Bob Clarida, *Ten Little Title Tunes: Towards a Musicology of Mass Media* (New York and Montreal, 2003), chs 1 and 2; Franco Fabbri, *L'ascolto tabù: Le musiche nello scontro globale* (Milan, 2005); and Theodore Gracyk, *Listening to Popular Music: Or, How I Learned to Stop Worrying and Love Led Zeppelin* (Ann Arbor, MI, 2007), particularly ch. 5.

[7]   There is a wealth of publications on audio technologies, but we would like to mention just some of the most relevant to our subject. On music reproduction, and particularly on actual contexts of production and consumption of records (in the United States), see William H. Kenney, *Recorded Music in American Life: The Phonograph and Popular Memory, 1890–1945* (New York, 1999) and Timothy D. Taylor, Mark Katz and Tony Grajeda (eds), *Music, Sound, and Technology in America: A Documentary History of Early Phonograph, Cinema, and Radio* (Durham, NC, 2012). On the radio, see Charles Hamm, 'Privileging the Moment of Reception: Music and Radio in South Africa', in S. Paul Scher (ed.), *Music and Text: Critical Inquiries* (Cambridge, 1992), pp. 21–37; Jody Berland, 'Contradicting Media: Toward a Political Phenomenology of Listening', in Neil Strauss (ed.), *Radiotext(E)* (New York, 1993), pp. 209–17; Susan J. Douglas, *Listening In: Radio and the American Imagination* (New York, 1999); Timothy D. Taylor, 'Music and the Rise of Radio in Twenties America: Technological Imperialism, Socialization, and the Transformation of Intimacy', in Paul D. Greene and Thomas Porcello (eds), *Wired for Sound: Engineering and Technologies in Sonic Cultures* (Middletown, CT, 2005), pp. 245–68; and Christina L. Baade, *Victory Through Harmony: The BBC and Popular Music in World War*

our object of study to be taken seriously has triggered mechanisms of aesthetic validation similar to those of classical music,[8] and probably has also prevented a stronger engagement with the 'dubious' – in the sense of 'not musical enough' – subject of ubiquitous musics.[9]

One might imagine that the study of music that accompanies other activities could provide some assistance, especially music in film, television, videogames, advertising and other media. In fact, however, most studies of film music have not focused on the listener's perspective (Kassabian's *Hearing Film* is one exception[10]), and studies of music in the other media are still developing. But because most disciplines are not focusing on these practices, most of the scholarship comes from canonically trained musicologists and thus centres on the sound and musical features rather than on reception or listening.

Psychologists of music have often accepted attentive (concert-hall-like) modes of listening as models, confounding their aims with those of musical analysis, and even taking on the task of validating its methods.[11] While it has lately become increasingly normal for them to pay attention to other listening situations, particularly to the use of music in daily life, their analysis of ubiquitous musics, when touched upon, rarely goes beyond contexts of consumption.[12] Other disciplines, like the sociology of music, media and communication studies or performance studies, have provided concepts – situations, practices, scenes and so on – that would be useful for studying the musical situations described at the beginning of

---

II (New York, 2012). On portable audio technologies, see Michael Bull, *Sounding Out the City: Personal Stereos and the Management of Everyday Life* (Oxford, 2000) and *Sound Moves: iPod Culture and Urban Experience* (London and New York, 2006); and Amit S. Rai, *Untimely Bollywood: Globalization and India's New Media Assemblage* (Durham, NC, 2009). On audio compression formats, see Jonathan Sterne, *MP3: The Meaning of a Format* (Durham, NC, 2012).

   [8]   See Franco Fabbri, 'What is Popular Music? And What isn't? An Assessment, after 30 Years of Popular Music Studies', *Musiikki*, 2 (2010): pp. 72–92; and Carys Wyn Jones, *The Rock Canon: Canonical Values in the Reception of Rock Albums* (Aldershot, 2008).

   [9]   See Jonathan Sterne, 'Sounds Like the Mall of America: Programmed Music and the Architectonics of Commercial Space', *Ethnomusicology*, 41/1 (1997): pp. 22–50; and Anahid Kassabian, *Ubiquitous Listening: Affect, Attention, and Distributed Subjectivity* (Berkeley, CA, 2013) would be exceptions in this sense.

   [10]   Anahid Kassabian, *Hearing Film: Tracking Identifications in Contemporary Hollywood Film Music* (New York and London, 2001).

   [11]   See Nicholas Cook, 'Perception: A Perspective from Music Theory', in Rita Aiello and John A. Sloboda (eds), *Musical Perceptions* (Oxford, 1994), pp. 64–95; and Eric Clarke, 'Music and Psychology', in Martin Clayton, Trevor Herbert and Richard Middleton (eds), *The Cultural Study of Music: A Critical Introduction* (New York and London, 2003), pp. 113–23.

   [12]   For recent examples, see Susan Hallam, Ian Cross and Michael Thaut (eds), *The Oxford Handbook of Music Psychology* (Oxford, 2009), and Eric Clarke, Nicola Dibben and Stephanie Pitts, *Music and Mind in Everyday Life* (Oxford, 2009).

this Introduction. But they have seldom been applied to them (DeNora's *Music in Everyday Life* is a notable exception[13]). And even if the industries most closely associated with ubiquitous musics have produced numerous research papers and patents – on musical radio programming, on the use of background music and so on – these have rarely been taken into consideration by musicologists repelled by their usual orientation to marketing.

In sum, a resistance to face the subject still persists in the general field of music studies, and we are convinced that this is linked to some basic assumptions about human subjectivity implied by the aesthetic paradigm that cannot be easily challenged – essentially, an image of human subjectivity as conscious (mainly mental, thus not bodily) and agentic, and of social order as a common (though not truly egalitarian) enterprise.[14]

On the other hand, the study of ubiquitous musics offers inherent difficulties, as, for a number of reasons, they defy a simple definition. First, as the opening of this Introduction demonstrates, the term covers a multiplicity of listening experiences. Second, if we consider radio, there has long been a wide range of musics that are listened to ubiquitously. Third, if we think of Muzak and other providers of programmed music, the kind of music that was associated with them – string orchestral arrangements, without voice or percussion, of nearly anything[15] – has been on the decline since the mid-1980s to the point that it is now very rarely heard. Fourth, the advent of new technologies, from CD writers to mp3 players, means that many people have unprecedented control over what they listen to in the background of everyday activities. Thus, in the abstract, any kind of music can be ubiquitous music given the proper circumstances, although perhaps Stockhausen and screamo are less likely candidates than less intense forms. Music with large dynamic ranges is often either difficult to hear or sometimes too loud, making a portion of the Western canon, especially the nineteenth-century symphonic canon, less useful than other parts. But there is no longer a set of musical details that characterizes ubiquitous music, and so there is no way of linking specific listening attitudes to distinct music styles, as Adorno did in his famous typology of listeners.[16] Even in the more social, contextual terrains of genre, we again reach a difficult impasse – as we have suggested above, the range of activities that are accompanied by ubiquitous musics is as varied as are people's everyday lives. Shopping, sleeping and secretarial work take place in such radically different contexts and across such radically diverse demographic or identity groups that there is no reasonable way

---

[13]   Tia DeNora, *Music in Everyday Life* (Cambridge, 2000).

[14]   On this, see especially Kassabian, *Ubiquitous Listening*.

[15]   See Joseph Lanza, *Elevator Music: A Surreal History of Muzak, Easy-Listening and other Moodsong* (New York, 1994).

[16]   Theodor W. Adorno, *Introduction to the Sociology of Music*, trans. E.B. Ashton (New York, [1962] 1976), pp. 1–20.

of labelling ubiquitous musics as a genre in any of the ways in which the term is generally used.[17]

Another characteristic of ubiquitous musics is that they are listened to allegedly with less attention than is generally deemed appropriate – by popular and art music aficionados alike – in Western Europe and North America. (We are unable to comment on discourses about listening and attention in the rest of the world.) In fact, this may be the most disturbing feature of ubiquitous musics for scholars, particularly whenever works of the classic canon are played as background music. On the other hand, common complaints about the undesired presence of ubiquitous musics in public spaces frequently point at the inconvenience of having a portion of personal attention occupied by unpleasant tunes. Therefore, it seems possible to define ubiquitous musics by their relationships to listening and attention.

At this point we could perhaps say something about attention. There has certainly been a widespread interest in attention over the past decade or two – the public debates around Attention Deficit Hyperactivity Disorder and the scholarly writing on the attention economy[18] are just two examples. As for music studies, Peter Gay's and James H. Johnson's books on the development of silent concert-hall listening in the nineteenth century discuss silence as a behaviour, but silence is no guarantor of attention.[19] In fact, it is unclear whether much music at all is *actually* heard in the way the arbiters of musical behaviour would approve. Conversely, it is simply impossible to know whether attention to ubiquitous musics is less than when music is ostensibly the primary focus of activity, as in concerts.

Finally, ubiquitous musics could be defined as those musical events that take place alongside other activities.[20] Some ubiquitous musics, such as CDs in the car, are chosen by the listener; some, such as listening to the radio while doing the housework, are semi-chosen; and some, such as music in shops and on telephone hold systems, are not chosen by the listener at all. But these musics are never intended for the sole purpose of aesthetic enjoyment – there always is something else going on. A direct consequence of this definition is that the study of ubiquitous musics must consider a wide scene, including musical and non-musical stimuli, the listener's attitude (a consequence of her present situation, musical competence,

---

[17]   See Franco Fabbri, 'Tipi, categorie, generi musicali. Serve una teoria?', in *Il suono in cui viviamo. Saggi sulla popular music* (Milan, 2008), pp. 121–36. Anahid Kassabian's 'Ubiquitous Listening', included in David Hesmondhalgh and Keith Negus (eds), *Popular Music Studies* (London, 2002), pp. 131–42, argues for considering ubiquitous music as a genre. However, she has since substantially rethought that argument; see Chapter 1 of her *Ubiquitous Listening*.

[18]   On the attention economy, see Georg Franck, *Ökonomie der Aufmerksamkeit* (Munich, 1998); and T.H. Davenport and J.C. Beck, *The Attention Economy: Understanding the New Currency of Business* (Watertown, MA, 2001).

[19]   Peter Gay, *The Naked Heart: The Bourgeois Experience Victoria to Freud, Volume IV* (New York and London, 1995); and James H. Johnson, *Listening in Paris: A Cultural History* (Berkeley, CA, 1995).

[20]   Kassabian, *Ubiquitous Listening*.

previous listening experiences), her body and also the physical environment and the social and cultural context, thereby challenging the status of the musical object. In fact, it is undoubtedly as a result of the conjunction of elements other than the music – as well as the absence of an attentional and aesthetic framework – that many perceptive and evaluative processes remain under the surface of consciousness.

Obviously, it would be impossible to provide a thorough account of all the elements involved even in the most banal of the situations reported at the beginning of this Introduction – ubiquitous musics are so entangled in the fabric of our everyday lives that they have proved to be a very elusive subject of research. However, no matter how difficult their study may be, we are convinced that ignoring them would be much more dangerous: ubiquitous musics are not only haunting or annoying melodies accompanying us all day long, but also a key to understanding how we are musically constituted as subjects. As phenomena like earworms prove,[21] the grey zone between consciousness and unconsciousness is already the place where most of our musical experiences begin.

About this Book

In this volume we intend, first, to offer an overview on a wide range of situations involving ubiquitous musics in order to make the case for their relevance as a research subject. Second, we aim to present some valuable and very diverse approaches to ubiquitous musics that have developed on and across different disciplinary fields – often on the edges of these fields. For the purpose of clarity we have divided the book into three Parts, summarized below in order. Part I, 'Histories', considers some historical antecedents of ubiquitous musics. Part II, 'Technologies', deals with ubiquitous musics associated with specific technical devices and with technology-related concepts: cell phones in India, the presence of visible playback technologies in films and portable digital players. Finally, Part III, 'Spaces', discusses some settings where ubiquitous musics are often present, such as malls, stores, gyms, offices and cars.

Histories

Part I offers three glimpses into the historical origins of the functional use of music, plus an overview of the theories on which the progressive diffusion of reproduced music, both in work and in leisure environments, was based. Even a glance at the summaries of the three essays makes it clear that our present understanding of the

---

[21]   See Victoria Williamson's research on earworms at Goldsmiths University, 'Earworm Project', Music, Mind and Brain Research Group at Goldsmiths, University of London <http://www.gold.ac.uk/music-mind-brain/earworm-project/> (accessed 15 June 2012).

role of music largely depends on past stances that tried to establish a grammar – articulated in different idioms depending on the historical context – of musical uses and effects, and fitted them into the social and economic scheme where, to a great extent, our contemporary lives still take place.

Lawrence Kramer's 'Caliban's Ear: A Short History of Ambient Music' (Chapter 1) traces a possible genealogy of ambient music (or, rather, of the use of classical music as ambient) through three moments that cover a long timespan, from early modernity to postmodernity: a passage from Shakespeare's *Tempest*, in which Caliban describes the noises and musics that reach his ear; a meditative fragment on the natural sounds of the night from James Agee's *Let Us Now Praise Famous Men*; and an autobiographical account of the effects of classical music piped in as background in New York's Penn Station. By juxtaposing these three episodes Kramer underscores a certain continuity of the idea of ambient music, although ultimately his gesture discovers a fundamental gap separating two different conceptions of music (and the world): from cosmological utopia to everyday soundtrack.

In 'Early Mood Music: Edison's Phonography, American Modernity and the Instrumentalization of Listening' (Chapter 2) Tony Grajeda reports on research conducted in the early 1920s under the direction of Dr Walter Van Dyke Bingham and sponsored by Thomas Alva Edison's company that aimed at classifying the effects of music on human moods. Although the Edison–Bingham project addressed the leisurely use of music at home and thus dealt mainly with music listened to as foreground, the author connects it with contemporary studies on the effects of background music in workplaces, placing it within the conceptual framework of the early twentieth-century discourses on Taylorization, the 'New Psychology' and ultimately within the ongoing process of the 'instrumentalization of listening'.

Christina Baade's 'Radio Symphonies: The BBC, Everyday Listening and the Popular Classics Debate during the People's War' (Chapter 3) recounts how surveys conducted after the Second World War confirmed that the number of people professing an appreciation for classical music had increased in the UK. This shift resonated with People's War ideologies of fairness, which held that the best of culture belonged to all, and was stimulated by the fresh energy devoted to music appreciation, supported by recordings, live performances and the radio. In particular, the BBC was praised for making the 'Common Man of the twentieth century' aware of music and its values, although the diffusion of classical music relied to a great extent on a repertoire of 'popular classics' and on older practices of transcription and adaptation, which were perceived by many as a threat to serious music. Baade's essay considers the BBC's attempts to resolve the conflict between cultural uplift and the need to reach a broad audience from the interwar period through to the onset of the war – when a new wartime wavelength, the Forces Programme, was created – until the formulation to the 1942 BBC Music Policy. It also examines the debates between advocates and critics of musical adaptations, as well as the BBC's efforts to regulate them.

Technologies

As has already been made evident in Part I, ubiquitous musics have been linked from the outset to the fresh listening possibilities offered by new sound technologies. However, Part II focuses specifically on sound technologies closer to the present: mobile phones in present-day India, the role of visible playback technologies in contemporary films and the subjective experiences triggered by listening to digital players. The variety of theoretical styles encompassed here bears witness to the difficulties in catching up with an intricate and ever-shifting reality.

In 'Sound, Perception and Mobile Phones in India' (Chapter 4) Amit S. Rai focuses on the overwhelming presence of voice over data in contemporary mobile usage in India today and on the growing importance of sound technologies for mobile telephony there. Employing a methodology adapted from Deleuze and Guattari and Manuel Delanda, he charts the shift in perceptual capacities in the movement from public to private sound, from the film screen talkie to the multiplex to the headset, and the deepening of privatized sound experiences in contemporary value-added services in mobile telephony. The essay pursues such questions as the following. How does sound get transformed through the micro-speakers of the contemporary handset? How do operators, value-added service providers and the everyday user negotiate this new technology? How have headsets (with both listening and microphone capacities) changed these negotiations? How is sound (as data and experience) secured through changes in perception as bodies assemble anew with mobile technology? Finally, how does sound interact, connect and disrupt other senses such as tactility, vision and proprioception that emerge through this body–machine assemblage?

Tim McNelis's and Elena Boschi's 'Seen and Heard: Visible Playback Technology in Film' (Chapter 5) addresses film soundtracks as an important element of people's everyday listening experiences, focusing on how visible playback technologies weave further meaning into the narrative construction of characters through songs. Private listening typically participates in the production of self-identity. However, when portable media and playback technology are present in films, they often serve social functions by facilitating projection of identities and bonding among characters. These devices can also diffuse music's potential to afford agency to characters by containing their musically projected identities or by reminding them – and audiences – that what they lack cannot be found through the music. Drawing on examples from a number of contemporary films made in Britain, Spain and the United States, this essay argues that visible playback technology is a key signifying element in films, serving functions beyond foregrounding the music and setting the historical period.

Finally, Marta García Quiñones' essay, 'Body and Context in Mobile Listening to Digital Players' (Chapter 6), offers an analysis of 'mobile listening', namely the listening situations made possible by the use of portable digital players or mp3 players, particularly in public spaces where they provide a continuous background to users engaged in everyday activities. The essay begins by tracing a brief history of music portability, from portable valve radios to portable cassette players (the Walkman), and later to portable digital players based on compressed formats. It moves then to compare the critical portrait of mobile listeners as isolated subjects, present in the public debate at least since the times of portable cassette players, to certain advertising campaigns depicting the use of digital players as an active, physically engaging activity, and to the experiences of users. Drawing also on some concepts elaborated in current neurobiological research into human perception and emotions, García Quiñones tries to explain how the mobile listener negotiates the relationship between her body, the shifting context and the music, at different levels.

Spaces

We tend to conceive of spaces as physical. But every space has its sound, be it music or the sound of its inhabitants, their objects and the outside world leaking through the windowpanes alongside light and colours. Aural spaces represent a fundamental component of everybody's daily lives. However, their sound is still often disregarded and – in a few cases – considered inappropriate. The essays in Part III seek to change the hitherto prescriptive approach to these listening practices and propose a shift towards a descriptive one instead, fostering a wider understanding of 'real' listening practices through a fresh theoretical ear.

Jonathan Sterne's contribution, 'The Non-aggressive Music Deterrent' (Chapter 7), discusses the way the outdoor aural space surrounding convenience stores and strip malls has changed after the 'non-aggressive music deterrent' phenomenon emerged in North America through the early 1990s. Sterne looks at instances where music is piped outside shops to prevent loitering by 'undesired' populations, examining how its purveyors imagine Muzak to work on these targets. Programmed music becomes 'sonic architecture', as he defines it – a product whose chief users are the retailers, who reclaim the outdoor space surrounding their store through music. Sterne focuses on the tacit race, class and age implications behind the 'non-aggressive' surface of these practices, unveiling the political and ethical dimension below the aesthetic surface of Muzak.

Serena Facci's essay, 'An Anthropology of Soundtracks in Gym Centers' (Chapter 8), focuses on the way the global diffusion of reproduced music has changed the use (for some, the abuse) of music. Through case studies on the music played in fitness centres in Italy, she combines ethnographic fieldwork and ethnomusicological approaches to discuss how and why some repertoires are chosen on the basis of the time of the day, the types of customer and the kinds of sport. Her study shows that music is essential not only for the organization of movements, but also for a complex mix of aesthetic, relational and psychological reasons.

To conclude, Franco Fabbri's piece, 'Taboo Listening (or, What Kind of Attention?)' (Chapter 9), addresses different instances of what he effectively describes as 'taboo listening', which encompasses all those listening practices outside the widely theorized – and idealized – attentive listening to good music. Fabbri unpacks several ideas surrounding the distinction between hearing and listening, and, after a sharp consideration of Adorno's typologies and their influence on musicology's (mis)understanding of the relationships between listening practices and music, takes us on a journey through music listening and attention while driving a car, working and – the taboo listening situation *par excellence* – making love. Finally, Fabbri argues that the attention model musicologists apply to listening is largely based on visual rather than acoustic stimuli, and calls for new directions in the study of ubiquitous musics.

As the diverse backgrounds of the contributors to this collection clearly show, the study of ubiquitous musics necessarily requires the combined effort of different disciplinary fields – musicology, communication studies, cultural studies, philosophy, sociology, among others – while allowing for a plurality of research styles, including historical inquiry, theoretical speculations, and ethnography. On the whole, the essays brought together here provide a wide range of theoretical and critical approaches, and ultimately aim – at least this is our hope as editors – at moving this young field a step forward.

PART I
Histories

Chapter 1
Caliban's Ear:
A Short History of Ambient Music

Lawrence Kramer

People today are awash in music from radios, television, elevators and super-markets. It is possible that the pervasiveness of music may lead to more hallucinations.

The New York Times, 12 July 2005[1]

The hallucinations in question are exaggerated forms of 'brainworms' – music stuck in the head. Scientists, the *Times* story reports, are currently investigating the strange phenomenon of an outbreak of 'musical hallucinations' among older people who have lost some hearing. These involuntary listeners find fully detailed music in their ears – music heard, not just imagined – when the segment of the brain that organizes sound into music operates on its own without auditory input.

The researchers plausibly enough suggest a cause-and-effect relationship between this phenomenon and ambient music, but the relationship may be more convoluted than that. If ambient music is now a fact of everyday perception – and it is – why speak of hallucinations when confronted with a continuation, at higher volume, of the music already in everyone's head: an echo, a resonance, an ensemble-playing by the brain, which knows quite well what world it is living in? (Do they have the same hallucinations in Cairo, where the decibel level of just living is reportedly about the same as standing next to a jackhammer?) Not for nothing is this volume (are you reading it in silence, or with music on?) called *Ubiquitous Musics*. When ambient music comes to be everywhere, following wherever technology has gone, it has no trouble worming its way into the fabled inside of the head.

In that locale, however, more is reorganized than just perception. Ambient music today tends to rinse away the subjective interiority that used to live between the ears. Why would it do that? Why has it *done* that? When did it start? In what follows I hope to float some answers in the air.

---

[1]　Carl Zimmer, 'Neuron Network Goes Awry, and Brain Becomes an IPod', *The New York Times: Science Times*, 12 July 2005, pp. 1, 6.

The Welkin

Ambient music is a modern phenomenon, born of the assembly line and the elevator and before that of the department store.[2] Commercial and industrial modernity coincide with its rise, and it has now handily survived their fall. But the idea of ambient music is much older. Music in the air, music heard across space, is a pastoral idea and a cosmological idea, in both cases with antique roots. At its most sophisticated in the era before its technological possibility, such music marked the intersection of the pastoral and the cosmological. This idea can be found working with undiminished force early in Thomas Hardy's novel of 1874, *Far from the Madding Crowd*:

> The sky was clear – remarkably clear – and the twinkling of all the stars seemed to be but throbs of one body, timed by a common pulse. The North Star was directly in the wind's eye, and since evening the Bear had swung round it outwardly to the east, till he was now at a right angle to the meridian … Suddenly an unexpected series of sounds began to be heard in this place against the sky. They had a clearness which was to be found nowhere in the wind and a sequence which was to be found nowhere in nature. They were the notes of Farmer Oak's flute.[3]

The sounds of the flute address nature from outside, not as an opposite, but as a supplement: the clearness of the notes to the clearness of the sky, the sequence of the notes to the rotation of the constellations. The music and the stars move to the same common pulse, even if the human pulse is, in a trope typical of Hardy, almost lost amid the grand but indifferent pulse of the cosmic whole. Farmer Oak's flute is of a piece with, in effect plays the same piece as, the shepherd's pipe of Virgil and Theocritus.[4]

---

[2]   For a brief account, with references to the extensive literature on this subject, see Herve Vanel, 'John Cage's Muzak-Plus: The Fu(rni)ture of Music', *Representations*, 103 (2008): pp. 96–106 and associated footnotes. For more extensive surveys, see Joseph Lanza, *Elevator Music: A Surreal History of Muzak, Easy-Listening, and Other Moodsong* (New York, 1994) and David Toop, *Ocean of Sound: Aether Talk, Ambient Sound and Imaginary Worlds* (London, 1995). For an intriguing interpretive foray, quite different in emphasis from mine here and thus a useful complement to it, see Ronald H. Radano, 'Interpreting Muzak: Speculations on Musical Experience in Everyday Life', *American Music*, 7 (1989): pp. 448–60. On the department store, see Linda L. Tyler, '"Commerce and Poetry Hand in Hand": Music in American Department Stores, 1880–1930', *Journal of the American Musicological Society*, 45 (1992): pp. 75–120. I should add the 'ambient music' of this chapter is any acousmatic music heard to cross and fill space; it is music in the air, and has nothing to do with the musical genre named 'ambient music' by Brian Eno.

[3]   Thomas Hardy, *Far from the Madding Crowd* (New York, 1971), pp. 19–20.

[4]   See Wendell Clausen, *A Commentary on Virgil: Eclogues* (Oxford, 1994), p. 36.

It ought to be possible, therefore, to compose a genealogy of ambient music. Not a chronicle, although that is possible, too, but a genealogy in the Nietzschean and Foucauldian sense, an indirect speculative history that re-conceives the phenomenon by exposing the antecedents to which it is linked, not by affiliation but by rupture. What follows is a fragment of one such genealogy. Others would have been possible,

> They learned
> Sweet plaintive songs, such as the pipe pours forth
> When pressed by player's fingers, heard through woods
> And brakes and pathless groves, through desert haunts
> And scenery of godlike calm.
>
> Lucretius, *De Rerum Natura*, V, 1385–1390

but perhaps not so many as one might think; the starting-point, at least – my title gives it away – is both a limit and a landmark. The destination is, too, though for different reasons – reasons in part idiosyncratic, in part symptomatic: they involve classical music, in the era of its cultural recession, finding a new career in ambient form. In a sense that destination is my true starting-point. Classical music, for better or worse, is the centre of my work, and its contemporary destinies have all too compelling an interest for me. The effect of its floating sound in a train station is the question, even the enigma, which I hope to unravel by taking it as the end-term in a sequence of moments, dispersed across time, of ambient music.

Three moments, to be exact: one fictional, one semi-fictional, one real; one early modern, one modern, one postmodern. The genealogical sequence resembles that of a literary genre, the progress poem, the speculative quasi-allegorical history by which a poem accounts the conditions of its own possibility. Three moments, then, as a Progress of Ambient Music in prose – only, to complicate matters, the early-modern moment that starts the sequence will not consent simply to pass but instead turns up again, and again, in later metamorphoses. Perhaps this proliferation is simply the means by which the allegory refuses to forget its own nature as artifice. Perhaps it suggests that, as a listening subject, the auditor of ambient music is (almost) always addressed as a Caliban. Nonetheless, the Progress moves (not *advances*, simply moves) through three emblematic moments: the first natural, the third technological, the second in transit between. That these categories will not survive the transition intact is only to be expected.

What did the listening subjects of these moments hear? In what sound-world did they hear it? How, in that world, did it matter that it was music that they heard, whether figuratively or literally? What, in that case, did the music, the musicality of music, (come to) mean?

The questions are posed of a liminal figure in liminal spaces and could hardly be posed otherwise. Liminality, too, is an acoustic issue; what is more liminal than the ear? So the questions are posed of Caliban, roaming an island that is no longer his except for its ambient music and its later echoes; of James Agee, caught between the metropolis and the backwoods in a dark time; and of myself, passing through the Bluebeard's Castle of New York's Pennsylvania Station to the sounds of disembodied Brahms and Mozart.

At this point we need descriptions of the moments in question. They will, of necessity, be partial descriptions (in both senses of the word), attuned to acoustic matters, devices for cupping the mind's ear.

The Island

Early in *The Tempest*, Prospero accuses Caliban of ingratitude for having been civilized, which, from Caliban's point of view, means dispossessed and subjugated. (Prospero, in exile from Europe, has appropriated the island from Caliban's mother. He rules there with the help of a book whose 'white magic' gives him power over the four traditional elements: water, air, earth and fire. All but water are personified, by Ariel, Caliban and Prospero himself, respectively.) The exchange between master and slave turns on the major instrument of civilization, namely language:

> Prospero:
> Abhorred slave
> Which any print of goodness will not take,
> Being capable of all ill! I pitied thee,
> Took pains to make thee speak, taught thee each hour
> One thing or other: when thou didst not, savage,
> Know thine own meaning, but wouldst gabble like
> A thing most brutish, I endow'd thy purposes
> With words that made them known: but thy vile race,
> Though thou didst learn, had that in't which good natures
> Could not abide to be with.
>
> Caliban:
> You taught me language: and my profit on't
> Is, I know how to curse.[5]

But Caliban has learned to do more than curse. His way with words may be one of the reasons why audiences, unlike Prospero (who nominally speaks for them), tend to find Caliban oddly endearing. (Perhaps another reason is because Caliban speaks for the audience's own resistance to docility in the name of virtue.) Nowhere is this truer than in the unique moment when Caliban speaks lyrically to convey his impression of the island's ambient music. His description even

---

[5] *The Tempest*, I, ii, 351–64. Text from William Shakespeare, *The Complete Works*, ed. Alfred Harbage *et al.* (Baltimore, MD, 1969). The Folio gives Prospero's speech here to his daughter Miranda, but the attribution is probably (I would say surely) an error or misprint.

anticipates the masque of plenty that Prospero will later invoke with magic. But Caliban's magic lies entirely in his speech:

> The isle is full of noises,
> Sounds and sweet airs that give delight and hurt not.
> Sometimes a thousand twanging instruments
> Will hum about mine ears, and sometime voices
> That, if I then had waked after long sleep,
> Will make me sleep again; and then, in dreaming,
> The clouds methought would open, and show riches
> Ready to drop upon me, that when I waked,
> I cried to dream again.[6]

The isle is indeed full of noises, in the form of songs, most of them sung by Ariel, the spirit of the air placing music in the air. The audience is supposed to imagine Ariel as invisible even as it sees him singing. Caliban's music alone is actually invisible, which imbues it with an inherent sense of distance and gives it a greater degree of wonder – a primary theme in the play – than can be found in Ariel's songs (for which some music survives). Shelley later, and Auden much later, would refer the play's music solely to Ariel – and Auden would ironically have Caliban speak in long-winded prose.[7] But Robert Browning, in 'Caliban upon Setebos' (ca. 1860, published 1864), heard things differently.

Browning remembered Caliban's ear and, in an important if disenchanting move, reconceived it as the ear of a purely natural being – Caliban as natural man. But then, Browning's is a post-Darwinian Caliban, caught up in the religious controversies of the Victorian era and portrayed as making a god in his own atavistic image. Browning's version of the island's music is therefore cruel and ominous. But it is still ubiquitous.

The Porch

Let Us Now Praise Famous Men, with photographs by Walker Evans and text by James Agee, is an account of life in the sharecropper South during the Great Depression, strangely divided between Evans's stark photos and Agee's rhapsodic prose. The text is punctuated by three meditative segments entitled 'On the Porch', each of which describes the sights and sounds that came to Agee and his hosts as

---

[6]   *The Tempest*, III, ii, 148–56. Shakespeare, *Complete Works*, ed. Harbage *et al.*

[7]   Percy Bysshe Shelley, 'With a Guitar: To Jane', *Shelley's Poetry and Prose*, ed. Donald H. Reiman and Sharon Powers (New York, 1977), pp. 449–51; W.H. Auden, 'Caliban to the Audience' from *The Sea and the Mirror*, in Auden, *Collected Poems*, ed. Edward Mendelssohn (New York, 1991), pp. 422–44.

they all lay on the porch at night. The third of these segments is an account of music in the air; it closes the book.

The music – and it is always treated as music, never as natural sound, never as cry – consists in a duet between two animal calls – one near, one distant. The singers are never verifiably identified, although Agee eventually decides to treat them as if they were foxes. Like the noises on Caliban's island, those in Agee's Southern woods are transporting; they create the space of a transient utopia in a world otherwise desperate and unforgiving. Agee and his companions are said to respond to the joining of these sounds with a silent laughter, a restorative joyousness, that Agee says he has 'experienced only rarely: listening to the genius of Mozart at its angriest and cleanest, most masculine fire; ... walking in streets or driving in country'; or in the early phases of tender sexual love.[8]

The source of this music's power is partly cosmological, as it is for Caliban and Farmer Oak, although the transport in this case is more chthonic than celestial – Agee is insistent on its corporeal and sexual qualities. But the power also derives from the ability of the ear and the word combined to hear, to have heard, these animal sounds as literal rather than merely figurative music, without even wasting a moment to deny the figurative hearing. So Agee will not only describe what has been heard simply as music – '[like a] low note on the clarinet. It ran eight identical times to a call or stanza, a little faster than allegretto'[9] – but he will even describe it as composed music, classical music: 'The first entrance of this call was as perfect a piece of dramatic or musical structure as I know of: ... the entrance of the mysterious principal completely unforeseen yet completely casual, with none of the quality of studiousness in its surprise which hurts for instance some of the music of Brahms'.[10]

This strange yet spontaneous indifferentiation of musical art and musical nature gives delight and hurts only a little. The effect of the 'drizzling confabulation of pastoral-nocturnal music'[11] cannot be communicated except by the music itself in its own fleeting interlude (Agee says that it lasted 20 minutes). But the 'grief' of this incommunicability pales before 'the frightening joy of hearing the world talk to itself'.[12]

The Portal

Penn Station pipes in classical music every day. I have always supposed that this choice, as opposed to standard 'elevator music', is motivated by a feeling that the

---

[8]   James Agee and Walker Evans, *Let Us Now Praise Famous Men* (Boston, MA, 1969), pp. 467–68. Agee also adds remembering a line of Shakespeare to the list, and, alas, 'watching negroes'.

[9]   Ibid., p. 464.

[10]   Ibid., p. 467.

[11]   Ibid., p. 470.

[12]   Ibid., p. 469.

music is tightly but pleasurably controlled, so that it offers a subliminal model for crowd behaviour in a problematic public space. (More on the architectural problem later; suffice it to say for now that no one *likes* Penn Station, and for good reason.) At any rate, the music is so much a part of the environment that it registers less as music, despite its high musical profile, than as an acoustic feature of movement regarded as flow. At least that happens when the environment is working right – that is, when people are moving through the station more or less on schedule and more or less without congestion, or without more congestion than usual.

On the day I am singling out, however, technical problems caused a large number of trains to be late, so that both conditions of neutrality broke down: nothing happened on schedule, and the density of the crowd grew constantly. It was in this context that the ambient music became audible, at least to me. And perhaps to others too, in varying degrees, if I was right in observing that the music helped stabilize the general atmosphere, conveyed a sense of order amid chaos and even guided the pace and pressure of movement in the increasingly cramped space.

The Penn Station episode is the most far-reaching of my examples because it is a case of ambient music doing perceptibly what is supposed to be done imperceptibly. In that regard, the episode re-enacts the originary scene enacted by Caliban, while it inevitably also redefines that scene. It brings the progressive allegory to a temporary close by recasting Caliban's sense of wonder as a sense of strangeness – a strangeness normally lost in a world where the technological means of producing ambient music is routine. Both the occasion and the specific music of the episode are purely accidental. There is no agency behind them, no intention to link them to the momentary, somewhat unusual, situation. What is being disseminated at the level of intention is not a work, not even a style, but a genre. Yet this is no reason not to consider the specifics. The effect of such a contingent harmony, a matching of music and situation that simply occurs, is present in both Caliban's and Agee's cases as well; it seems to be a part of the originary concept of ambient music. As a trope, ambient music is an accidental sound that reveals an essence.

In all three cases, the ambient music has an effect that it shares with interactive media, which two of the cases nonetheless antedate: the ambient music violates the classic model of communication whereby a message is transmitted from a sender to a receiver. Music in the air is an expressive form, but it does not come from a personifiable source and is not addressed to a listener as recipient. It does not act like a voice on Roland Barthes's model of voice as innately coercive,[13] even though for both Caliban and Agee the music is at least evocative of song. The music in the air attracts, but does not compel, attention. Besides, this music is indifferent to any attention it attracts or, perhaps more accurately, tolerates.

---

[13] 'Listening', in Roland Barthes, *The Responsibility of Forms: Critical Essays on Music, Art, and Representation*, trans. Richard Howard (Berkeley, CA, 1991), pp. 245–60.

Yet there is a key difference among the cases. In the early-modern and modern examples, this sourceless music does not interpellate the auditor as a subject. (The *auditor*, not the *listener*: the listener is a participant, the auditor an accident.) The music, that is, does not follow the model of ideology proposed by Louis Althusser, who, like Barthes, finds an essential coerciveness in voice: here, a voice that hails (interpellates) its addressee as a particular type of subject.[14] The voice prevails when the subject accepts the hail by answering it. Perhaps the non-interpellative character of Agee's ambient music represents a modernist nostalgia for Caliban's ear, a wish at least to eavesdrop on a premodernity already long since lost. Caliban himself has already lost it, except in his one recurrent moment as an auditor.

The nostalgia arises because the history of ambient music in modernity, especially if the radio and even more especially the car radio are included in it, might well be defined as a learning how to interpellate. But the postmodern instance is peculiar and, in some sense, also Caliban-like. The classical music piped into Penn Station is certainly interpellative, unsurprisingly so, but it lacks the structure of address on which interpellation is supposed to depend. In this it differs markedly from non-ambient classical music, which does depend on a structure of address, albeit a dialectical or dialogical one.[15] This music in the air is closer – just how close is one of our questions – to traditional Muzak, which developed as a means of interpellating the worker or elevator passenger or shopper without addressing anyone at all. Fully ambient music, classical or not, seems to take the ideologically determined modern subject for granted or else to regard it as beside the point.

What effect does this change have? What effect does it register? What new mode of subjectivity does it sponsor?

The Woods

The answers may begin with a question posed by the end: the sounds of the finale of the Brahms Second Piano Concerto followed, without transition, by the finale of the Mozart Clarinet Quintet: music heard while I followed the announcement, by the disembodied and perhaps computerized voice of the station announcer, to 'assemble' by a certain gate to await the arrival of a train delayed by equipment

---

14   See Louis Althusser, 'Ideology and Ideological State Apparatuses', in *Lenin and Philosophy*, trans. Ben Brewster (New York, 1971), pp. 170–86.

15   On interpellation and address in listening to (classical) music, see my 'The Mysteries of Animation: History, Analysis, and Musical Subjectivity', *Music Analysis*, 20 (2001): pp. 159–66; *Classical Music and Postmodern Knowledge* (Berkeley, CA, 1995), pp. 21–5; and *Interpreting Music* (Berkeley, CA, 2010), pp. 47–51. In a critique of Althusser, Judith Butler observes that address (along with its symbol, voice) is only one interpellative means among many others available; see her *Excitable Speech: A Politics of the Performative* (New York, 1997), pp. 1–42.

failure. The assembly, a large one, was composed of exasperated people – people not only delayed but beset by the weather of a brutally hot and humid day: they, we, were all Calibans for the moment, reduced to a creatureliness too dependent on technical manipulations not subject to understanding and control, and yet, for all that, quite remarkably orderly and peaceable. How cynical would one have to be to credit, or, put otherwise, to blame the music for this?

Caliban may hold the answer, but only if we pose a further question. In staging the pertinent scene in *The Tempest*, did Shakespeare, and should we, let the mysterious music remain unheard or provide it from above or below the stage? (It would have to be live music even in a modern production; piped music would have the effect of exposing the apparatus, which is exactly what is not wanted. The music must sound as if enchanted, and the only way it can do that is by preserving the 'live' sound of performance while denying, visually, any source to the sound.) The effects would be quite different: with no music, a proto-Cageian attentiveness to ambient sound as such in its musicality; with music, a questioning of the enigmatic place of music between nature and culture, the heavenly spheres and the earth – precisely the kind of questioning that the technology of later ambient music suspends, since there is never any mystery about where the music comes from.

This suspension is gradual; it forms the 'plot' of the historical trajectory. This trajectory follows a familiar pattern – familiar enough, indeed, to invite suspicion. The suspicion will come, but the pattern must be traced first.

The music that Caliban hears is edged with magic and enchantment – and the magic is not metaphor, since Prospero is literally a thaumaturge, although knowing this fact does not render the music less mysterious or expose its source. Depending on production values – do *we* hear anything in this scene? Is it Ariel we hear? Should the 'airs' be vocal or instrumental? – we do not even know that the sounds come at Prospero's bidding; all we can do is surmise. And if we do hear something, be it voice or instrument, we are caught between contrary modes of knowing what we hear. Are we drawn more to the factual truth that the sound originates in the motions of an unseen body behind the apparatus of theatrical illusion or to the phenomenological truth that the music is simply there, in the air, both if we hear it and (perhaps even more) if we do not?

Browning's Caliban hears less than Shakespeare's and surmises more. He inhabits a world where music as such has vanished but where music in nature has become metaphor; as we have already heard, this is the very metaphor that will be rendered literal in Agee's narrative. In the case of Browning's Caliban, the metaphorization is a material process: the cry of a bird becomes a kind of rough music as a result of its reproduction on a pipe – in effect a panpipe – that Caliban has devised for himself. The music appears as a cry of pain, because everything this Caliban sees and hears is measured by a private utilitarian calculus of pleasure and pain. Yet the same music, imagined as if the pipe were sentient and had vocalized the sound, also becomes a cry of Promethean defiance. Caliban's ear hears itself in Caliban's surrogate voice. The sound in the air becomes musical only after it has been mechanically reproduced, in a travesty of the pastoral sound of the shepherd's pipe:

> Hath cut a pipe of pithless elder-joint
> That, blown through, gives exact the scream o' the jay
> When from her wing you twitch the feathers blue:
> Sound this, and little birds that hate the jay
> Flock within stone's throw, glad their foe is hurt:
> Put case such pipe could prattle and boast forsooth
> 'I catch the birds, I am the crafty thing,
> I make the cry my maker cannot make
> With his great round mouth; he must blow through mine![16]

The mystery here is no longer magical but purely natural: the mystery of animal sentience. Browning's great feat is to have his Caliban *speak* for animal sentience – the very thing that animal sentience as such is incapable of doing. In the speech also resides a certain musicality, a bodily-material music mimicked by the rough magic of Browning's style in this text.

The potential for enchantment that nonetheless persists can best be gauged if we shift our attention to a different Caliban, the Caliban-like figure of Wagner's young Siegfried. The Wagnerian hero-to-be notoriously begins as a natural – all too natural – man in the music drama named after him. He not only rivals Caliban for brutishness, but may even be partly modelled on Shakespeare's Caliban. Like Caliban, Siegfried is a solitary misfit in a remote, primitive natural world, raised by an exiled and disaffected 'father' and distinguished by unruly urges partly qualified by intimations of a finer sensibility.

That sensibility first manifests itself in *Siegfried* in the 'Forest Murmurs' scene of act 2, in which the musicalization of nature portends Siegfried's coming of age as a hero. Reflecting on the mystery of his parentage, Siegfried hears sounds and sweet airs and the song of a little bird amid the rustle of the forest, a locale that is, of course, pregnant with enchantment in the German tradition. Unlike Caliban, he does not hear music as such but the murmurs of the forest *as* music. Only we, in the audience, hear music literally, and the music we hear is itself metaphorical, a representation of natural sound in its becoming musical. The music in the air does not cross into nature from the sphere of magic, but instead possesses a natural magic, or more exactly renders nature itself both musical and magical.

---

[16] 'Caliban upon Setebos'. Text from *The Shorter Poems of Robert Browning*, ed. William Clyde Devane (New York, 1934), pp. 238–44. But the text is easily accessible online. Note that Caliban speaks of himself in the third person; the start of the first quoted line, 'Hath' (for 'He hath'), thus refers to Caliban himself, to whom the imaginary speaking or singing pipe, cast as a little Caliban, stands exactly as the big Caliban stands to the imaginary god Setebos.

Within the opera's diegesis, there is no music except the song of the wood bird in a forest otherwise full of natural sounds. Within the opera's extradiegetic space, the forest scene appears as a becoming-music, even, perhaps, insofar as it does so, as a becoming-invisible, a scene heard but not seen, less a place than a distance that becomes a proximity. (The sound of ambient music as such is a distance rendered proximate, even over-proximate.) The audience simultaneously listens to Wagner's music as performed for the occasion, and hears the

A little breeze, perchance
Escaped from boisterous winds that rage without,
Has entered, by the sturdy oaks unfelt,
But to its gentle touch how sensitive
Is the light ash! that, pendent from the brow
Of yon dim cave, in seeming silence makes
A soft eye-music of slow-waving boughs,
Powerful almost as vocal harmony
To stay the wanderer's steps and soothe his thoughts.

William Wordsworth, 'Airey-Force Valley' (1842)

diegetic forest murmurs *as* a music that no one performs. Siegfried, at this point half in and half out of the diegesis, hears the same murmurs as musicalized, and therefore encrypted, speech. His question is how to understand the wood bird's song.

In this context, given the skill of Browning's Caliban with a reed, it is interesting that Siegfried, too, crafts a reed and tries, but fails, to imitate the bird's song. The sound of the reed or the shepherd's pipe or 'oaten flute' is a realization of the distance innate to music 'in the air'. When both Berlioz, in the 'Scène aux champs'

Berlioz, 'Scène aux champs'

from *Symphonie fantastique*, and Wagner, in act III of *Tristan und Isolde*, want to invoke that sound, they place the piper offstage. But Siegfried is bewildered by distance; he experiences everything close up. He can make music only on his horn, which he uses only to announce and declare himself, to close rather than to open distance. It is the horn that, when the reed fails, shifts Siegfried's register from pastoral to heroic and summons forth his antagonist Fafner as an ambivalent 'good companion'.

In contrast to what technology would soon amply demonstrate, ambient music for Siegfried is precisely a music that cannot be made: not played, not manufactured. It can only be heard, and heard only on condition of not being understood. The enchantment here is, so to speak, a product of pure, rather than material, metaphor, inaccessible except to Caliban's ear. Or ears, since what the audience hears incorporates but also exceeds what Siegfried hears, the audience having a capacity for nostalgia, based on the idea of natural magic, that the naive and uncouth Siegfried lacks. Siegfried hears the ambient music as a riddle; the audience hears it as an idyll.

A similar effect famously arises with the offstage singing at the beginning of *Tristan*, where Caliban's ear has mutated to Isolde's wrath, a form of selective deafness nonetheless penetrated by the disembodied song of a lovesick offstage sailor. In this case the positions of audience and character as established in *Siegfried* are equalized or even reversed. Isolde, painfully self-aware and self-evasive, hears an enchantment that she repudiates precisely because she wants it too much; the audience hears an old song.

But enchantment is always in the air along with the music. For Wagner, one might speculate, with the covered orchestra pit at Bayreuth in mind, the musicalization of space, space becoming the emanation of music in the air, is the fundamental form of enchantment itself in a modern era that renders all ears Caliban's ears. To invoke a still later Wagnerism, it is not time that becomes space in *Parsifal*, but music. In yet another instance of metaphors becoming literal, this transformation happens – invisibly – on stage at the conclusion of the opera when serried voices from above the scene ('from the middle and the topmost height') float down to reconsecrate the grail after Parsifal has healed Amfortas's wound and assumed his office.[17]

Wagner, *Parsifal*, act 3, mm. 1014–1016

Such a musicalization of space also resounds, a sonorous legacy in air, through the text of James Agee. As already noted, Agee's forest of the night is already nostalgic just as a location – even more so, we might add now, than Wagner's murmuring groves or Browning's version of Caliban's island. Agee's forest is a wilful–wistful archaism because technology has already long since intervened in it. It is no longer the forest primeval; it is not even the forest that Siegfried shares with his counterparts in the Brothers Grimm. It is no longer a place apart. The classical composers Agee mentions in his own version of the forest murmurs

[17]   On this topic see my 'The Talking Wound and the Foolish Question: Symbolization in *Parsifal*', *Opera Quarterly*, 22 (2006): pp. 208–29, and David Lewin, 'Amfortas's Prayer to Titurel and the Role of D in *Parsifal*: The Tonal Spaces of the Drama and the Enharmonic C-flat/B', *19th-Century Music*, 7 (1984): pp. 336–49.

are as likely to be heard on radio or shellac disk as in a concert hall. Ambient music has already become technological, so that the only way to retain any sense of enchantment is to displace the sound of the music back again into the sounds of nature – Bach to a fox, gradus *ex* Parnasso.

Manhattan (or The Island)

The postmodern situation carries this condition to its logical terminus in the liminal but purely pragmatic and (not even dis- but) unenchanted locale of a railway terminal, in particular the utterly banal Penn Station. The collapse of enchantment is so complete that one doesn't even notice it until it unravels for a moment and a note of magic sneaks guiltily back. This is an environment in which the music (except to that involuntary musicological ear, and not always to that – even I didn't really hear the Brahms until I joined the gathering at the gate) is as much absent as present: unheard melodies, not sweet but utterly bland.

But this terminal is too familiar; surely we didn't travel all this way just to arrive again at the stale revelation of modernity as disenchantment, alienation, mechanization and, more lately, digitalization? Or rather: just why is that exactly what seems to have happened? The real question here is not about the credibility of this scenario – some form of it is still indispensable to our descriptive repertoire; it's familiar for a reason – but about how to avoid invoking the scenario too easily, too glibly, so that it loses its significance before we can even finish repeating its formulas.

The remedy for such glibness is exactness. So it's important to observe that Agee's description is not a register of loss but a celebration of an evocative power that can still be found. And although the Penn Station anecdote characteristically involves the nameless modern crowd, the everyday pandemonium long since anatomized by the likes of Poe and Baudelaire and Benjamin, there is still something in it for Caliban's ear. The scene could not be transformed by music in the air; it negated such evocativeness along with anything more than a purely acoustic audibility, so that my listening to the Brahms and Mozart amid the crowd in Penn Station was purely clinical. It had no emotional dimension at all, no aesthetic character. Yet this technological flatlining can also be understood as having supplied a horizon line to the containing, overcrowded space. It served as a humanization, even if it was, so to speak, a humanization without humanity. If the music could not address me as a subject, and especially not as the richly endowed interior subject for whom (or to constitute which) it had been composed, it could at least remind me that I had not (not yet, not all) been extinguished as a subject. All one has to do is imagine Penn Station without the music – low ceilings, no windows, invisible exits, narrow corridors linking splotches of unoccupied space accompanied only by the shuffle of feet and the babble of voices – to see the music's value.

A comparison to Grand Central Terminal, which has no such music and needs none, is pertinent here, because the design of Grand Central supplies the horizon line almost literally in the famous vault of the star ceiling with its constellated figures, and the framing of the central arena with marble staircases that mirror each other in leading upward and out. It is next to impossible to feel claustrophobic in Grand Central, next to impossible not to in Penn Station. The ambient classical music in Penn Station remedies the site's spatial chokehold, not in spite of the music's lack of magic and of real audibility, but by means of them.

The Penn Station episode is a classic study in why classical music 'relaxes' you. As noted in my *Musical Meaning*, the basis of this 'relaxation' is probably the absence of a rhythm track; except to people with classical-music expertise, the piped-in classics make no appeal to the body.[18] The paradoxical result is that this allows the music to direct the body unnoticed; the metrical regularity of classical music, doubled by its periodic phrase structure, models the orderly movement of the crowd in space and an underlying condition of calm, choreographed motion.

The subjectivity effect of the music follows from this choreography. It is created in the collective response of what Foucault might have called the docile body, but a body that need not, and probably does not, acknowledge itself as docile. The effect of the music as 'melodic surveillance' (Nick Groom) or an acoustic 'police situation' (John Cage) is countered, albeit not erased, by its effect as a pliable 'sonorous envelope' (David Schwarz):[19] a faint but palpable presence, a kind of musical aether that buoys up bodily movement by yielding to it. The social calculus in this situation is too complex to resolve. The Muzak Corporation long since gave up the notion that only a certain bland type of 'light' music could exercise a pacifying power over public space; virtually any music can act as an opiate. But when the music incorporates a certain resistance to its own pacifying function, as the design of classical music makes almost inevitable, even docility may become something else, something more. It is quite hard to say. And one can't really ask the people involved, who are assumed to be affected by sounds hovering at or beneath their threshold of awareness.

In the case of the particular pieces by Brahms and Mozart recalled by my anecdote, the social modelling extends to the place of the person in the collective. The concerto mobilizes the piano–orchestra relationship in its traditional or proverbial guise of integrating self and society, and the quintet does something similar in the division between clarinet as solo and strings as ensemble.

In Mozart's case, too, the contrast between the rather angular and dry string sound and the liquidity of the clarinet activates an unspoken sense of well-being,

---

[18]   Lawrence Kramer, *Musical Meaning: Toward a Critical History* (Berkeley, CA, 2001), p. 50.

[19]   Nick Groom, 'The Condition of Muzak', *Popular Music and Society*, 20/3 (1996): p. 8; Groom ascribes the phrase to Joseph Lanza's *Elevator Music* but it does not appear there; Cage, quoted in Vanel, 'John Cage's Muzak-Plus', p. 103; David Schwarz, *Listening Subjects: Music, Psychoanalysis, Culture* (New York, 1997), pp. 7–22.

something also attained in the Brahms via the broadly cantabile second theme of the movement. The fact that the pieces are finales – that is, loosely integrated forms – continues the modelling at another level. The music avoids tension and drama; it brings its varied themes and episodes into a loose confederacy; it moves at a good clip, but clearly walks rather than runs.

Absolutely none of this needs to be recognized or processed consciously in order to be effective under normal circumstances. We need, in fact, another word for the normal experience of ambient music today than *hearing* or *listening* – the terms needed by Caliban and Agee, who train their ears on the source of sound even as it eludes them. History has caught up with the formula passed down from a Muzak executive who described the company's product as music designed to be heard but not listened to.[20] We are too used to this music to hear it; we are

On the Nature of Things is a spatial orchestral tone poem [that] ... takes as its point of departure Lucretius' poem *De Rerum Natura*. The general atmosphere of the piece is intended to evoke a sense of classical pastoral antiquity. ... For the intended spatial effect on which this work substantially depends, only the violins, violas, and cellos should occupy the stage. ... The solo flute has its own sequestered location, well apart from the strings and from the other winds, and high up if feasible.

Henry Brant (1956)

better at hearing its absence. Latter-day ambient music is simply absorbed by the ambling subject; it is diffused in the general habitation of public space; it registers more as sensation than as perception. Its ubiquitous presence has fostered a new sensory mode.

Classical music yields itself to that mode well enough, but not unreservedly. It performs uneasily as what Ronald Radano calls 'consensus music', the umpteenth recycling of *The Four Seasons* or *Eine kleine Nachtmusik* or 'Für Elise' notwithstanding.[21] Classical music cannot be entirely parted from its own history or from the history of the kind of subjectivity it addresses – or, indeed, from the historical force of address that is basic to its operation. When classical music is in the air, those who cross its acoustic space are caught in an interpellative tug-of-war. On one side is the resonant-resonating subjective depth to which the music was originally addressed, and to which it is still normatively (if perhaps anachronistically) addressed;[22] on the other side is the flatness of the animated figure who (that?) moves to the music precisely insofar as the music escapes or repels notice. As I implied by speaking of a reminder (which is also a remainder), this splitting actually constitutes a recovery of traditional subjectivity at the site

---

[20]   The phrase was coined by Donald O'Neill; see Stanley Green, 'Music to Hear but Not to Listen To', *Saturday Review*, 28 September 1957, p. 56.

[21]   Radano, 'Interpreting Muzak', p. 455.

[22]   For more on the relationship of classical music to the history of subjectivity, see my *Why Classical Music Still Matters* (Berkeley, CA, 2007), pp. 18–22.

of its presumptive absence. A link to that subjectivity might be said to become available, if only as nostalgia, to the extent that the absorption of ambient music is interrupted and so becomes self-aware. If, that is, it should happen at all.

Ambient classical music thus occupies an ambiguous intermediate zone. It is not only unusual but in its way disturbing that, on the day of my anecdote, ambient Brahms and Mozart became floating presences like Caliban's island noises and that I (though with how many others I cannot say) found myself hearing, listening to, this music, not automatically via the trained listener's reflex arc, but attentively. The sound of this familiar music became a species of estrangement. Yet it was the estrangement that unravelled the acoustic cocoon and brought the music uncannily (back) to life.

This and my other modern instances of ambient music all involve a temporary symbolic reversal of the mythic history emblematized by Caliban's island noises. Music in the air originates (so we imagine) as audible breakthrough, something that literally airs – that is, reveals, uncovers itself. But as it passes from myth to history and technology, such music merges with the air itself: the airs become the air; the music becomes audible but unheard. It becomes, we might say, *audited.* As Richard Middleton notes:

> Until relatively recently, music punctuated life; often the performed time of the musical event stood in a dissociated, even liminal relationship to the time of surrounding existence. The shift is not absolute … [M]usicalized life and lived music interact. Nevertheless, the *specialness* of the musical event that we can recognize in many traditional contexts – its capacity to interrupt – has been attenuated.[23]

The history of this attenuation may be measured by the moments that rub against its grain, those increasingly rare interludes or interruptions in which the music comes to be noticed, noted, and not merely audited. Precisely because classical music has a marginal position on the soundtrack of modernity, especially late modernity, it may also have the greatest potential to restore the capacity of music in general for interruption. It may reaffirm, even newly reveal, musical meaning as interruption and punctuation and liminal passage. Precipitated out of ambient sound, classical music may thus – oddly, a bit uncannily – find a new role for itself in auditory culture as the true (if piped-in) heir of the shepherd's piping.

---

[23]   Richard Middleton, *Voicing the Popular: On the Subjects of Popular Music* (New York, 2006), p. 175.

Chapter 2

Early Mood Music:
Edison's Phonography, American Modernity
and the Instrumentalization of Listening

Tony Grajeda

Well before the development of systematic studies on the influence of background music on the behaviour of consumers, before the arrival of 'functional music' in the workplace designed to increase productivity and 'industrial efficiency', before even George Owen Squire came up with the idea for Muzak, there was Thomas Edison's research in 'mood music'. Indeed, the so-called 'father of the phonograph', that towering figure of the first half-century of recorded sound, sponsored research in the early 1920s for 'the purpose', he proclaimed, 'of ascertaining and classifying the effects of music on the minds and moods of mankind'.[1]

In 1920 William Maxwell, President of the Phonograph Division of Thomas A. Edison, Inc., persuaded Edison to underwrite a series of scientific experiments on 'what music will do for you'. Conducted under the direction of Dr Walter Van Dyke Bingham, Director of the Department of Applied Psychology at what was still known as the Carnegie Institute of Technology, the project attempted 'to develop the true psychology and philosophy of music', as well as 'establish by comparison the difference between the emotions aroused by the New Edison and those provoked by ordinary talking machines'.[2] The two-year research project produced a number of studies, including a 1921 paper titled 'A Classification of 589 ReCreations [that is, recordings] According to Their Effects Upon the Hearer', culminating in a short publication simply called *Mood Music*, described as 'a compilation of 112 Edison Re-Creations according to "what they will do for you"'. The company also built a sales campaign around the research, encouraging phonograph dealers to hold what were called 'mood change parties'. The 'parties' as such were organized around auditing specific Edison records, with listeners subsequently invited to fill out a 'mood change chart' in order to document their 'mental reactions to music', with such reactions listed on the chart as 'serious to gay' and 'worried to carefree'.

---

[1] Ad copy, 'Over 55,000,000 Readers Will See This Ad in the February Issues of Leading Magazines', *Edison Diamond Points*, 4/2 (January 1921): p. 11.

[2] See George L. Frow, *The Edison Disc Phonographs and the Diamond Discs: A History with Illustrations* (Sevenoaks, 1982), p. 247.

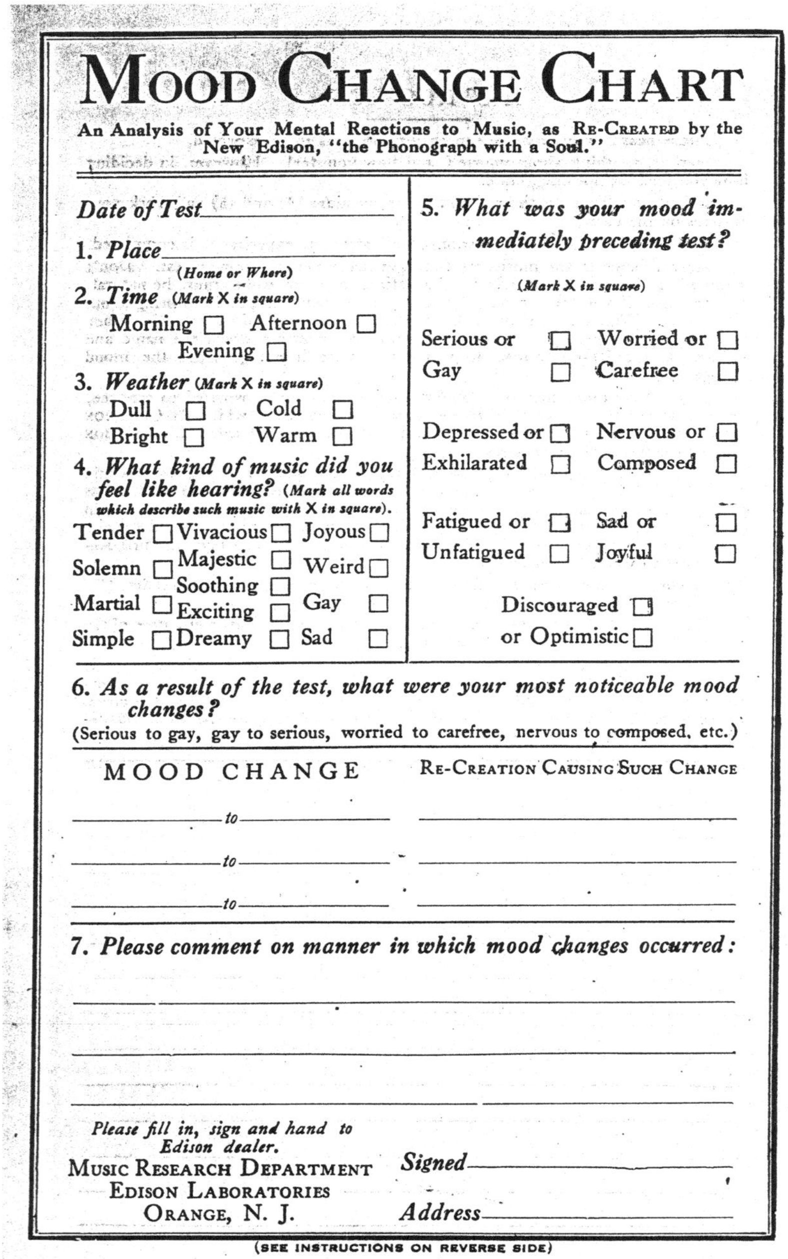

MOOD CHANGE CHART

An Analysis of Your Mental Reactions to Music, as RE-CREATED by the New Edison, "the Phonograph with a Soul."

Date of Test_____

1. *Place*_____
   (Home or Where)

2. *Time* (Mark X in square)
     Morning ☐   Afternoon ☐
         Evening ☐

3. *Weather* (Mark X in square)
     Dull ☐   Cold ☐
     Bright ☐   Warm ☐

4. *What kind of music did you feel like hearing?* (Mark all words which describe such music with X in square).
   Tender ☐ Vivacious ☐ Joyous ☐
   Solemn ☐ Majestic ☐ Weird ☐
   Martial ☐ Soothing ☐
         Exciting ☐ Gay ☐
   Simple ☐ Dreamy ☐ Sad ☐

5. *What was your mood immediately preceding test?*
   (Mark X in square)

   Serious or ☐   Worried or ☐
   Gay   ☐   Carefree ☐

   Depressed or ☐   Nervous or ☐
   Exhilarated ☐   Composed ☐

   Fatigued or ☐   Sad or ☐
   Unfatigued ☐   Joyful ☐

   Discouraged ☐
   or Optimistic ☐

6. *As a result of the test, what were your most noticeable mood changes?*
   (Serious to gay, gay to serious, worried to carefree, nervous to composed, etc.)

   MOOD CHANGE   RE-CREATION CAUSING SUCH CHANGE

   _____to_____   _____

   _____to_____   _____

   _____to_____   _____

7. *Please comment on manner in which mood changes occurred:*

   _____

   _____

   _____

   Please fill in, sign and hand to Edison dealer.
   MUSIC RESEARCH DEPARTMENT
   EDISON LABORATORIES
   ORANGE, N. J.

   *Signed*_____

   *Address*_____

(SEE INSTRUCTIONS ON REVERSE SIDE)

Figure 2.1   Mood Change Chart. Courtesy of US Dept of the Interior, National Park Service, Thomas Edison National Historical Park.

In what follows I explore this fascinating moment in early 'mood music' by building on the only academic treatment of the subject to date, Eleanor Selfridge-Field's essay 'Experiments with Melody and Meter, or the Effects of Music: The Edison-Bingham Music Research',[3] along with my own research of company documents at the Thomas Edison National Historical Park.[4] As I aim to demonstrate here, a thorough consideration of the Edison–Bingham project requires positioning it within the discourse on social and cultural modernity, a period in which scientific practices, such as those informing the emerging field of behaviouralism for example, inflected certain artistic practices throughout many industrialized societies during the early decades of the twentieth century. Hence, I connect Edison's 'pioneer scientific research into the mental effects of music', as it was put in a company publication,[5] to early attempts at 'synchronizing routine factory operations',[6] such as the 1921 case of a phonograph used in a postal operation, in which it was claimed that recorded music in the workplace dramatically increased productivity of the workers.

Besides signalling a shift in musical experience and apprehension from the realm of aesthetics to a concern with functionalism (that is, from standards to standardization), what can be heard in the 'mood music' project, I want to suggest, is the early murmur of what would become, by the century's end, the sheer instrumental rationality of music – from Muzak to the 'Mozart effect'.[7] More specifically, I want to speculate on how this research aimed to classify 'types of listeners' (and this well before Adorno's typology of listeners in his *Introduction to the Sociology of Music*), research that posited a new science and rationality of listening through mood assessment and emotional responses which could be said to have contributed to the instrumentalization of listening.

---

[3]   Eleanor Selfridge-Field, 'Experiments with Melody and Meter, or the Effects of Music: The Edison–Bingham Music Research', *The Musical Quarterly,* 81/2 (Summer 1997): pp. 291–310. The mood music project is also touched on briefly in William Howland Kenney, *Recorded Music in American Life: The Phonograph and Popular Memory, 1890–1945* (New York, 1999) and Steve J. Wurtzler, *Electric Sounds: Technological Change and the Rise of Corporate Mass Media* (New York, 2007).

[4]   I wish to thank the archival staff, and especially Douglas Tarr at the Thomas Edison National Historical Park, West Orange, NJ, for their generous and invaluable assistance during my research visits in 2002 and 2003.

[5]   *Mood Music* (Orange, NJ, 1921), p. 9.

[6]   Ad copy, 'The Thomas A. Edison Prize' for the 'most meritorious research on THE EFFECTS OF MUSIC [to be] submitted to the American Psychological Association before June 1, 1921', quoted in Selfridge-Field, 'Experiments with Melody and Meter', pp. 295–96.

[7]   For an incisive critique of the 'Mozart effect', see Gwenyth Jackaway, 'Selling Mozart to the Masses: Crossover Marketing as Cultural Diplomacy', *Journal of Popular Music Studies,* 11/12 (1999/2000): pp. 125–50.

The Social and Cultural Conditions of American Modernity

In order to grasp what led to the emergence and tentative formation of early 'mood music', we need to at least briefly consider a larger context beyond the modernization of sound – one that would include contemporaneous developments in the sphere of industrial production (Fordism and Taylorization), as well as the New Psychology of the early twentieth century (Freud's reception in America). To begin with, we should recall that the mechanical reproduction of sound through early phonography was not only a project of cultural modernity, but also one of social modernity. As Anson Rabinbach argues in *The Human Motor*, a kind of 'confluence' between social and cultural modernity takes shape in the late nineteenth century – a confluence between the endeavours of science and those of art. The work of Etienne-Jules Marey and Eadweard Muybridge, for example, sought to apply 'new scientific modes of perception to social questions', especially questions about the body and its functioning. Their experimental use of photography to 'freeze' motion and document 'instants of time', as Rabinbach conveys, involved subjecting 'the body to a series of objective, scientifically determined norms and economies of motion'.[8] These attempts to measure and analyse movement through technologies of representation did not go unnoticed by Edison.

In 1888, after nearly a decade-long hiatus from work on sound, Edison presented his 'perfected' phonograph to the world, now more deliberately conceived as an apparatus of science, as a means to revealing certain objective truths about the world:

> The most skillful observers, listeners and realistic novelists, or even stenographers, cannot reproduce a conversation exactly as it occurred. The account they give is more or less generalized. But the phonograph receives, and then transmits to our ears again, every least thing that was said – exactly *as* it was said – with the faultless fidelity of an instantaneous photograph. We shall now for the first time know what conversation really is; just as we have learned, only within a few years, through the instantaneous photograph, what attitudes are taken by the horse in motion.[9]

---

[8]   Anson Rabinbach, *The Human Motor: Energy, Fatigue, and the Origins of Modernity* (Berkeley and Los Angeles, CA, 1992), pp. 86–7. Along the same lines, Jonathan Crary explores the development of optical devices earlier in the nineteenth century that contributed to 'a complex remaking of the individual as observer into something calculable and regularizable and of human vision into something measurable and thus exchangeable'. See Jonathan Crary, *Techniques of the Observer: On Vision and Modernity in the Nineteenth Century* (Cambridge, MA, 1990), p. 17.

[9]   Thomas A. Edison, 'The Perfected Phonograph', *The North American Review*, 146/379 (June 1888): pp. 648–9.

As his choice of words here suggests, Edison, who in fact had come in contact with both Marey and Muybridge, considered his research in acoustics consistent with their time–motion studies.[10]

Moreover, as photography and phonography assisted the drive for rationalization of the body, rendering it a quantifiable and thus more instrumentalized object, these optical and auditory devices also brought about perceptual changes in the subject, ushering in new ways of seeing and hearing.[11] For, as Edison claimed, the phonograph is capable of capturing 'what conversation really is', disclosing a reality of speech 'unattained by any other means'. And since 'it imparts to us the gift of hearing ourselves as others hear us',[12] the phonograph is uniquely qualified to produce a form of self-consciousness with empirical force – a mechanical sounding board to a more modern notion of a self.

Edison's still primitive study in acoustics throughout this period – the treatment of sound as distinct, 'atomized' units rather than the more commonplace sense of a flow of auditory phenomena – grounded his attempt to establish music on a 'scientific basis'. As he once said, 'I am like a phonograph', listening to sound 'from a mechanical point of view'.[13] As one of the leading authors, or perhaps

---

[10]   On Muybridge's 1888 zoopraxiscope demonstration at Edison's Orange, NJ laboratory and Edison's likely meeting with Marey during his visit to the 1889 Paris Universal Exhibition, see Neil Baldwin, *Edison: Inventing the Century* (New York, 1995), pp. 208–12, and Ronald W. Clark, *Edison: The Man Who Made the Future* (New York, 1977), pp. 172–5. See also Tom Gunning, 'Doing for the Eye What the Phonograph Does for the Ear', in Richard Abel and Rick Altman (eds), *The Sounds of Early Cinema* (Bloomington and Indianapolis, 2001), pp. 13–31.

[11]   'Recording has transformed music', asserts Michael Chanan, 'by changing the experience of the ear.' This point corresponds to Walter Benjamin's observations on how 'the entire spectrum of optical, and now also acoustical, perception' has been altered by the apparatus of film: 'With the close-up, space expands; with slow motion, movement is extended. The enlargement of a snapshot does not simply render more precise what in any case was visible, though unclear: it reveals entirely new structural formations of the subject.' See Walter Benjamin, 'The Work of Art in the Age of its Technological Reproducibility', in *Illuminations*, ed. and intro. Hannah Arendt, trans. Harry Zohn (New York, 1969), pp. 235–6. In much the same way, the idea here that audio technologies alter not just what we hear but *how* we hear remains a pertinent aspect to my analysis of the mood music project. For more on Benjamin's analysis applied to musical perception, see Michael Chanan, *Repeated Takes: A Short History of Recording and Its Effects on Music* (London and New York, 1995), pp. 9–10.

[12]   Edison, 'The Perfected Phonograph', p. 650.

[13]   Quoted in John Harvith and Susan Edwards Harvith (eds), *Edison, Musicians, and the Phonograph: A Century in Retrospect* (Westport, CT, 1987), pp. 10–11. See also Edison, 'The Perfected Phonograph': pp. 641–2. Edison's theory of sound as composed of discrete, isolated tones was influenced by the work of Hermann von Helmholtz, who, in *Sensations of Tone as a Physiological Basis for the Theory of Music* (1863, English translation 1875), posited a rational fundament for musical perception (see Baldwin, *Edison: Inventing the Century*, p. 320). By tapping into 'the conception of Pythagoras that number and harmony

composers, of what we might call the sound of modernity, Edison was surely caught up in the scientific thought of his times. While the nature of sound undergoes an evaluation informed by the empirical research of applied science, the phonograph, a novel machine testing those nascent theories, begins to transform the experience of sound, setting new conditions for a listening subject.[14]

Such conditions included the modernization of sound manifested in and constituted by the built environment, which is the subject of *The Soundscape of Modernity: Architectural Acoustics and the Culture of Listening in America, 1900–1933*, Emily Thompson's thorough examination of the ways in which the American soundscape experienced a dramatic transformation in the early part of the twentieth century. As Thompson convincingly demonstrates, this period witnessed the emergence of what was being called the New Acoustics, a science of sound authored by physicists, engineers and technicians associated with the telephone, radio and motion picture industries – figures who designed and utilized increasingly sophisticated electro-acoustic technologies to theorize and understand the behaviour of sound energy. These efforts contributed to the construction of such modern architectural spaces as the Symphony Hall in Boston and Radio City Music Hall in New York. Thompson argues that new electro-acoustic technologies and architectural design informed by scientific models, along with the development of acoustical materials to eliminate what was considered noise and to control sound, produced an unprecedented sound that was distinctively modern. This modern sound was defined equally by an aesthetic of efficiency (relatively free of noise, clear and controlled), by its status as a product or commodity to be purchased and consumed, and by its 'perceived demonstration of man's technical mastery over his physical environment'.[15] By the 1920s such technical mastery had taken hold through the acoustical design of such 'modern' auditoriums as the Eastman Theater in Rochester, New York, providing evidence, as Thompson emphasizes, of the mathematical and ultimately scientific rationalization of spatial relations within which the production and reception of sound could now be heard.[16]

---

constituted the principle of the Universe', Edison placed his machine within a long tradition relating mathematics to music, one that extends to the digitalization of sound. See Tony Grajeda, 'The Sound of Disaffection', in Henry Jenkins, Tara McPherson and Jane Shattuc (eds), *Hop on Pop: The Politics and Pleasures of Popular Culture* (Durham, NC, and London, 2002), pp. 357–75. See also Mark Katz, *Capturing Sound: How Technology Has Changed Music* (Berkeley, CA, 2004), especially ch. 7, 'Music in 1s and 0s. The Art and Politics of Digital Sampling' (pp. 137–57); and Aden Evens, *Sound Ideas: Music, Machines, and Experience* (Minneapolis, 2005).

[14]   For a pathbreaking account of the nineteenth-century scientific study of sound by such major figures as Alexander Bell and Hermann von Helmholtz, see Jonathan Sterne, *The Audible Past: Cultural Origins of Sound Reproduction* (Durham, NC, and London, 2003).

[15]   Emily Thompson, *The Soundscape of Modernity: Architectural Acoustics and the Culture of Listening in America, 1900–1933* (Cambridge, MA, and London, 2002), p. 3.

[16]   See especially ch. 6 of Thompson, *The Soundscape of Modernity*, 'Electroacoustics and Modern Sound, 1900–1933' (pp. 229–94). While Thompson underscores the spatial

Parallel to the New Acoustics taking place elsewhere, the Edison Company's research on early 'mood music' by the late 1910s and early 1920s was quite deliberately articulated to scientific methods of the day. As stated in the Foreword to the company's published study:

> It is based, not upon arbitrary arrangement or opinion, but upon scientific experiments, instituted by Mr. Thos. A. Edison, and conducted by a corps of noted American Psychologists ... It treats music from an entirely new viewpoint – the viewpoint of *what it will do for you*.[17]

In a short essay that concludes the *Mood Music* pamphlet, titled 'Research on Moods and Music', Bingham elaborates on the methodology employed by the research team:

> One difference, between scientific knowledge of the effects of music and unscientific statements, or opinion, is that the evidence for the scientific statements is gathered systematically, under controlled conditions, instead of resting on occasional observation, anecdote, or arm-chair speculation. Moreover, we wanted to determine not how the subject *acts*, but how he *feels* while listening to various selections. We wanted to know which ones made him sad, and which made him exhuberant [*sic*] – and so on.[18]

What is striking about the 'mood music' project from its very inception, as Bingham's statement reveals, is this concern with the psychology of listeners and the affect of listening. Although the Edison Company had concentrated its efforts to date on the technologies of sound and on achieving an aesthetic of 'realism', the research on music and moods marked a notable shift from social space to psychic space – in other words, it staged a turn from the scene of the object to that of the subject. Thus, with its stress on systematically classifying both recordings and listeners, valorizing efficiency in both choosing and responding to music, the 'mood music' project was clearly bound up with the social and cultural currents of the time, implicated in, as already suggested, the general movement towards greater rationalization of both work and leisure in the early twentieth century.

---

configurations of modern sound, Jonathan Sterne's *The Audible Past* focuses more on 'techniques of listening', or what he calls 'audile technique', described as 'a concrete set of limited and related practices of listening and practical orientations toward listening'. Yet Sterne's work aligns with Thompson's in that both insist on the crucial role played by sound and listening in the larger project of modernity, with Sterne's book chronicling 'a set of practices of listening that were articulated to science, reason, and instrumentality and that encouraged the coding and rationalization of what was heard'. See Sterne, *The Audible Past*, pp. 90, 23.

[17] *Mood Music*, p. 3 (emphasis in original).

[18] Ibid., p. 29.

Accordingly, while the organization of production and labour with Ford's assembly line by 1910 and Frederick Taylor's *Principles of Scientific Management* (1911) exemplified the 'science' of human engineering in the modern industrial workplace, thus instantiating the rationalization of mass production,[19] a coextensive development in the sphere of 'leisure' was also taking place. Indispensable to the expansion of this sphere was the field of advertising, which throughout this same period was taking shape as a full-blown industry and had started to employ 'mass psychology'. By the 1920s, as Raymond Williams notes, 'advertising had developed into an art and science', partly by wedding more familiar powers of persuasion with new-fangled notions of 'psychological' advertising.[20] As Stuart Ewen argues in *Captains of Consciousness*, the economic imperative of mass production necessarily required mass consumption, and mass consumption required a far more efficient means of organizing and channelling desire than had previously been attained. Similar to the way 'mood music' work refocused on a listening subject, the advertising world began to turn its sights away from the supposed attributes of the product to be sold and towards the consumers themselves, who were now found to be wanting and in need of the very products conveniently available to cure their (modern) ailments. One such proponent of this budding behavioural psychology, Edward Bernays, considered by Ewen to be 'a founder and leader of modern commercial public relations', is quoted as saying:

> If we understand the mechanism and motives of the group mind, is it now possible to control and regiment the masses according to our will without their knowing it … Mass psychology is as yet far from being an exact science and the mysteries of human motivation are by no means all revealed. But at least theory and practice have combined with sufficient success to permit us to know that in certain cases we can effect some change in public opinion … by operating a certain mechanism.[21]

One such mechanism, which would become much more obvious later in the century with the pervasive presence of Muzak and the use and abuse of rock songs in car commercials, would be music itself and 'what it will do for you' – newly conceived by Edison as 'the working value of music'.

Finally, given the discursive tone and tenor in which the 'mood music' project was constructed, it appears to have been symptomatic of what social historians have dubbed the New Psychology – the dissemination of Freud's work in America where, by 1915, psychoanalysis had become 'a general intellectual

---

[19] For a thorough account of Taylorization, see Martha Banta, *Taylored Lives: Narrative Productions in the Age of Taylor, Veblen, and Ford* (Chicago, IL, and London, 1993).

[20] Raymond Williams, 'Advertising: The Magic System', in *Problems in Materialism and Culture* (London, 1980), p. 179.

[21] Edward Bernays, cited in Stuart Ewen, *Captains of Consciousness: Advertising and the Social Roots of the Consumer Culture* (New York, 1976), pp. 83–4.

phenomenon'.[22] In addition to its assimilation into the realm of modern advertising, demonstrated by Ewen and other scholars, the New Psychology had begun circulating as a discourse; as 'periodical coverage increased dramatically' with articles on Freud and psychoanalysis appearing in, for example, *Good Housekeeping*. Moreover, as John Burnham points out, '[e]xperimenters in art and literature were seeking ways to move beyond surface appearances and discover underlying elements in the same way that social scientists explored a scientific approach to the human mind and character'.[23] Of course, Edison's 'mood music' research was not the first serious study in the psychology of music, since Professor Bingham himself had already published in the nascent field.[24] But it is certainly one of the earliest attempts to analyse 'the effects of music' through scientific method in the service of a market – in short, to rationalize the reception and consumption of music and thus prepare the ground for the eventual commodification of listening itself.

Early Mood Music and the Instrumentalization of Listening

The project was formally initiated in 1920 when Bingham was contracted by the Edison Company to begin research on determining 'the mental effects of music'. Among the goals were the following:

1. 'Classification of musical selections according to their psychological effects'
2. 'Types of listeners'
3. 'Modification of moods by music'.

The researchers also conceived this 'experimental study of music as an aid in synchronizing routine factory operations'.[25]

Such work was undertaken at a time when a number of stories had begun to circulate in the culture on the use of music in the workplace. For example, the 1921 case of a phonograph used in a postal operation was heralded with the following headline: 'A New Edison in the Minneapolis Post Office Lightens Labor and Speeds Up the Energy of the Men.'[26] A similar tale is told in a 1921 issue of *Industrial*

---

[22] John Burnham, 'The New Psychology', in Adele Heller and Lois Rudnick (eds), *1915, the Cultural Moment* (New Brunswick, NJ, 1991), p. 121.

[23] Ibid., p. 123.

[24] See Selfridge-Field, 'Experiments with Melody and Meter', pp. 292–3.

[25] Ibid., pp. 295–6.

[26] Addressing the organizational structure of Edison's factory system, *Scientific American* remarked how 'it is noticeable that order and system reign in every department. Everything is done upon the American, or "piece", system'. Indeed, the larger shape of Edison's 'system of manufacture', according to Andre Millard, involved a shift from skill-based 'craft culture' to a more assembly-line model organized around 'a calculated division

Management in which a phonograph is introduced in a printing shop: 'Without the music the workers plow along at the same old speed. But when the music starts, their fingers fly at a greater speed over the cases and they feed their jobs faster than they ever fed them without the music.'[27] Another item on 'increasing production' through the use of music quotes one Gordon Gray, identified as a 'well-known writer', who is said to have 'great faith in the assistance music can render to labor':

> Pronouncing music an aid to industry, the efficiency fiends have recommended that manufacturing concerns engage tuneful artists whose stimulating selections will urge the employe [*sic*] on to the performance of Herculean labors – the laborer being worthy of his harmony ... Music has power to electrify the laziest employe [*sic*]. Therefore, Mr. Manufacturer, if you see bankruptcy ahead, don't get discouraged; get a piano-player, belt it in and build up your business.[28]

The anecdotal nature of these stories – which the Edison promotional machine was all too eager to press into service – appears to have motivated a side project to the research on mood music. According to company documents, one member of the research team, Esther L. Gatewood of Columbia University's Teachers' College, authored an unpublished paper, 'An Experimental Study of the Use of Music in an Architectural Drafting Room', which began with the somewhat apocryphal reputation of its own subject:

> Many old fables tell of the effect of music upon the feeling and emotions of the hearer, and frequent allusion is made to this fact in more recent literature. Certain studies have been made, confirming the belief that music does have an effect upon the hearer. These investigations, however, have dealt with the passive listener, from the standpoint of enjoyment, of musical pleasure. The effect of music upon work produced or upon people at work has not been systematically studied, altho [*sic*] occasional references to its possible effect have been made.[29]

---

of labor'. Thus, the manufacture of the phonograph, crucial to a cultural history of consumer society, also played a part in the economic history of capital's relations of production. See 'Edison's Phonographic Doll', *Scientific American*, 62/17 (26 April 1890): p. 263. See also Andre Millard, *Edison and the Business of Innovation* (Baltimore, MD, 1990), p. 75. A short notice in a Minneapolis newspaper, 'Phonograph Stirs Postoffice Clerks to Increase Speed' (13 September 1921), was featured in one of the company's monthly publications: 'Real Music and Hard Work', *Edison Diamond Points*, 4/9 (September 1921): pp. 9, 12.

[27]   The *Industrial Management* article by Frank H. Williams, 'Phonograph Reduces Labor Turnover', was quoted in full in 'What Music Does For Labor', *Edison Diamond Points*, 4/11 (November 1921): pp. 16–17.

[28]   'Music Tonic for Workers', *Edison Diamond Points*, 3/5 (April 1918): p. 10.

[29]   Esther L. Gatewood, 'An Experimental Study of the Use of Music in an Architectural Drafting Room', unpublished ms, n.d., Esther Gatewood folder, Box 24, Phonograph Division, Thomas Edison National Historical Park, p. 1.

In order to retell these 'old fables' in the script of social science research, Gatewood outlined the major questions comprising the study:

1. Is music of any help in this particular situation, namely, the actual work of getting out plans in an architectural drafting room?
2. Is music on the contrary a distraction to the work?
3. What type of music is *most* preferred under such circumstances?
4. In what way does the worker feel that music helps, providing, of course, that he does consider it a help?
5. If music were constantly available, in what time units would it be used most advantageously?[30]

Gatewood's findings revealed that the vast majority of the 56 workers surveyed responded that music made work easier, while only six workers 'declared that music distracted them from their work'.[31] In its summary of conclusions, the study highlighted this *lack* of distraction, along with a more far-reaching explication of its findings:

> Music lends aid in two different ways. Many feel that it actually speeds movement, and *most* all workers feel that it has a beneficial effect on the mood of the worker, which in turn is reflected in his work. Some declare that it performs both these functions.[32]

The conclusions to Gatewood's research are interesting for being both behaviouralist – that the music increased the speed of a working body – and psychological – that the music contributed to the well-being of the workers.[33]

Seemingly consistent with the 'mood music' project, the Gatewood study can nonetheless be differentiated from the larger study in its focus on a labouring body and specifically on what should or should not be heard while that body is at work. As with the previously noted instances of music in the workplace, the core purpose behind such efforts was to provide background music that would not distract workers from their work but rather energize a labouring body, alleviate a fatigued

---

[30] Ibid., pp. 3–4.

[31] Ibid., p. 8.

[32] Ibid., p. 16.

[33] It is worth noting that in a letter accompanying Gatewood's report, Bingham wrote Maxwell to underline the kinds of music purportedly having such effects: 'The men working for long periods under high tension find that they need the New Edison music "early and often" to keep themselves in a favorable mood and in a proper condition for rapid, effective work. We may not like to face the facts that the most desired type of music for this purpose is jazz and the least desired, vocal solos. But such are the returns.' W.V. Bingham, letter to William Maxwell, dated 17 March 1921, Box 19, Phonograph Division, Thomas Edison National Historical Park.

body and, perhaps, 'lift the spirits' of a body otherwise preoccupied. The 'mood music' project, to the contrary, shifted its attention from the workplace to that of leisure – the domestic sphere. Moreover, it inverted the figure–ground relation by pushing the role of music from background to foreground not only by offering a form of respite from work itself, but also by directly interpellating listeners – 'what music will do for *you*'. In other words, 'mood music' was intended not to be ignored, but precisely to be heard; 'mood music' had to be heard if it was to *work* on a body exhausted from labouring and the overall strain of modern life.

Akin to the research agenda for the unpublished study on the use of music in an architectural drafting room, the research method for the *Mood Music* work involved a number of listeners, this time subjected to some 589 selections – recordings that, according to Bingham, 'included almost every kind of vocal and instrumental selection, popular and classical, brilliant and subdued, simple and elaborate'.[34] Reports of the listeners fell into three groups: 1) mixed responses; 2) 'selections which produced little or no effect'; and 3) those which 'produced marked effects'.[35] This last group was, of course, precisely what the Edison Company was after. It was determined that 135 selections had 'exerted a marked and definite effect' – that is, much the same effect upon 'numerous different normal listeners'. 'These were the Re-Creations, which could be depended upon to produce desired Mood Changes', wrote Bingham, 'and, as such, they were set aside, classified and arranged in lists, according to the moods which they produced'.[36]

The classifications included 'Moods of Wistfulness', 'Jolly Moods and Good Fellowship', 'Love – and its Mood', 'Moods of Dignity and Grandeur', 'The Mood for Tender Memory', and, lest we forget, 'Devotion is Also a Mood'. In order 'To Make You Joyous', another category that promised to 'change [your] gloomy mood into one of cheerfulness', one might listen to Grieg's 'Butterfly' or Rossini's 'William Tell – Fantasie'[37] (see Figure 2.2). 'To Bring You Peace of Mind', listen to soprano Anna Case's version of 'Home Sweet Home'.[38] 'To Stimulate and Enrich Your Imagination', the 'mood of invention' could be inspired by selections from Bizet's *Carmen* or an evening with Rachmaninov's 'Serenade in B Flat Minor'.[39]

The openly functionalist imperative notwithstanding, it was Bingham's and Edison's hope that 'these lists' would 'start the people of America thinking about and using music in this new, practical and helpful way'.[40] If nothing else, the

34   W.V. Bingham, 'Research on Moods and Music', *Mood Music* p. 29.
35   *Mood Music*, p. 30.
36   Ibid., p. 31.
37   Ibid., p. 14.
38   Ibid., p. 13.
39   Ibid., p. 11.
40   Ibid., p. 31.

Figure 2.2   'A bad jolt in the market. Steadied by music', from the *Mood Music*
              pamphlet.

categories of 'mood music' suggest another way of thinking about genre, in which
the organizing principle had less to do with style than it did with the emotional
state of the listener. In other words, the 'mood music' project consciously engaged
a listening subject – one clearly held to be an effect of specific sounds generating
quite specific responses. What the Edison team imagined, then, was a listening
subject attuned to the commodity experience itself. Picture, they ask in the
publication,

> A tier of shelves in the living room of your house. On each shelf, a row of neat
> volumes. On each volume, a label, perhaps like this:
> 'Ave Maria'
> Play when worried and nervous
> Brings you peace of mind
> You, the mistress of the house, enter. You have been shopping and your nerves
> are on edge. You step to the shelf. It is as simple to choose the music needed to
> soothe your spirit, as it is to find the right seasoning ingredients in your well-
> ordered pantry.[41]

If the situation here seems a touch naive, with a rather predictable concatenation
of gendered signifiers (shopping – home – pantry), the problems that gave rise to
such needs are drawn in the publication as an implacable fact of life:

---

[41]   Ibid., p. 8.

Think of the millions of women who have been suffering with loneliness, exhausted by house-work, torn with the nerve-racking experiences of modern life. Music would have cheered their loneliness, relieved their fatigue, soothed their raw nerves. Think of the millions of men who have been worried with business cares, worn out by work, kept at nervous tension by the struggle for a living. Music might have banished their worries, supplied renewed vigor, brought back the contented frame of mind. Think of the millions of young folks, still in their formative stages, filled alternately with nebulous, soaring ambitions and with puzzled, overpowering discouragements. Music would have inspired them with truer ideals and stimulated their finer instincts. Why, then, has the power of music not been harnessed to the service of man? [42]

Nervous and exhausted from shopping

Soothed and refreshed by music

Figure 2.3   'Nervous and exhausted from shopping. Soothed and refreshed by music', from the *Mood Music* pamphlet.

At the very least, then, the 'mood music' project grounded its purpose in full recognition of the turmoil of modern life, that the subjects of modernity were unduly ravaged by capitalist competition, suffering from the utter exhaustion of consumer society (see Figure 2.3), or paralysed by conflicting influences and impulses beyond the ken of wayward youth. Even as it predictably offered a form of compensation that could only reconcile one to the existing state of things, the 'mood music' effort

---

[42]   Ibid., p. 6.

still acknowledged the toll that modernity took on bodies without exception – bodies that could perhaps be restored only by listening to an Edison recording.

Lastly, the work on 'mood music' also took on a more public face in the form of what the Phonograph Division designated as 'mood change parties', hundreds of which were held during the course of the two-year research project. Auditing Edison records (of course), listeners were encouraged to fill out a 'mood change chart', described as 'an analysis of your mental reactions to music', which documented one's potential change of mood: serious to gay, worried to carefree, nervous to composed (see Figure 2.4). A few high-profile 'mood change experiments' were even conducted at Yale, Harvard and Columbia universities. A newspaper account of the 'mood change test' given to a class in Yale's Psychology Department in 1921 remarked how the tests were 'directed toward alleviating neurotic conditions, with a view of discovering psychological antidotes for depressed conditions of mind whether due to fatigue or disappointment'.[43] While these Ivy League 'mood change' events lent an air of legitimacy to the proceedings, company documents reveal that Thomas A. Edison, Inc. had few illusions about the project's scientific merits. In a letter to Edison, William Maxwell highlighted that two 'mood change demonstrations' had taken place at Columbia University, with four more arranged at City College, adding, 'Don't know that these College demonstrations will lead to many sales, but they certainly dignify the proposition and make it easier to book in homes.'[44] In a follow-up letter, Maxwell wrote:

> ... even if this research work was actually of no value, it provides us with a background and gives us an atmosphere, which is of incalculable value. I think scientists and the public at large now concede to us unquestioned leadership in the field of developing and providing the true benefits of music ... So long as we keep these psychologists at work for us, I think we have the field largely preempted, and their work provides a splendid background for practical sales promotion work, such as the Mood Change Chart, which is a very good example of what I mean. I prepared the Mood Change Chart and got Dr. Bingham to approve it. We were thus able to present it to the public, as a piece of research work, and not as a sales promotion scheme.[45]

---

[43]   'Note Changes in Mood Caused By Hearing Music', *New Haven Sunday Register*, 22 May 1921, clipping file folder, Box 20, Phonograph Division, Thomas Edison National Historical Park. See E.C. Boykin, 'Putting Over Mood Change Parties: Sophisticated New York City Finds Them Unique and Refreshing – Educational Institutions Co-Operate on This Big Psychological Experiment', *Edison Diamond Points*, 4/5 (April 1921): pp. 6–7. See also 'Mood Change Parties a New Sensation', *Edison Diamond Points*, 4/4 (March 1921): pp. 14, 18.

[44]   William Maxwell, letter to Edison, dated 14 March 1921, Box 19, Phonograph Division, Thomas Edison National Historical Park.

[45]   William Maxwell, letter to Edison, dated 19 March 1921, Box 19, Phonograph Division, Thomas Edison National Historical Park.

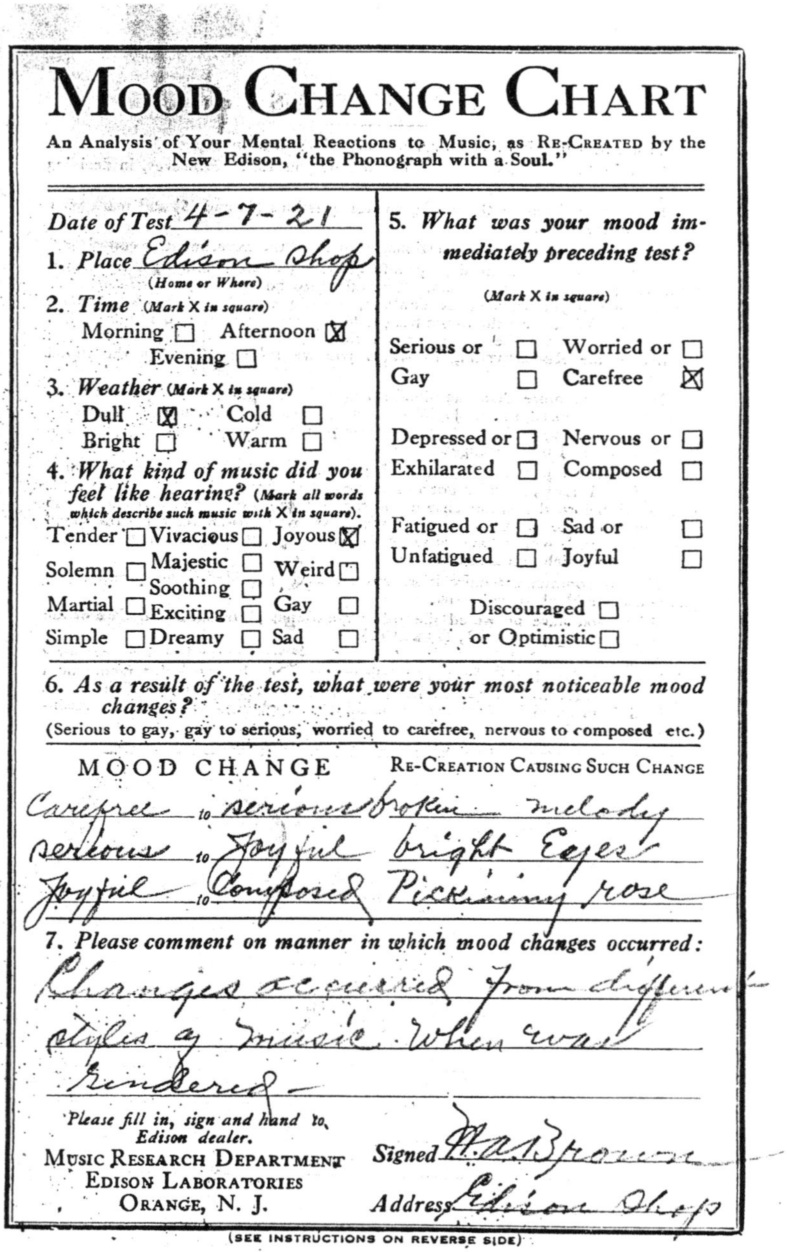

Figure 2.4   Mood Change Chart filled out. Courtesy of US Dept of the Interior, National Park Service, Thomas Edison National Historical Park.

For the most part, then, the 'mood change experiment', under the guise of high-minded empirical research, was yet another Edison sales campaign – cleverly pitched as a form of 'parlor entertainment'. 'We live in an age of self-analysis', states the trade publication promoting the 'mood change parties', 'and the Edison Mood Change Chart offers one of the most fascinating means of studying emotional reactions'.[46]

In trying to rationalize the market in music by analysing the psychic experience of listening, thereby contributing to the instrumentalization of listening itself, the Edison research in early mood music could be heard as a kind of pre-echo of developments to come. For if we now, nearly a century later, find ourselves immersed in a sea of sound – ambient music, background, foreground, surround sound, what Anahid Kassabian calls 'ubiquitous music'[47] – then we are also immersed in a sea of science – drowning in countless studies and research on the effects and influences of music on the behaviour of restaurant patrons, supermarket patrons, shoppers everywhere. As Kassabian points out, such conditions provoke a question of aural subjectivity, resonating with our now accustomed mode of listening. Yet we are not only dispersed and distributed, as she argues, throughout a network of noise, pulsing along an endless electronic environment in a kind of pre-Oedipal flow, but we are also positioned, I would suggest, situated and structured as objects of study in a kind of dialectical dance of social and cultural (post)modernity.

---

[46]   'Mood Change Parties a New Sensation', p. 14.

[47]   Anahid Kassabian, 'Ubiquitous Listening', in David Hesmondhalgh and Keith Negus (eds), *Popular Music Studies* (London, 2002), pp. 131–42.

Chapter 3

Radio Symphonies: The BBC, Everyday Listening and the Popular Classics Debate during the People's War[1]

Christina Baade

The preference for Tchaikovsky among radio listeners is as significant a commentary on the inherent nature of the radio voice as on the broader social issues of contemporary listening habits.

Theodor W. Adorno (1941)[2]

Thanks to 'Our Love' and 'Moon Love' for introducing me to Tchaikovsky – in fact thanks to the whole BBC for all my worldly knowledge.

Letter to *Radio Times*, 17 November 1939[3]

In Humphrey Jennings's and Stewart McAllister's 1942 documentary, *Listen to Britain*, the audience is guided, ear first, through a series of sounds and images in the wartime British landscape. The diversity of music genres and environmental sounds is striking, as is the fluidity with which the film moves across lines of social class, traverses sites of work and leisure and shifts between depicting live and broadcast performances. These juxtapositions are amplified in the film's climactic sequence, which features Dame Myra Hess and the RAF Symphony Orchestra performing Mozart's Piano Concerto No. 17 in a lunchtime concert at a transformed National Gallery, its permanent collection replaced for the duration by sandbags and war art. Guided by what David Rosen calls 'the roving eye of the camera', we observe a range of attentive and inattentive listening practices as we ourselves listen: an audience member follows the performance in her score, shop girls eat sandwiches, members of the forces examine paintings and the

---

[1]   An earlier version of this chapter was presented at 'The Proms and British Musical Life' conference at the British Library in 2007. Many thanks to the head archivist Jacquie Kavanagh and that invaluable resource, the BBC Written Archives Centre, for permission to quote BBC copyright material.

[2]   Theodor W. Adorno, 'The Radio Symphony' (1941), in *Essays on Music*, ed. Richard Leppert (Berkeley, 2002), p. 266.

[3]   (Mrs) B. Taylor, letter to *Radio Times*, 17 November 1939, p. 14.

Queen closely observes the performers from her front-row seat.[4] While it depicts classical music's diverse wartime audience, the Mozart sequence also ensounds its new role as an accessible morale-booster, set, as it is, between another lunchtime performance – the popular duo Flanagan and Allen performing their song, 'Underneath the Arches', for workers in a factory canteen – and industrial noise.[5] The use of harmonic modulation from song to concerto and an audio dissolve from Mozart into noise integrates the concert into the everyday wartime soundscape, rather than setting it apart in the ritualized space and time of the concert hall.

The concerto sequence in *Listen to Britain* embodied two powerful and contradictory understandings of classical music and its role in Britain's war effort. On the one hand, it represented a democratic vision of 'great' music, reaching and appealing to a diverse audience of forces and civilians, workers and royalty. In 1942 symphonic music seemed ubiquitous in wartime Britain: on the BBC; in women's films, where concertos populated the soundtracks; in variety theatres; and even in the repertory of dance bands and theatre organs, where it appeared in special arrangements and in popular songs like 'Moon Love'.[6] Surveys by Mass-Observation and BBC Listener Research confirmed that classical music had gained in popularity during the war while the press reported that 'orchestra mania' was sweeping the country.[7] The rise of the 'popular classics', as the repertory of well-known classical and romantic symphonic works by Tchaikovsky, Beethoven and others was known, resonated with People's War ideologies of fairness, which held that the best of culture belonged to all.[8] Especially in a war against Germany, whose national image involved a proprietary relationship with great music, the notion of the popular classics countered the epithet applied to Britain as 'the land without music' and offered a hopeful vision of a future in which Britain would be a musical leader. For those invested in bringing the benefits of classical music to the masses, the popular classics confirmed the effectiveness of their campaign.

---

[4]   David Rosen, 'The Sounds of Music and War: Humphrey Jennings's and Stewart McAllister's *Listen to Britain* (1942)', in Cliff Eisen (ed.), *'Coll'astuzia, col giudizio':* *Essays in Honor of Neal Zaslaw* (Ann Arbor, MI, 2009), p. 420.

[5]   *Listen to Britain* (UK, 1942), dir. Humphrey Jennings and Stewart McAllister, reissued by Image Entertainment (2002). Also available online: 'LISTEN TO BRITAIN, 1942?', uploaded by PublicResourceOrg, 2 December 2009 <http://www.youtube.com/ watch?v=6h8pHumy7NE> (accessed 25 April 2012).

[6]   Ivan Raykoff, 'Concerto con Amore', *Echo*, 2/1 (2000) <http://www.echo.ucla.edu/ volume2-issue1/raykoff/raykoff-article.html> (accessed 25 April 2012); and 'Hylton Saves the Phil. Orch.', *Melody Maker*, 3 August 1940: p. 1.

[7]   Mass-Observation Archive, File Report 1138, 'Music: Effect of the War on the Musical Tastes of Panel', 6 March 1942; BBC Written Archives Centre, 'Listener Research Bulletin No. 103', 12 September 1942, R9/1/2; and A.K.H., *Liverpool Post*, quoted in 'Notes and News', *The Musical Times*, January 1943, p. 27.

[8]   Sonya O. Rose, *Which People's War? National Identity and Citizenship in Britain 1939–1945* (Oxford, 2003), pp. 25, 31.

On the other hand, for many critics, the popular classics and their mass audience promised not a democratic utopia but an active threat to serious music. At the heart of their concern was the way the popular classics could transform the 'complete and satisfying metaphysical world' of serious music into mere anodyne entertainment.[9] By their very accessibility, both in intellectual terms and in convenience, the popular classics 'trivialized' serious music (to use Adorno's term), tearing it from the site of ritual and depositing it into the everyday.[10] Meanwhile, the ignorant enthusiast became a figure of concern for serious music critics and listeners. The ignorant enthusiast embodied the challenges of 'gaining adherents' to good music without diluting the composer's intentions, suffocating diversity in the repertory or having music degenerate from a 'cultural force' into a 'mere spiritual sop'.[11] From this perspective, the threat embodied in *Listen to Britain*'s National Gallery sequence lay not in its cheap tickets, but in its tolerant depiction of inattentive listening, the way it cut Mozart's score to serve the dramatic aims of the film and in the equivalence it implied between Mozart and music-hall song. The audio dissolve into factory noise punctuated this strikingly modern depiction of music instrumentalized for war.

Whereas the demographic trends towards classical music appreciation were understood as a new wartime phenomenon, the concerns about inattentive listening and trivialization were not. In many ways, such concerns were a symptom of modernity as it had developed during the preceding decades: they were a reaction to sound technologies that brought recorded and broadcast performances into domestic spaces; to the growth of leisure time and the commercialized entertainment to fill it; to progressive ambitions for universal education, cultural uplift and true democracy; and to the expanding divide, in practice and discourse, between high culture and mass commercial culture.[12] The wartime embrace of music as a morale-builder heightened the urgency of resolving what many regarded as the incompatible aims of expanding the audience for classical music while preventing its trivialization. Indeed, the debate over the popular classics hinged more upon whether trivialization and ignorant enthusiasts could be tolerated or were a problem to be combated.

---

[9]   'The Fortress of the Spirit', *The Listener*, 28 September 1939, p. 606; and Scott Goddard, 'Broadcasting and the Teaching of Music', *The Listener*, 20 July 1939, p. 153.

[10]   Adorno, 'Radio Symphony', p. 261.

[11]   BBC Written Archives Centre, 'Music Policy', BBC Internal Circulating Memorandum, from the Director of Music to the Controller of Programmes, 14 November 1939, R27/245/1.

[12]   See D.L. LeMahieu, *A Culture for Democracy: Mass Communication and the Cultivated Mind in Britain between the Wars* (Oxford, 1988); Andreas Huyssen, 'Mass Culture as Woman: Modernism's Other', in *After the Great Divide: Modernism, Mass Culture, Postmodernism* (Bloomington, IN, 1986), pp. 44–62; James J. Nott, *Music for the People: Popular Music and Dance in Interwar Britain* (Oxford, 2002); and Mark Katz, 'Making America More Musical through the Phonograph', *American Music*, 16/4 (1998): pp. 448–75.

No organization in Britain was more implicated in these debates than the BBC, which played a central role in the nation's musical life. By the beginning of the war, it was the nation's top employer of musicians while its fees for compositions and popular songs represented 54 per cent of the Performing Rights Society's income. Its ensembles, most notably the BBC Symphony Orchestra, set the standard for well-rehearsed performances while appearing on its wavelengths helped establish the careers of theatre organists, dance bandleaders and popular singers. Reaching between 70 and 80 per cent of the population by the late 1930s, the BBC had become part of the nation's everyday life.[13] Although it could not ignore entertainment, the public-service corporation emphasized education and cultural uplift in its programming – a mission that expanded during the war to include the support of morale and national unity. Critics, listeners and musicians responded by subjecting the BBC's wartime music policy and programming decisions to careful scrutiny and, often, vigorous debate. This was particularly the case with the 1942 'BBC Music Policy', written by the Controller of Programmes Basil Nicolls and the new Director of Music, the composer and conductor Arthur Bliss, which attempted to resolve the conflict between 'the cult of maximum audience' and 'purely musical consideration' in the BBC's wartime programming.[14]

For some observers, like Theodor Adorno, who in his 1941 essay, 'The Radio Symphony', interrogated the project of serious music broadcasting, the conflict was impossible to resolve. Although Adorno offered penetrating insights into the musical and social ramifications of situating symphonic music into the everyday, the BBC's policy decisions, grounded as they were in broadcasting practice and wartime necessity, were arguably more revealing of the 'broader social issues of contemporary listening habits'. To investigate the uneasy alchemy of classical music, broadcasting and the everyday, this essay focuses on two issues at the heart of the wartime popular classics debate: the repertory and rituals of the BBC's symphonic broadcasting and the corporation's regulation of popular arrangements and adaptations of classical repertory.

'An Enobling Spiritual Force': Converting Listeners to 'Great Music'

In 1943, on the occasion of the BBC's twenty-first birthday, *The Times* reflected, 'Now a farm labourer near Land's End, a tram driver in Newcastle, a shopkeeper in Abergavenny can and do say what they think of symphony, song, and chamber

---

[13]   Christina L. Baade, *Victory Through Harmony: The BBC and Popular Music in World War II* (New York, 2012), p. 3.

[14]   BBC Written Archives Centre, 'BBC Music Policy', draft by the Controller of Programmes amended in accordance with suggestions made by the Director of Music [Sir Adrian Boult], the Deputy Director of Music and Arthur Bliss, 1 April 1942, R27/73/1. Arthur Bliss replaced Adrian Boult as Director of Music on 1 April 1942; Boult continued at the BBC in his role as conductor of the BBC Symphony Orchestra.

music ... Music, an aristocratically developed art, has been democratized by radio.' *The Times* acknowledged the limitations of the shift, particularly in the 'crude and intolerant' response of many listeners and the ways broadcasting distorted the sonorities of large performing forces, but it praised the BBC for spreading 'the seed of musical experience, appreciation, and knowledge'.[15] Such qualified praise was precisely the type with which Adorno took issue in 'The Radio Symphony'. For Adorno, radio's dampening of dynamic and timbral subtleties in symphonic performance, along with the substitution of a mono-aural, domestic medium for the encompassing concert-hall experience, were only the start of the problem. Radio listening transformed the symphony into aural wallpaper; it converted the work from a structural totality into a series of 'pre-digested' themes that rewarded the 'passive sensual and emotional acceptance' of commodity fetishism rather than active musical thought. Although romantic works of 'melodic inventiveness' and 'structural poverty' fared well over radio, the medium did violence to Beethoven's symphonies; 'moreover', Adorno noted, 'it is very likely that Beethoven is listened to [via radio] in terms of Tchaikovsky'.[16] He concluded: 'No ... educational attempt is worth undertaking that does not give the fullest account of the antagonistic tendencies promulgated by serious music in radio.'[17]

As Richard Leppert has pointed out, Adorno's critiques emerged in an American context, where he heard 'great music' promoted as such by the commercial networks.[18] On American commercial radio, symphonic broadcasts were 'prestige' programming, set among popular fare aimed at a mass audience, whereas on the non-commercial, public-service BBC, they were at the heart of its mission of education and cultural uplift. For Sir John Reith, the BBC's first Director General, it would have been a travesty to devote the service to lowest-common-denominator entertainment. During the 1920s and 1930s the BBC Music Department pursued a three-pronged approach in its programming. First, it aimed to educate all listeners about serious music by featuring regular performances of the standard classical repertory and music appreciation talks. Second, it programmed challenging repertory aimed at the musically knowledgeable.[19] Finally, its administration also came to encompass light music ensembles, brass bands and military bands, which played salon music, marches and approachable classical music (often in arrangement); such respectable fare could serve as a gateway to better things. Although they may have regarded serious music as a transcendent value, Music Department staff did not delude themselves about the transparency of the medium or their institutional power. As the 1942 'BBC Music Policy' insisted, '[t]he BBC

[15] 'Broadcasting and Music', *The Times*, 19 November 1943, p. 6c.

[16] Adorno, 'Radio Symphony', pp. 253–66.

[17] Ibid., p. 269.

[18] Richard Leppert, 'Commentary', in Theodor W. Adorno, *Essays on Music*, ed. Richard Leppert (Berkeley, CA, 2002), pp. 216–17.

[19] Jenny Doctor, *The BBC and Ultra-modern Music, 1922–1936: Shaping a Nation's Tastes* (Cambridge, 1999), pp. 81–9.

exists to further the cause and develop the art of music *through broadcasting* ...
even when at times loyalty to the requirements of broadcasting seems to conflict
with non-broadcasting musical and professional considerations'.[20] The following
sections will examine how the BBC 'further[ed] the cause' of classical music
during the interwar period, at the onset of war and on its new wartime wavelength,
the Forces Programme.

Inventing Classical Broadcasting: The Interwar Period

During the 1920s and 1930s the BBC was, essentially, in the process of inventing
serious music broadcasting, and Music Department staff devoted considerable
energy to addressing 'the antagonistic tendencies' of broadcasting serious music.
The major challenge was that programmers and audiences conceptualized the role
of radio in very different terms: whereas BBC staff regarded music broadcasting
as an analogue to concert attendance, many listeners conceptualized the wireless
as blending the domestic convenience of the gramophone with the continuous,
live background music offered in modern sites of leisure, such as tea shops, dance
palais and cinemas. For these listeners, radio offered a steady stream of music
and entertainment, which they could audit in states of awareness that ranged from
close attention to distraction.[21] The BBC opposed 'tap' listening, but it could
only encourage – not compel – listeners to cultivate what the music education
broadcaster Percy Scholes called the 'habit of Attention'.[22] As the *BBC Yearbook*
of 1930 exhorted, 'Listen as carefully at home as you do in a theatre or concert
hall. You can't get the best out of a programme if your mind is wandering, or if you
are playing bridge or reading. Give it your full attention.'[23] The BBC also engaged
in a number of 'guerrilla' tactics to discourage unplanned listening. Most notably,
it avoided regular time slots, necessitating listeners to consult the programme
guide and plan their listening in advance. The practice relaxed only in the late
1930s when the BBC 'lightened and brightened' its programming in response to
competition from English-language commercial radio from continental Europe.[24]

Although the BBC eschewed time slots, it cultivated other temporal rhythms.
In the Music Department the privileged scheduling unit was the live concert
(and recital). As Jenny Doctor has shown, serious music programming, ranging
from small to large ensembles, was organized into daily and weekly cycles,

---

[20]   BBC Written Archives Centre, 'BBC Music Policy', 1942.

[21]   Paddy Scannell and David Cardiff, *A Social History of British Broadcasting,
Volume 1: 1922–1939: Serving the Nation* (Oxford, 1991), p. 373.

[22]   Percy Scholes, *Music Appreciation: Its History and Techniques* (New York, 1935),
p. 117.

[23]   *BBC Yearbook* (1930), p. 60, quoted in Scannell and Cardiff, *A Social History of
British Broadcasting, Volume 1*, p. 371.

[24]   Baade, *Victory Through Harmony*, p. 21.

which culminated in a concert broadcast by the BBC Symphony Orchestra in the prime evening hours.[25] The BBC also reinforced yearly cycles, particularly after it assumed the sponsorship and organization of Sir Henry Wood's Promenade Concerts in 1927, transforming them into a national music festival that attracted large audiences with affordable tickets, exposed concertgoers to both standard and new repertory and celebrated British culture.[26] The Proms highlighted another key aspect of the BBC's mission: to attract audiences to live performances by the BBC Symphony Orchestra and other ensembles. Radio was a critical tool in disseminating music, but no Music Department member would have regarded it as a replacement for concert attendance. Indeed, the BBC's efforts to educate listeners and promote concert organizations did much to solidify the modern concept of the symphony concert as a site of highbrow, sacralized culture. Between the 1890s and 1920s, as Christopher Small and Lawrence Levine have shown, concert rituals and the relationships underpinning them became increasingly formal, characterized by professional musicians playing complete works, dedicated spaces, dimmed lighting and a docile, attentive audience, which had been schooled not to whisper, nap, eat, fidget, arrive late or leave early.[27] The BBC's instructions for listeners at home echoed those that had been used to tame concertgoers during the preceding three decades.

In addition to combating inattentive listening, Music Department staff emphasized training listeners in how to engage actively and intellectually with serious music, rather than treat it with 'passive sensual and emotional acceptance'.[28] The BBC's extensive, often adventurous, repertory was noted by *The Times*, which observed, 'It ransacks the byways of the orchestral repertory and it gives first performances of new works of every school with a proper disregard of what its wireless listeners think.'[29] It was the Music Department's responsibility to advance the cause of the art and to serve the needs of the minority that understood and appreciated serious music; administering lesser (if still respectable) fare like dance bands and cinema organs fell to the Variety Department. Music Department staff greeted the 1936 arrival of systematic audience research as a threat to artistic integrity, for the value of its music broadcasts could not be measured in terms of audience size.

---

[25]   Jenny Doctor, '"Virtual Concerts" – The BBC's Transmutation of Public Perform-ances', paper presented at the conference 'Britannia (Re-) Sounding: Music in the Arts, Politics, and Culture of Great Britain', organized by the North American British Music Studies Association, Oberlin, OH (June 2004), unpublished.

[26]   David Cannadine, 'The "Last Night of the Proms" in Historical Perspective', *Historical Research*, 81/212 (2008): pp. 315–49.

[27]   Christopher Small, *Musicking: The Meanings of Performing and Listening* (Hannover, NH, 1998); and Lawrence W. Levine, *Highbrow/Lowbrow: The Emergence of Cultural Hierarchy in America* (Cambridge, MA, 1988), pp. 190–91.

[28]   Adorno, 'Radio Symphony', pp. 266–7.

[29]   'Broadcasting and Music', p. 6c.

'In Defense of Civilization': Symphonic Music for a Nation at War

The declaration of war on 3 September 1939 made urgent a reassessment of the relationship between serious music broadcasting and listeners, a process that had tentatively begun during the late 1930s. In what was regarded widely as 'a war in defense of civilization', the Music Department's primary responsibility continued to be 'the presentation of the best music of all categories, planned in a comprehensive scheme and performed under the best possible conditions', as the Director of Music Adrian Boult asserted in a policy statement issued in November 1939.[30] These aims had to be balanced with the BBC's broader wartime priorities of supporting national unity and boosting morale, which entailed not only the 'permanent strengthening and underpinning' of great music, but also light entertainment that offered 'relief and relaxation'.[31] Unfortunately, both quality and morale-boosting had suffered in the first weeks of the war when, as part of required air-raid precautions, the BBC cancelled the Proms, evacuated the BBC Symphony Orchestra to Bristol, replaced most live performances with gramophone recitals and reduced its service to a single wavelength.

As live music broadcasting regained its feet, the single wavelength continued to pose a challenge: listeners who sought alternatives to the BBC's signal were likely to turn to enemy stations, so it was vital to appeal to a mass audience. Boult and his department aimed to broaden serious music's appeal, according to the new 'Music Policy' document, by 'the shortening of programmes where artistically possible, and the rigorous ruling-out of the mediocre'. Responding to 'the prevailing psychological conditions' (that is, in order to boost morale), they emphasized 'the great classics, as this literature contains the finest and most inspired musical thinking'. Rather than attempting to confound distracted listening, as it had before the war, the BBC now accommodated thematic (as opposed to structural) modes of listening, so deplored by Adorno, which depended on familiarity, melodic detail and emotion. During the week of 26 November 1939, which Boult's document presented as a model for the new policy, few serious music concerts or recitals ran over 45 minutes, and nearly all focused on the standard repertory.[32] For example, Wednesday's concert by the BBC Symphony Orchestra, which was performed before a live audience in Bristol and represented the 'backbone' of the Corporation's orchestral broadcasting, featured Elgar's *Enigma Variations* and Rachmaninov's *Rhapsody on a Theme of Paganini*.[33] Other orchestral broadcasts featured well-known works by Mozart, Beethoven, Mendelssohn, Dvořák and Smetana. More recent symphonic music, such as Honegger's *Pastorale d'été*, tended to be tuneful.

---

[30]   'Wireless in War', *The Listener*, 7 September 1939, p. 464; and BBC Written Archives Centre, 'Music Policy', 1939.

[31]   'The Fortress of the Spirit', p. 606; and 'Wireless in War', p. 464.

[32]   BBC Written Archives Centre, 'Music Policy', 1939.

[33]   Programme Listings, *Radio Times*, 24 November 1939; and Ralph Hill, 'Radio Music in 1940', *Radio Times*, 29 December 1939, p. 6.

Interspersed with popular variety shows like *Itma*, concerts by the BBC Salon Orchestra, 'outside broadcasts' of dance bands from West End hotels, detective dramas, war-themed talks, the news and religious services, such concerts promised to interest – or, at least, not drive away – non-specialist listeners. The risk was that the BBC might alienate 'purists', who themselves might turn to enemy stations, and fail to sustain the continued development of the art.[34]

The single wavelength remained in place until January 1940, and during that time the BBC struggled to resolve the tension between appealing to a broad audience while placating purists. Throughout the autumn, music critics and individual listeners excoriated the BBC for its reductions in serious music, particularly during the prime evening hours. 'Lovers of café music, light music, variety music … these folks got what they wanted. But … one could not but feel that the authorities were forgetting the existence of the musically intelligent', wrote Scott Goddard in *The Listener*.[35] In December the BBC finally began to defend itself, drawing upon the new 'Music Policy' document and its analysis of programming during the week of 26 November 1939. This 'average week' featured 18 orchestral concerts and 25 recitals, with eight programmes in each category scheduled during 'evening or "high spot" periods'.[36] In total, the BBC had aired 26 hours of serious music, which, exclaimed Ralph Hill, the serious music critic for the BBC programme guide *Radio Times*, was 'more than a fifth of the whole week!'.[37] According to *The Listener*, the 'nightly average of seventy-five minutes' met 'the average man's – even the trained musician's – ability to listen attentively' without overwhelming him (or her) with 'musical indigestion'. Music-lovers who complained about sharing the wavelength were being 'unconsciously Nazi-minded' in their demand for *Lebensraum* in the airwaves.[38]

Scolding aside, Hill, *The Listener* magazine, and Boult himself in a broadcast talk, promised that serious offerings would improve in 1940. The BBC would reintroduce concerts of contemporary and early music, feature more 'outside concert organizations', like the Hallé Society, and begin a new series of public concerts by the BBC Symphony Orchestra.[39] The revival of pre-war approaches

---

[34]   BBC Written Archives Centre, 'Music Policy', 1939; and Compton Mackenzie, 'Editorial: The BBC', *Gramophone*, February 1940, p. 307.

[35]   Scott Goddard, 'Broadcast Music during 1939', *The Listener*, 28 December 1939, p. 1296.

[36]   'The Musical Table d'Hôte', *The Listener*, 28 December 1939, p. 1264; and Hill, 'Radio Music in 1940', p. 6.

[37]   Hill, 'Radio Music in 1940', p. 6.

[38]   'The Musical Table d'Hôte', p. 1264. *Lebensraum* (literally, 'living space') was the German foreign-policy objective that justified the invasion of Poland and precipitated the war. Published by the BBC, *The Listener*, which printed radio talks, editorials and new content, advanced the corporation's educative mission with a more literate segment of the listenership than the populist *Radio Times*. See Debra Rae Cohen, 'Intermediality and the Problem of the *Listener*', *Modernism/Modernity*, 19/3 (2012): pp. 569–92.

[39]   Ibid.; and Hill, 'Radio Music in 1940', p. 6.

to repertory and concert (as opposed to studio) performances was enabled by the Forces Programme, which began broadcasting on an experimental basis during the evening hours on 7 January and expanded to a 12-hour a day service on 18 February.[40] With the Forces Programme providing a light alternative, the Home Service could finally carry longer programmes requiring sustained concentration. No longer did the BBC have to hold the entire nation's attention all of the time.

The Popular Classics, Soldier-Listeners and the Forces Programme

Although it functioned for programmers and listeners as a light alternative, the Forces Programme, as its name suggested, was promoted as being especially designed for the forces. Soldiers, sailors and airmen listened communally in 'billets, dug-outs, messes, and canteens', where listening was by necessity distracted and subject to interruption, whether by 'conversation or by the call of duty'.[41] 'No man can listen to chamber music or a serious play in those conditions, even if his companions will let him', explained *The Listener*.[42] The Forces Programme featured content that could withstand inattentive listening: sport, light and popular music, and news, all presented in a less formal manner. It was the listening conditions that necessitated the change, the BBC was careful to clarify, not the men themselves: 'they are a special section of the old listening public transferred to new and peculiar surroundings. Bodies of men need an approach different from that most suitable for the family circle.'[43] That the circumstances were special should not obscure the fact that the BBC was embarking upon a radically new programming approach, in which inattentive and 'tap' listening were not only recognized, but also actively supported. The Forces Programme developed a large following among civilian listeners, who themselves were encountering 'new and peculiar surroundings' on the home front, but the BBC justified the shift by emphasizing potent wartime tropes of masculine bonding and 'the soldier-hero'.[44] Framing the audience in these terms helped legitimate experimentation in light-entertainment formats and even in programming for distracted listening.

The regard for the Forces Programme as the primary service for the troops also led to the expectation that it should serve the full spectrum of forces' listening interests. Thus, the Forces Programme included token offerings for those with minority tastes, although programmers emphasized the light and popular music favoured by the majority. The category of light music was expansive: comprising

---

[40] Baade, *Victory Through Harmony*, p. 48.

[41] 'Special Programmes for the Forces beginning this Week', *Radio Times*, 5 January 1940, p. 5; and 'Full-Time Programmes for the Forces', *Radio Times*, 16 February 1940, p. 3.

[42] 'The Stuff to Give the Troops', *The Listener*, February 1940, p. 308.

[43] Ibid.

[44] Rose, *Which People's War?*, p. 160.

roughly half of the music broadcast each week and ranging from brass bands to small 'tea shop' ensembles, it was appreciated by both officers and enlisted men.[45] In contrast, preferences for classical and popular music split along lines of class, age and rank, with more officers preferring classical music and more enlisted men preferring dance music; the fortunes of these genres on the wavelength changed as the BBC moved from prioritizing morale-boosting entertainment to education.[46] During the first two years of the Forces Programme, popular music was a significant presence and represented, by early 1941, more than half of all music on the wavelength, whereas vanishingly little classical music was aired, ranging from 3 per cent in May 1940 to 6 per cent in February 1941.[47]

In its most distinctive classical programmes, *Orchestral Half Hour*, *These You Have Loved* and *Forces Music Club*, the Forces Programme departed from the model of concerts and recitals that had characterized serious music broadcasting on the pre-war BBC and wartime Home Service. Adopting formats that were unique to radio and emphasizing familiar selections from the lighter classical repertory, the programmes contributed to the wartime rise of the popular classics. *Orchestral Half Hour* aired almost monthly between February 1940 and mid-1942; as the name implied, it continued the wartime policy of offering classical music in short doses. It tended to feature overtures and ballet music, rather than symphonic movements, and favoured well-known romantic composers like Tchaikovsky. By offering continuous live music uninterrupted by announcements, the programme not only forestalled the perception of 'lecturing', but also facilitated its use as background listening in communal settings.[48] As Listener Research Department studies confirmed, communal, distracted listening remained the rule in the forces throughout the war: 'The Forces do not listen to the wireless – they hear it … the general hubbub makes it impossible to "listen" except when very close to the set, sitting on someone else's bed with one's greatcoat on!' wrote one soldier.[49]

These You Have Loved, which ran intermittently throughout the war, contrasted strikingly with *Orchestral Half Hour*, for it was a gramophone-records programme

---

[45]   According to analyses of sample weeks in the Programmes as Broadcast logs conducted by Rob Greenway, the figures ranged from 61 per cent in May 1940 to 41 per cent in February 1941 and back to around 50 per cent from August 1941. Rob Greenway, 'A Balance of Music on the Forces Programme' (BA thesis, University of York, 2007), pp. 17, 44.

[46]   According to a 1944 survey, 17 per cent of officers preferred classical music as opposed to only 7 per cent of enlisted men. Twenty-one per cent of enlisted men preferred dance music against only 3 per cent of officers. BBC Written Archives Centre, 'Type of Entertainment', October 1944, R34/185, quoted by Greenway, 'Balance of Music', p. 47.

[47]   Greenway, 'Balance of Music', pp. 17, 44, 51.

[48]   Ibid., pp. 40–41.

[49]   BBC Written Archives Centre, Listener Research Weekly Report No. 60, 15 November 1941, R9/1/1.

based around the personality of its commère, Doris Arnold.[50] Her 'refined taste' and careful selection of recordings created a strikingly cohesive programme of 'everybody's favourite songs and melodies', encompassing repertory from Sibelius's *Finlandia* to Handel's 'Largo', its signature tune.[51] Although *These You Have Loved* began airing in November 1938, the programme gained new significance on the Forces Programme, where the attractive and sympathetic Arnold gained an enthusiastic following among the troops: 'any number of portraits of Doris have been given places of honour in billets in France and elsewhere', reported the *Radio Times*.[52]

Orchestral Half Hour and *These You Have Loved* inhabited a liminal terrain between light music and the popular classics, well suited to a wavelength that served as a light alternative to the Home Service. In 1941, however, the BBC began to increase the proportion of classical music represented on the Forces Programme. Major Richard Longland, a BBC army liaison officer and a critical figure in the shift, explained, 'However generally popular the programme may be now, we are quite likely to be shot at in the future for not having provided any really substantial musical fare for the Forces, or rather for not having made a very definite effort to improve the taste.'[53] Indeed, classical music advocates had criticized the programme since its inception for its steady stream of 'Forces bilge'.[54] In early 1941 Longland convened a meeting between BBC staff and forces representatives to learn what classical music 'would be acceptable to the swing and theatre-organ devotees, but which would also satisfy both the middle-brows and those who liked really good music'.[55] The committee determined that the route to raising tastes lay in presenting familiar works (that is, popular classics), such as Handel's *Water Music*, Tchaikovsky's *Swan Lake* and Wagner 'concert selections', in 'invigorating' programmes with presentation that was 'simple and direct, never patronizing or quasi educational'.[56]

---

[50]   Having entered the BBC as a shorthand typist, Arnold was the first woman 'to produce and present her own radio show, *The Melody Is There*, in 1937'. See Catherine Murphy, '"On an Equal Footing with Men?" Women and Work at the BBC, 1923–1939' (PhD thesis, Goldsmiths College, University of London, 2011), p. 193.

[51]   M.N. White, letter to *Radio Times*, 26 September 1941, p. 8; Cover, *Radio Times*, 22 August 1941, p. 1; and Doris Arnold, 'These You Have Loved', *Radio Times*, 10 May 1940, p. 10.

[52]   'The Broadcasters', 'Both Sides of the Microphone', *Radio Times*, 19 April 1940, p. 8; and Arnold, 'These You Have Loved', p. 10.

[53]   BBC Written Archives Centre, Major Longland, letter to Mr. Isaacs, 24 May 1941, R27/228.

[54]   Robin Hull, letter to *The Musical Times*, September 1941, p. 345.

[55]   BBC Written Archives Centre, 'Good Music in the Forces Programme', BBC Internal Circulating Memorandum from Richard Longland to the Controller of Programmes, c. 1941, R27/228.

[56]   BBC Written Archives Centre, 'Music for the Forces Programme', BBC Internal Circulating Memorandum from Richard Longland to the Director of Music, 24 April 1941, R27/228.

The series that most effectively implemented the strategy was *Forces Music Club*, developed by Alec Robertson. From September 1941 each instalment featured a handful of forces men and women, who discussed musical activities in their unit, and the BBC Symphony Orchestra, which played the music that they selected. Like the popular jazz show *Radio Rhythm Club*, whose name it echoed, *Forces Music Club* was designed to serve a special musical minority in the forces – in this case, those who appreciated classical music but '[found] it hard to exercise their tastes in the close company of scores who do not share them'.[57] Although classical music continued to be a minority taste, its proponents in the forces, among civilians and within the BBC were influential, and its representation in the Forces Programme had increased to over 11 per cent by August 1942. Meanwhile, the quantity of popular music fell to 38 per cent of musical programming on the Forces Programme, a counterintuitive development for a light wavelength – and one not supported by the BBC's own listener research.[58]

The shifting ratios of classical to popular music on the Forces Programme were the result of a sea change in BBC policy during 1942, signalled by a new 'Music Policy' document issued on 1 April, which coincided with the arrival of Arthur Bliss as the new Director of Music. In the wake of serious military setbacks in North Africa and Asia, Bliss asserted a muscular new vision for serious music to an admiring press. Playing upon his status as 'a towering ex-Grenadier Guardsman', the *News Review* evoked Bliss's uncompromising attitude: 'Vowed he: "I want to make great music the finest entertainment it is possible to have. The Fighting Services should be treated like princes and given only the best in music."'[59] Not only did the 1942 'BBC Music Policy' enshrine Bliss's optimistic belief that 'the best possible broadcast performance of all worthy music' was compatible with 'winning the largest possible audience, thereby continually raising public taste', but the BBC's programming during that year seemed to prove it.[60] *The Musical Times* noted 'a greatly improved state of things' for classical music on the Forces Programme and, reflecting upon the repertory that had aired during 1942, it observed, 'The listener with a fair amount of leisure time is probably better able to gain an education in the masterpieces than at any previous time.'[61]

The changes at the BBC coincided with accounts describing the ubiquity of public concerts, particularly those focusing on the 'popular classics', and a growing sense that the nation's tastes were improving. Early in 1942 the social survey organization Mass-Observation asked its voluntary National Panel 'what effects, if any, the war

[57] C. Gordon Glover, 'This Week's Miscellany', *Radio Times*, 29 August 1941, p. 5; and Greenway, 'Balance of Music', p. 37.

[58] Greenway, 'Balance of Music', pp. 44–50.

[59] 'Radio: For the Princes', *News Review*, 16 April 1942, BBC Written Archives Centre Press Cuttings.

[60] BBC Written Archives Centre, 'BBC Music Policy', 1942.

[61] 'Notes and News', *The Musical Times*, December 1942, p. 378; W. McN., 'The BBC Comes of Age', *The Musical Times*, December 1943, p. 367.

had had upon their musical tastes'. It reported that, among the 'largely middle and artisan class' respondents, 'the main lines of change are towards a greater appreciation of "classical" music or a decreased appreciation of dance music'.[62] The findings of the BBC Listener Research Department echoed those of Mass-Observation: according to its longitudinal wartime surveys, appreciation of classical music was growing while violent hostility towards it was shrinking (the opposite was true for dance music and cinema organs).[63] The most dramatic change was the 1941–1942 decline of individuals who professed 'hostility' to symphonic concerts – from 40 per cent to 28 per cent.[64] Despite the rise of the popular classics and their associations with the People's War virtues of democracy and inclusion, popular and classical music continued their binaristic dance. At the BBC, the reassertion of serious music as 'an ultimate value' and masculine, patriotic, pursuit correspondingly cast popular music as a problematic, even effeminate, area of musical endeavour, requiring careful supervision. As the next section will explain, the pursuit of 'the best possible performance' entailed a renewed policing of the boundaries of classical music, a reweighing of the aims of education and entertainment, and the identification of a new wartime deviant: the ignorant enthusiast.

'The Best Possible Performance': The Trouble with Transcription

On 1 April 1942, his first day as Director of Music, Arthur Bliss banned 'Concerto for Two', a swung classic based on Tchaikovsky's Piano Concerto No. 1 in B-flat.[65] Written in 1941 by the American Jack Lawrence, the song capitalized on the recent Bette Davis melodrama *The Great Lie* (1941), which featured both a concert pianist and the concerto itself. Extending the theme, the introduction in the December 1941 recording of the song by the well-regarded bandleader Carroll Gibbons evoked the realm of the concert hall, featuring both a solo piano and a harmonic reworking of the memorable four-note brass motive that opened the work. The bombast quickly gave way, however, to a chorus, which offered the first movement's opening theme, refashioned as a foxtrot.[66] Bliss was unimpressed. In

---

[62]   Mass-Observation Archive, 'Music: Effect of the War on the Musical Tastes of Panel'. Mass-Observation qualified its findings, explaining that '58% of the sample said their tastes were unchanged, and 11% never had any interest in music to speak of'.

[63]   BBC Written Archives Centre, Listener Research Bulletin No. 103, 12 September 1942, R9/1/2.

[64]   Robert Silvey, 'Paper on Listener Research for Royal Statistical Society', BBC Internal Circulating Memorandum, from the Listener Research Director to the Controller of Programmes, 23 May 1944, R9/15/1, BBC Written Archives Centre.

[65]   BBC Written Archives Centre, '"Concerto for Two" and "Tchaikovski's B Flat Concerto (Modern Dance Band Arrangement)"', BBC Internal Circulating Memorandum from the Director of Music, 1 April 1942, R27/73/1.

[66]   Carroll Gibbons and the Savoy Hotel Orpheans, *Time Was ...* (Empress Music, 1996).

his memorandum forbidding the broadcast of 'Concerto for Two', he described the song as an affront to music-lovers and the 'Russian people', comparing Lawrence's treatment of the concerto to the Germans' rumoured destruction of Tchaikovsky's home and manuscripts.[67] He noted that the song was the first to be banned under the new music policy, which classified most jazzing of the classics as 'definitely offensive and musically harmful'.[68]

Bliss's objections to 'Concerto for Two' echoed those of numerous *Radio Times* correspondents: 'This war is bad enough, but when one of man's most valuable compensations – music – is pilfered, robbed, and dressed up in the disreputable garb of "Tin Pan Alley", things are going from worse to worst', fumed one writer.[69] Widely understood as an American import, swung classics developed as a way of circumventing the 1939 American Society of Publishers, Authors and Composers' ban on the broadcast of its catalogue; big-band arrangers soon realized that basing new works on public-domain pieces was an excellent way of earning additional royalties, and swung classics became an important popular subgenre.[70] Although critics cast them as violating the sanctuary of classical music, swung classics could also be seen as existing at the edge of a continuum of classical adaptations, arrangements and transcriptions; they were a striking reminder of the porous boundary between popular and classical music, everyday listening and the concert hall. Indeed, with themes drawn from works by Tchaikovsky, Mozart and Rimsky-Korsakov, swung classics (and other popular adaptations) existed symbiotically with the rise of the popular classics in orchestral contexts, each reinforcing the recognizability and marketability of the other.

Despite language that cast swung classics as a new offence against classical music, the boundaries between classical and popular music had long been fluid. In the nineteenth century, parlour song adopted bel canto opera accompaniment styles, minstrel shows featured opera burlesques and working men's brass bands played arrangements of symphonic movements and opera overtures.[71] In an era before widespread sound reproduction, such popular adaptations (as well as more faithful piano transcriptions) were an important means for listeners to explore the classical repertory. Music appreciation advocates from the 1920s embraced phonography and radio as providing the opportunity to study the repertory in its 'original' form; however, light music ensembles, brass bands, military bands, dance bands and theatre organs, continued to play classical arrangements.[72] Thus, even as new

---

[67]   BBC Written Archives Centre, '"Concerto for Two" and 'Tchaikovski's B Flat Concert"'.

[68]   BBC Written Archives Centre, 'BBC Music Policy', 1942.

[69]   P.H. Mack, letter to *Radio Times*, 10 November 1939, p. 5.

[70]   David W. Stowe, *Swing Changes: Big-Band Jazz in New Deal America* (Cambridge, MA, 1994), pp. 94–5.

[71]   Levine, *Highbrow/Lowbrow*, pp. 92, 96; and Trevor Herbert, *The British Brass Band: A Musical and Social History* (New York, 2000), p. 55.

[72]   See Scholes, *Music Appreciation*; and Katz, 'Making America More Musical'.

technologies offered listeners direct access to the work as the composer intended, the interwar expansion of live music – in cinemas, tea shops and dance palais – also made the experience of classical music in arrangement an everyday experience.

For Adorno, even the most faithful transcription destroyed the structural integrity of the work. Indeed, his critique of the radio symphony lay in the fact that broadcasting transformed the 'original' version into something like 'the softened chamber music arrangement, which, by virtue of its mere arrangedness, easily approaches the sound of the so-called salon orchestra'.[73] Arrangements encouraged 'quotation listening', in which a theme was heard in a setting that removed it from the context intended by the composer. A theme in quotation became banal and entered into the commoditized realm of popular music, where the act of recognition – rather than engaged, structural listening – was the driving force. In turn, exposure to adaptations and arrangements changed listeners' approach to the original work, which they would begin to hear as a string of quotations, the recognition of which would 'prove [listeners] to be small cultural owners within big ownership culture'.[74] Ownership was, of course, a mirage and a sad substitute for true agency and cultural knowledge.

Adorno's discussion of quotation listening helps explain why Bliss regarded swung classics as 'musically harmful'. Particularly for less educated listeners, they promoted a mode of listening that would yield only a superficial understanding of classical music. The objections of Bliss and other classical music advocates went deeper, however: for them, popular music inhabited the category of the abject (that is, both irredeemably low and disavowed by the symbolic order).[75] As the 1942 'Music Policy' explained, '[t]he BBC ... accepts [dance bands and cinema organs] as a musical activity of a low order and should see to it that they are adequately controlled and directed and are as good of their kind as possible'.[76] For such ensembles to play classical music, whether transcribed or adapted, amounted to a desecration. The practice, however, was pervasive at the BBC in ensembles, including cinema organs and dance bands, as well as light orchestras, military and brass bands, and small light combinations.

The 1942 'Music Policy' and Transcription

The reason for the pervasiveness of classical transcription at the BBC was not only fashion, but also, as the 'Music Policy' document affirmed, the fact that

---

[73]   Adorno, 'Radio Symphony', p. 260.

[74]   Ibid., pp. 263–4; and Theodor Adorno (with the assistance of George Simpson), 'On Popular Music' (1941), in *Essays on Music*, ed. Richard Leppert (Berkeley, CA, 2002), p. 453.

[75]   See Julia Kristeva, *Powers of Horror: An Essay on Abjection*, trans. Leon S. Roudiez (New York, 1982), pp. 1–2.

[76]   BBC Written Archives Centre, 'BBC Music Policy', 1942.

live performance was its 'preferred' mode for music broadcasting. Transcription was contentious, however, and much of the sweeping new music policy was devoted to establishing the bounds of acceptability for the practice. Whereas Basil Nicolls, the Controller of Programmes, asserted that audience size was 'almost paramount' in serious music broadcasting, even if it meant performing the classics in transcription, Bliss and other Music Department staff maintained that the BBC's priorities included sustaining high musical standards, thus limiting the priority given to attracting large audiences and the role of musical transcription and adaptation.[77] The final document reflected a compromise between the two positions: 'The BBC's policy is to accept what purists would regard as unwarranted transcriptions of the classics in order to further the ultimate objective [of gaining "adherents"]. There are limits however to this acceptance.' Transcriptions had to maintain 'faithfulness to the original text', and the standard of performance had to be excellent. Military and brass bands, both of which had long traditions of playing classical transcriptions, fulfilled the criteria.[78] Not incidentally, they were also ensembles associated closely with the masculine and solidly British terrains of martial culture and working men's associations.

Forms of live entertainment that had expanded during the interwar years fared less well under the new criteria. These included dance bands with their repertory and instrumentation imported from America, theatre organs associated intimately with the popular pastime of the cinemagoing, and even light music ensembles, whose numbers expanded exponentially to provide background music for leisure. According to the new 'Music Policy' document, the problem with light music transcriptions arose when light music ensembles abandoned their repertory of operettas, Strauss waltzes and pieces like Bucalossi's 'Grasshopper's Dance' for more ambitious works, 'e.g. the Overture to "Tannhauser" – by octets, etc.'. Especially in the case of small ensembles, this was not only unfaithful to the original text; it was 'absurd'. Indeed, the light music output, which comprised roughly half of all music broadcast by the BBC, had come to be dominated by small ensembles, leading to 'a certain lack of virility'.[79] As another report put it, '[t]he sounds they produce are generally thin and listless, and their programmes consist mainly of abbreviated, emasculated versions of music originally written for a full orchestra, or dainty little pieces written for teashop ensembles'.[80] The solution implemented throughout 1942 involved using larger ensembles, encouraging 'a vigorous and healthy idiom' and vetting programmes to ensure the use of 'more robust material'.[81]

---

[77]   Nicholas Kenyon, *The BBC Symphony Orchestra: The First Fifty Years, 1930–1980* (London, 1981), pp. 193, 175.

[78]   BBC Written Archives Centre, 'BBC Music Policy', 1942.

[79]   Ibid.

[80]   BBC Written Archives Centre, 'Light Music Investigation' [1942], R27/172/1.

[81]   BBC Written Archives Centre, 'BBC Music Policy', 1942.

Although dance bands did not carry the same associations with effeminacy, their commercial, mass appeal rendered their interpretations of the classics problematic in the new music policy. From the 1920s, inspired by Paul Whiteman's symphonic jazz, dance bands frequently integrated light classical numbers into their programmes. The BBC's house bandleaders Jack Payne and Geraldo enthusiastically continued the practice, both on and off the air, and often employed string complements. For example, in a 1941 Albert Hall charity extravaganza, 'Music in the Modern Form', Geraldo conducted a 70-strong orchestra in 'one of the most mixed programmes ever heard at that august venue': the selections included the 'Polovetsian Dances' from Borodin's *Prince Igor* and the *William Tell* overture, along with 'Tea for Two' and 'St. Louis Blues'.[82] *Melody Maker*'s 'Mike' (the critic Spike Hughes) deplored the practice as pretentious and criticized bandleaders who had 'appointed themselves educators-in-ordinary to the semi-musical public', but others celebrated the role that dance bands played in advancing the cause of music appreciation.[83] In *Kings of Rhythm*, Peter Noble argued that dance versions of classical music had resulted in

> ... a steady increase of interest in 'straight' classical music from listeners whose first contact with the great melodies of all time came through dance-band 'transcriptions'. Whatever may be one's owns views on this question, there can be no argument but that dance-music has brought in its wake an understanding and high regard for music from masses of people who in the 'nineties', for example, would not have considered themselves 'musical' in any sense of the word.[84]

Classical music advocates warned, however, that popularizing the classics risked making them intellectually moribund. One listener wrote to the *Radio Times*:

> Those who advocate 'music for the people' and an ever diminishing allotment for more cultivated listeners must face an inescapable fact. If the spearhead of progress is dulled and flattened by neglect and indifference no more great music will be created. It will die of suffocation by the majority.[85]

In the months leading up to the BBC's new music policy, a debate over classical adaptations for the theatre organ raged in the pages of the *Radio Times*, culminating in an on-air debate between its two belligerents: the music critic Ralph Hill and the variety columnist C. Gordon Glover. The catalyst was an all-Tchaikovsky recital

---

[82] 'Geraldo's Super Albert Hall Concert', *Melody Maker*, 13 December 1941, p. 1; and Peter Noble, *Kings of Rhythm: A Review of Dance-Music and British Dance-Band Personalities* (London, n.d. [1944]), p. 24.

[83] 'Mike' [Spike Hughes], 'Stop the Jazzing-Up Pop-Song Process!', *Melody Maker*, 7 February 1942, p. 5.

[84] Noble, *Kings of Rhythm*, p. 7.

[85] Ralph Hill, 'Some Music – and Letters', *Radio Times*, 27 August 1943, p. 4.

by the theatre organist Reginald Foort, given on Sunday 21 September 1941, which opened with 'Waltz of the Flowers' from the *Nutcracker Suite* and closed with the *1812 Overture*. In an anticipatory column, Glover observed that, despite the objections by serious musicians, the public responded more favourably when introduced 'to the symphonic gospel' by theatre organists than by 'direct assault'. He concluded: 'On the whole it seems to me that the playing of certain classics on the theatre organ is not only justifiable but laudable.'[86] Hill responded by distinguishing popular adaptations from respectful transcriptions, bemoaning the growth of the 'cheapjack approach to great music'. He continued in high dudgeon:

> What musicians would object to is a cinema organist playing, say, the slow movement of Tchaikovsky's Fifth Symphony with the original harmony and rhythm jazzed up, and all the slimily vulgar mechanical 'effects' ... substituted for the original orchestration.[87]

Radio Times readers soon entered the fray, with one pronouncing Foort's version of Tchaikovsky's *1812 Overture* to be 'a rare musical feast'.[88] Hill scoffed at such hapless musical taste and declared the theatre organ, 'with its stops for puling babies, thunderstorms, ack-ack guns, and tanks (water and other)', to be the 'ideal medium' for the bombastic overture while 'Two Hopeful Schoolgirls' expressed dismay that the BBC allowed adaptations 'for the enjoyment of ignorant people'.[89]

The debate became personal when Hill excoriated Glover's musical tastes, and Glover responded that Hill and his 'orchidaceous' supporters preferred to enjoy their music in 'priggish' isolation.[90] Hill gleefully accepted the mantle of closed-mindedness, but defended himself against the charge of priggishness:

> If 'a breath of the lusty air of the ordinary world' of music means listening to some emasculated crooner mouthing 'Will this be moonlove, nothing but moonlove ...' to the first theme of the slow movement of Tchaikovsky's Fifth Symphony, I prefer infinitely the atmosphere of the hot-house.[91]

Hill effectively inoculated the appreciation of serious music from the 'taint' of queerness.[92] Although serious musical pursuits in Britain had long been regarded

---

[86] Glover, 'This Week's Miscellany', *Radio Times*, 19 September 1941, p. 5.

[87] Ralph Hill, 'This Week's Radio Music', *Radio Times*, 26 September 1941, p. 5.

[88] W.E. Payne, letter to *Radio Times*, 2 October 1941, p. 8.

[89] Ralph Hill, 'This Week's Radio Music', *Radio Times*, 10 October 1941, p. 4; and 'Two Hopeful Schoolgirls', letter to *Radio Times*, 10 October 1941, p. 8.

[90] Hill, 'This Week's Radio Music', 10 October 1941, p. 4; and C. Gordon Glover, letter to *Radio Times*, 17 October 1941, p. 4.

[91] Hill, letter to *Radio Times*, 24 October 1941, p. 4.

[92] Alan Sinfield coined the term 'inoculation' to describe how playwrights like Noël Coward preserved the likability of the leading characters for mainstream audiences: 'the

as unmanly, Hill displaced charges of effeminacy on to popular crooners, reinforcing the masculinity of serious musical pursuits. Indeed, the vehemence of his response, and the energy with which the BBC defended canonical works from the 'abuses' of theatre organ and dance bands, betrayed the difficulties of asserting the inherent value, virility and straightness of classical music while also promoting it as a uniting force for British listeners.

In the matter of transcriptions, the 1942 'Music Policy' document limited theatre organs to 'lesser classics' and instructed that they observe 'good taste in registration', reflecting the moderating influence of the BBC theatre organist Sandy Macpherson, rather than that of Hill or Glover.[93] Like other advocates for adaptations of classical repertory, Macpherson took as self-evident the superiority of great music in its original form, although he regarded categorical opposition to adaptation as elitist. In his own act of inoculation, he distinguished between careful adaptations that might lead listeners to seek 'better' music and the 'jazzing up' of a theme or movement. The latter, Macpherson charged, was the prerogative of 'the dance-band and Charing Cross Road [that is, British popular music publishers] community', not – apparently – theatre organists.[94]

The 1942 'Music Policy' and Swung Classics

The claim that swung classics could promote classical music appreciation was an almost indefensible position at the BBC. In his comments on Nicolls's 'Music Policy' draft, Bliss was firm: '"Mr Christ comes to town" [an oblique reference to Alec Templeton's popular "Bach Goes to Town"] will win no more adherents to the Sermon on the Mount. The missionary aim is defeated by the vulgarity of the Hollywood setting.'[95] For their critics, swung classics not only failed to convert listeners; they were an abject genre and threatened to pollute both the classics and the minds of their audiences. Elements of anti-Americanism and racism characterized some of the critiques of the practice, such as when 'Playfellow' observed, '[I]t bears all the characteristics of a primitive negro outlook. In its love of high-lights alone … it is a form of mental infantilism'.[96] Swung classics drew upon serious music's catchiest melodies and set them in a popular context, leaving development, lengthy movements and harmonic complexity behind. They debased the field of serious music by treating its repertory as raw material, rather

---

principals may be somewhat effeminate, but the really despicable queer is someone else'. See Alan Sinfield, *Out on Stage: Lesbian and Gay Theatre in the Twentieth Century* (New Haven, CT, 1999), pp. 104–5.

[93]   BBC Written Archives Centre, 'BBC Music Policy', 1942.

[94]   Sandy Macpherson, letter to *Radio Times*, 10 October 1941, p. 8.

[95]   Arthur Bliss, *As I Remember* (London, 1970), p. 150.

[96]   'Playfellow', '"Swinging" of the Classics', *Huddersfield Daily Examiner*, 22 January 1942, BBC Press Cuttings.

than approaching individual works reverently on their own terms. Moreover, they expanded the field of who could consider himself or herself a lover of Tchaikovsky or Ravel, without doing the necessary music appreciation homework.

Unsurprisingly, the new music policy took its hardest line in the matter of classical adaptations with dance bands, which were to be confined 'to their own genre', and swung classics, which were to be prohibited except in the cases of 'serious experiments ... aris[ing] from a sincere artistic impulse'. Implementing the policy consistently would require diligent effort, and Nicolls soon established the Dance Music Policy Committee, with members drawn from the Music, Variety, and Programme Planning Departments, to enforce the new rules. Although most of its energy was devoted to enforcing the BBC's wartime ban on male crooners, overly sentimental female singers, sentimental songs and songs that were offensive to Allied sensibilities, the Committee also enforced a strict ban on swung classics, beginning with its first meeting on 31 July when it banned five swung classics, including Glenn Miller's arrangement of the 'Anvil Chorus' from *Il Trovatore*.[97] The prohibition of swung classics was, according to *The Star*, the Committee's 'one inviolable rule', and it remained in place even after the war.[98]

The Committee also worked to maintain the distinctions between performances by dance bands and light music ensembles, reflecting the 'Music Policy''s position on 'confining ... dance-bands to music in their own genre'.[99] Although bandleaders and many Variety Department producers regarded classical transcriptions as a legitimate component of their repertory, Music Department staff objected to dance bands performing light classical music in what they regarded as an inept and tasteless manner.[100] Variety Department staff soon recognized that a double standard was at work. Whereas dance bands were forbidden from playing classical adaptations in the name of 'good taste', the Music Department poached '[Variety's] own artists – Noel Gay, Phil Green, Noel Coward, and so on' for its programmes, leading to unwelcome duplication. 'If this sort of encroachment doesn't stop', the producer Cecil Madden wrote, 'I shall be forced to engage Toscanini ... in self-defense!'[101] In response to backlash from the Variety Department, by late 1942 the Dance Music Policy Committee moved to a strict limit on the amount of popular

[97] BBC Written Archives Centre, Dance Music Committee Minutes, 31 July 1942, R27/74/1.

[98] Untitled article, *The Star*, 22 December 1942, BBC Written Archives Centre Press Clippings.

[99] BBC Written Archives Centre, 'BBC Music Policy', 1942.

[100] BBC Written Archives Centre, 'Committee on Dance Music Policy, etc.', BBC Internal Circulating Memorandum from Overseas Music Director (K.A. Wright) to the Assistant Controller of Programmes, 6 May 1942, R27/73/1.

[101] BBC Written Archives Centre, 'Who Does What?', BBC Internal Circulating Memorandum from Mr. Cecil Madden to Empire Music Supervisor, 12 June 1942, R27/416/1.

music that light ensembles could play.[102] Enforcing the segregation of repertory into classical and popular remained a challenge, however, for the potpourri repertory of many light music ensembles and dance bands mapped uneasily on to the BBC's bipartite structure for music administration (Music versus Variety) and broadcasting (Home versus Forces). Something-for-everyone programming might embody People's War ideals of diversity and inclusiveness, but it also threatened the broadcasting-specific imperatives of avoiding the overduplication of repertory, maintaining the best possible performance and preserving the logic of choice between serious offerings on the Home Service and popular material on the Forces Programme.

Even as the BBC struggled to establish clear distinctions between serious, light and popular music broadcasting, the familiar works favoured by popular and light music ensembles figured with increasing prominence in popular classics programmes of symphony orchestras, 'cashing in on the market for orchestral music'. Nothing symbolized the new popularity – and commodification – of the popular classics better than the ubiquity of Tchaikovsky's Piano Concerto No. 1 in B-flat Minor, from which 'Concerto for Two' had taken its theme. In his discussion of the 'orchestra mania' sweeping the country, A.K.H., the *Liverpool Post* music critic, cited the example of the London Philharmonic Orchestra and 'another southern orchestra', both of which performed the piece at their Nottingham concerts in the same week. For the discerning, mass popularity tainted Tchaikovsky's First and other concertos, including Rachmaninov's Second and Gershwin's *Rhapsody in Blue*. A.K.H. warned that the growth of such audiences led to 'a dead monotony ... enveloping the concert scene all over the country', but others argued that the popularity of such repertory, given judicious programming, could help expose neophytes to a much broader range of the symphonic literature.[103] Although purists debated the implications of ignorant enthusiasts joining the ranks of concertgoers, they all conceded that the war had changed the orchestral landscape.

Conclusion

In June 1944 the music publisher Ralph Hawkes speculated on the causes of the unprecedented 'boom' in music during the war:

> I think the present popular popularity of orchestral music is largely due to its sedative qualities, its power to refresh minds and nerves jaded by the privations and anxieties of war ... But there is another factor: public education by radio ... the activities of [the BBC], over a period of fifteen years, have resulted, by and

---

[102]   BBC Written Archives Centre, Dance Music Committee Minutes, 13 November 1942, R27/74/1.

[103]   A.K.H., *Liverpool Post*, quoted in 'Notes and News', p. 27; and letter to *The Musical Times*, March 1943, p. 91.

large, in a higher standard of taste and have brought into being a considerable new public for serious music.[104]

The Mozart concerto sequence in *Listen to Britain* celebrated the ability of classical music to engage and boost the morale of a wide range of wartime citizens, who engaged with the music in many different ways. And yet, the depiction of music's powerful impact was not unique to the Mozart sequence; rather, it was apparent throughout the film for a wide range of contexts and musical genres.

This equalization of musical genres and engagement resonated with Adorno's ultimate concern in 'The Radio Symphony'. Radio, as a medium, forced listeners to engage with orchestral music much as they engaged with popular music: as a commodity, in a mode of 'passive sensual and emotional acceptance'.[105] Although it embraced the broadcasting of orchestral music, the BBC itself struggled against uncritical modes of listening, the commodification of serious music and classical adaptations that altered the original text too much. Since its founding, the BBC had striven to promote the values of the concert hall to a wide audience, and during the war it finally seemed to have succeeded. Not only did audiences flock to popular concerts, but popular arrangements of classical works, and even swung classics, offered a simulacrum of 'great' music. Concert halls became not simply a sacralized realm, but also everyday spaces that could be accessed as a part of the wartime democratization of culture – or its commodification. The problem of swung classics and ignorant enthusiasts, however, was not that they transformed classical music into a commodity; rather, it was that they revealed the interpenetration of the everyday and the sacralized, popular and classical, live and broadcast, as well as the ways in which all musicking was both communal and transactional. The music educational experiment of the BBC had succeeded in a wave of People's War idealism, but not (as Adorno might have predicted) in the manner its proponents had hoped.

---

[104]   Ralph Hawkes, 'Music in the Open Air', *Tempo*, June 1944, p. 10.
[105]   Adorno, 'Radio Symphony', pp. 266–7.

PART II
Technologies

Chapter 4
Sound, Perception and Mobile Phones in India

Amit S. Rai

This essay attempts a sort of science fiction of sound in India's new media assemblage. Speculative fiction is the best mode, I argue, to capture the biomorphic unconscious of media assemblages.[1] Employing a 'machinic phylum' methodology adapted from Deleuze and Guattari[2] and Manuel Delanda,[3] I chart the shift in perceptual capacities in the movement from public to private sound, from the single-screen talkie to the multiplex to the headset, and the deepening of privatized sound experiences in contemporary value-added services in mobile telephony.

The concept of 'machinic phylum' developed a techno-vitalism running through Simondon, Leroi-Gourhan, McLuhan, Parisi, Goodman and, of course, Hansen, Massumi and Deleuze and Guattari. The attributes of this concept are immanence and conjunction, both understood as different orders of movement. In other words, the concept allows for a kind of dynamic typology of machines. John Marks notes that the 'originality of Deleuze's materialism' is closely tied to the terms 'machine' and 'machinic'. According to Marks, Deleuze, in his book *Foucault*,[4] considers that new human forms opened up through the combination of the forces of carbon and silicon. However, argues Marks, this statement should not necessarily be read in 'terms of the human body being supplemented or altered by means of material prostheses'. The machine that Deleuze invents is a speculative fiction with a material history, an 'abstract phenomenon that does not depend entirely upon physical and mechanical modifications of matter'. The machine is instead 'a function of what might be thought of as the "vital" principle of this plane of consistency, which is that of making new connections, and in this way

---

[1]   Matteo Pasquinelli, *Animal Spirits* (Rotterdam, 2008); Steve Goodman, *Sonic Warfare: Sound, Affect, and the Ecology of Fear* (Cambridge, MA, 2009).

[2]   Gilles Deleuze and Félix Guattari, *A Thousand Plateaus*, trans. Brian Massumi (Minneapolis, MN, 1987 [1980]); Gilles Deleuze, *Spinoza: Practical Philosophy*, trans. Robert Hurley (San Francisco, CA, 1988 [1970]); Gilles Deleuze and Félix Guattari, *What is Philosophy?*, trans. Hugh Tomlinson and Graham Burchell (New York, 1994 [1991]).

[3]   Manuel Delanda, *Intensive Science and Virtual Philosophy* (New York, 2002); Manuel Delanda, *Deleuze: History and Science* (New York, 2010).

[4]   Gilles Deleuze, *Foucault*, trans. Sean Hand (Minneapolis, 1988 [1986]).

constructing what Deleuze calls "machines"'.[5] Gary Genosko, in his article on Félix Guattari, generates the other image of the machinic phylum:

> [Guattari's] *Cartographies schizoanalytiques* and *Chaosmose* elaborated nonrepresentational maps of the self-engendering processes of subjectification, pragmatically attending to the specific ways in which singularities come together, through four ontological functions of the unconscious, their interfaces, and the character of their components: material fluxes and machinic phylums; existential territories and incorporeal universes.[6]

However, we can grasp all four aspects of this ontology as simultaneously actual and discursive on the plane of expression, and virtual and non-discursive on the plane of content. It is this counter-actualization towards the virtual that we will explore with this speculative fiction.

Given the overwhelming prevalence of voice over data in contemporary mobile usage in India, this chapter pursues a set of interrelated questions: what happens to the social and habitual experience of sound through the micro-speakers of the contemporary handset? How do operators, value-added service providers and the everyday user negotiate this new technology? How have headsets (with both listening and microphone capacities) changed these negotiations? How is sound (as data and experience) secured through changes in perception as bodies assemble anew with mobile technology?[7] Finally, how does sound interact, connect and disrupt other senses such as tactility, vision and proprioception that emerge through this body–machine assemblage?

To Begin

First were my mother's VCRs. I say VCRs for, I suppose, obvious reasons, but her pirated library found many lives in my immigrant childhood of 1980s Orange County, California (behind the Orange Curtain). I see this vitalism of the machine as something that shifts analysis beyond the relation between diasporic identity and the narrative form of Hindi filmic melodrama. Indeed, it is one thing to say we

---

[5]   John Marks, 'Materialism', in Adrian Parr (ed.), *The Deleuze Dictionary* (Edinburgh, 2005), pp. 156–7.

[6]   Gary Genosko, 'Guattari, Pierre-Félix (1930–92)', in Parr (ed.), *The Deleuze Dictionary*, pp. 121–3.

[7]   'Body' here refers to a non-coinciding resonant unity, a moving whole, whose durations, intensities, tactility, vibrations and perceptions are resonant with each other across a whole set of functions, fluxes and phase transitions. It is the body of affectivity, or capacities and tendencies, which have a reality and a virtuality, a mode of capture. This body, like Lucretius' 'clinamen' (a swerve of atoms), has habits of becoming: a swerve within a statistical reality.

lived the melodramas; but if we grant the machinic phylum its fully ontological status, diasporic video piracy is a form of machinic becoming. From around that time I recall the necessary relation between practice, perception and movement.

How does sound, through the micro-speakers of the contemporary handset, feed back with the experience of embodied movement itself?

The mobile phone is a convergent, cross-platform, multi-use device that is portable, intimate and dynamically networked.[8] What is the scale, pattern and speed of this dynamic networked device in India?[9] In diagramming media effects, the speed, scale and pattern of interactions of a given media are each qualitative multiplicities that change in kind by dividing themselves through intensive variation. As the speeds of information flow – the scale of mobile uptake and the habits of information technology – affected the everyday lives of diverse populations in India, a qualitative difference in perceptual capacities was produced. Since the deregulation of the telecom industry in 1997, the mobile has emerged as a catalyst for economic growth and new consumerist practices, as well as the resurgence of government sponsored fraud, corruption and nepotism on a massive scale. Used to support social and economic development initiatives ranging from disease surveillance to increasing access to financial services (that is, neoliberal debt), mobile phone connections are approaching 700 million in India today. Since 2004, when the cost of a mobile subscription dropped dramatically and thus became accessible to more and more Indians, the subscriber base has grown on average by 6 million a month, adding 19 million users in December 2009; as of May 2012 the number of mobile phone subscribers was at 929.37 million.[10] The average cost of a mobile phone in India is less than INR 10,000 (ca. USD 180), with Motorola offering the lowest at INR 800 (ca. USD 14), and India's own Micromax at INR 980 (ca. USD 17);[11] Micromax sells a phone that can last up to a week on one charge and up to a month on standby mode, targeting rural populations with limited access to electricity. Indeed, agricultural development and increasing the productivity of rural populations have been two of the much-touted benefits of mobile phones in India,[12] even though the lack of an effective policy and regulatory environment, as well as the poor availability of ICT and mobile infrastructure in rural areas,

---

[8]   Mizuko Ito, Daisuke Okabe and Misa Matsuda (eds), *Personal, Portable, Pedestrian: Mobile Phones in Japanese Life* (Cambridge, MA, 2005).

[9]   Marshall McLuhan, *Understanding Media: The Extensions of Man* (New York, 1964).

[10]   IMAI (Internet and Mobile Association of India), *Report on Mobile VAS In India: 2010* <http://www.iamai.in/rsh_pay.aspx?rid=TyuYXL2OyFA=> (accessed 10 June 2012).

[11]   With 208 handsets with an aggregate price of INR 2,089,945 this averages to INR 10,048, the lowest being Motorola WX180 at INR 800 and the second lowest Micromax x100 at INR 980 (November 2010 figures). See 'Mobile Phone Prices and Price List for India', *Fonearena* <http://www.fonearena.com/mobile_phone_pricelist.html> (accessed 1 November 2011).

[12]   IMAI, *Report on Mobile VAS In India: 2010*, p. 1.

is widely acknowledged. Despite the fact that average revenue per user declined by over 50 per cent from 2006 to 2009, according to some estimates mobile networks are contributing nearly 6 per cent to GDP in India, and that is a fairly conservative figure. (For comparison with an economy that had over 80 per cent mobile phone usage in the early 2000s, consider the Philippines, where the contribution of mobile networks was close to 10 per cent of GDP.[13]) Industry observers insist that 3G mobile telephony, already launched in India in the wake of several controversies of corruption, will accelerate the transmission of data, creating new opportunities for economic development, media consumption, gaming and value-added services.[14]

My ethnographic research in Mumbai, Delhi and Bhopal confirms that the adoption of the mobile in the major cities is increasingly focused on connectivity to various information platforms (Internet, governmental, regional, gaming and so on), displacing voice telephony as its most important function. In India these mobile information connectivities ingress – to use Whitehead's notion – into more and more imbricated bodily and cultural processes.[15]

Today, in the contemporary mobile handset (as industry and as cultural practice) in India the quality of sound is generally thought of as secondary or supplementary to the network or optical features of the device. So, for instance, on the popular *The Mobile Indian* website, a typical phone review notes:

> Galaxy Nexus (GT-I9250) has a 4.65-inch Super Amoled HD screen with 1280x720 pixel resolution and is devoid of any hardware or even capacitive buttons in the front.
>
> Under the 8.94 mm slim form factor, it houses a dual-core 1.2 GHz Texas Instruments OMAP 4460 mobile processor coupled with 1 GB RAM and 16 GB onboard memory and PowerVR SGX 540 graphics chip, clocked at 384 Mhz.
>
> It has a 5 megapixel auto-focus camera with LED Flash at the rear and a 1.3 megapixel camera in the front. For connectivity, it has 3G capability with 21

---

[13]   Ibid. p. 3.

[14]   See, for instance, *The Mobile Indian* <http://www.themobileindian.com> (accessed 10 June 2012).

[15]   In Alfred North Whitehead's theory of perception of actual entities, 'ingression' is the objectification of one actual entity through the prehensions of another actual entity. See Alfred North Whitehead, *Process and Reality: An Essay in Cosmology*, corrected ed. David Ray Griffin and Donald W. Sherburne (New York, 1978), pp. 48, 62, 219–21. On the other hand, for Whitehead a 'prehension' is an interaction of a subject with an event or entity that involves perception but not necessarily cognition. A prehension is both virtual and actual, both event and process. It is constituted by different sets of interactions between at least two multiplicities, whose variations are real and potential depending on its ecology. See Whitehead, *Science and the Modern World* (New York, 1967 [1925]), p. 69.

Mbps speed, Bluetooth 3.0, dual-band WiFi (802.11 a/b/g/n) support and NFC (Near Field Communication) chip.

Samsung has added a 1750 mAh battery to power the Galaxy Nexus. We expect it to be priced at close to Rs. [INR] 30,000 mark.[16]

This secondary or marginal status of mobile sound quality suggests something about the dominance of the tacto-visual (for example, touch screens) in contemporary mobile cultures in India (and globally).

And yet the sound experience of a given device is unquestionably important to consumers – especially in youth markets – given the rise of several pop musical genres over the past 20 years (Indipop, neo-spirituals, new Bollywood), the emergence of peer-to-peer networks of file-sharers in India, the proliferation of DJ cultures and the explosion of micro-speaker media assemblages (increasingly common headsets that range from relatively inexpensive in-ear buds to the new emergent market for designer over-the-ear headphones such as Bose, Shure, Dr Dre and so on). Moreover, I would argue that bodily movement (GPS), tactility (the mobile's vibration setting, for example) and sound (voice, buzz, music) are closely linked together in contemporary mobile practices in India.

Proximations of Mobile Desire

As we know, in cultures of abstract informationalism algorithms find functional lives in doubling, serializing, compressing, sampling and virally proliferating throughout an ecology of sensation.[17] If perception has become newly machined in the era of interactive, user-generated digital media, the experience of sound has undergone its own transformations. Certainly, the aim of contemporary value-added services and mobile marketing is to bring within the range of every mobile more goods, services, brands, products, sensations, connections and synergistic experiences than ever before.[18] What happens to the phenomenon of sound in mobile networks given this intensification, amplification and acceleration of consumption, all readily available through a palm-sized 'life-line'? In feminist theories of assemblages – for instance, in the work of Patricia Clough,[19] Luciana Parisi,[20] Steve Goodman,[21] Jasbir

---

[16]   Nilabh Jha, 'Upcoming Phones Worth Waiting for', *The Mobile Indian*, 26 April 2012 <http://www.themobileindian.com/news/6275_Upcoming-phones-worth-waiting-for_full> (accessed 10 June 2012).

[17]   Anna Munster, *Materializing New Media: Embodiment in Information* (London, 2006), p. 66.

[18]   On 'brand synergy' see Naomi Klein, *No Logo* (New York, 2009), pp. 143–64.

[19]   Patricia Tiniceto Clough (ed.), with Jean Halley, *The Affective Turn* (Durham, NC, 2007).

[20]   Luciana Parisi, *Abstract Sex* (New York, 2004).

[21]   Goodman, *Sonic Warfare*.

Puar[22] and Elizabeth Grosz[23] – heterosexist and masculinist assumptions of the constitution of desire around 'lack' or naturalized sex are critiqued for their inability to conceptualize desire as anything more than an effect of abstract repression. These feminists, drawing on the work of Gayatri Spivak, Judith Butler, Michel Foucault, Gilles Deleuze and others, have sought to bring desire into a consideration of how the body-in-capital functions in terms of its material compositions, its regulatory and normalizing regimes, its molecular and molar flows and lines of flight.[24] Sound in this critical discourse assumes its properly ontological status. My own concept of ecologies of sensation is genealogically rooted in this feminist analysis of embodiment through the affirmation that every form of gender and sexual domination has an evolving history of force, value and sense.

If we define desire as a force of proximation that arises from confused, habituated passions, we can analyse sound in mobile phone cultures in terms of the kinds of combinations and feedbacks between bodies, movement, capital, media and technologies that actually do, and potentially could, emerge from the tactical deployment of sound in such ecologies.[25] By 'force of proximation' we

---

[22]   Jasbir K. Puar, *Terrorist Assemblages: Homonationalism in Queer Times* (Durham, NC, 2007).

[23]   Elizabeth A. Grosz, *Chaos, Territory, Art: Deleuze and the Framing of the Earth* (New York, 2008).

[24]   Deleuze defines 'assemblages of desire' in this way: 'For me, an assemblage of desire indicates that desire is never a natural or spontaneous determination. For example, feudalism is an assemblage that inaugurates new relationships with animals (the horse), with land, with deterritorialization (the knight riding away, the Crusades), with women (courtly love and chivalry) ... etc. These are totally crazy assemblages but they can always be pinpointed historically. I would say for myself that desire circulates in this heterogeneous assemblage, in this kind of symbiosis: desire is one with a determined assemblage, a co-function. Of course, an assemblage of desire will include power arrangements ... but these must be located among the different components of the assemblage. Along one axis, we can distinguish states of being and enunciation in the assemblages of desire ... Along another axis, we would distinguish territorialities or re-territorializations, and movements of de-territorialization that lead into an assemblage. Power arrangements would surface wherever re-territorializations, even abstract ones, take place. Power arrangements would therefore be a component of assemblages and yet these assemblages would also include points of deterritorialization. In short, power arrangements would not assemble or constitute anything, but rather assemblages of desire would disseminate power formations according to one of their dimensions'; see Gilles Deleuze, 'Desire and Pleasure', in *Two Regimes of Madness: Texts and Interviews 1975–1995*, ed. David Lapoujade (New York, 2006), pp. 124–5.

[25]   Following Spinoza, Deleuze reminds us that joy or sadness are both passions, or confused ideas, insofar as a person's 'power of acting is not increased to the point' where the conception of self and its action is adequate. This critique of inadequate passions prepares, says Deleuze, for another very different distinction, between passions and actions: 'An idea of *affectio* always gives rise to affects. But if the idea is adequate instead of being a confused image, if it directly expresses the essence of the affecting body instead of

mean a conscious or non-conscious drive bringing us closer to a given person, thing or state of things (via digital proxies or avatars),[26] blurring the lines between self and other, public and private, intimate and impersonal (experiences of virtual presencing). As Munster puts it:

> Proximity is a form of connection that results from differential relations, that is, relations in which the ongoing variation of things from each other produces both convergence and divergence. Proximate relations provide a mode for understanding and living in the world as a folding out onto other things – something edging close to something else – but these things do not quite line up with the objects they are attempting to reach.[27]

So the force of proximation can actualize potentialities (converge and merge differential timescales), and it can deterritorialize in passionate (habituated, mnemonic) rituals of consumption, possession and aggression. Furthermore, this force of proximation is instrumentalizing in that such desire renders the person, thing or state of things into a means of enjoyment. The mobile phone in dominant discourses in India is metaphorized into a digital 'Swiss Army knife', whose various components maximize both the productivity and pleasures of the user and the capacities of the information network. Soon, very soon, the discourse

---

involving it indirectly in our state, if it is the idea of an internal *affectio*, or a self-affection that evinces the internal agreement of our essence, other essences, and the essence of God (third kind of knowledge), then the affects that arise from it are themselves actions (III, 1). Not only must these affects or feelings be joys or loves (III, 58 and 59), they must be quite special joys and loves since they are no longer defined by an increase of our perfection or power of acting but by the full, formal possession of that power or perfection. The word *blessedness* should be reserved for these active joys: they appear to conquer and extend themselves within duration, like the passive joys, but in fact they are eternal and are no longer explained by duration; they no longer imply transitions and passages, but express themselves and one another in an eternal mode, together with the adequate ideas from which they issue' (Deleuze, *Spinoza*, pp. 50–51). Without necessarily following Spinoza into his naturalistic pantheism, what we can affirm in Deleuze's analysis is the crucial distinction between confused passions, which arise from an inadequate sense of how compositions between bodies are mutually affected by variable intensities, and the expressive activity of an affection that spontaneously modulates intensive relations in terms of their critical thresholds.

[26]   Emily Apter, in a Lacanian register, notes the increasing importance of this proxy or avatar: 'The avatar haunts media and cyberspace in multiple guises. Nested in online chat rooms and seminars, internet commodity arcades, art installations, game worlds, architectural models, data-shadows, and program algorithms, the avatar has become the face of it-ness, who-ness, and what-ness mediating community and unseating the subject's *Eigentlichkeit* (self-possession, the "having" of what is my own).' See Emily Apter, 'Technics of the Subject: The Avatar-Drive', *Postmodern Culture*, 18/2 (2008) <http://pmc. iath.virginia.edu/text-only/issue.108/18.2apter.txt> (accessed 10 June 2012).

[27]   Munster, *Materializing New Media*, p. 68.

screams, the mobile will bring the (networked) world within reach of every user: 'Reliance Communications, among the first private operators to launch 3G mobile telephony in the country, is planning to provide 3G services in 140 cities by March 31 [2011].'[28] Messaging, GPS and other location-based services, mobile commerce, social media, web browsing and downloading, mobile productivity tools, advertising, gaming, radio, music, TV, films, video – all intensify the desire to own a mobile as a force of proximation. As an example, consider this response on flirting and dating through the mobile phone by an 18 year-old living in a young men's hostel in south Mumbai:

> Like if I like a particular girl, and if I am attracted to her and if I have infatuation, so obviously I will talk more to her through the cell phone. If I don't know you that much then I can only express my feelings through cell phone, some of the things which I really want to tell you and which I can't tell in front of everybody, I can tell this through cell phone. Like I want to tell somebody sorry, so I don't feel ashamed, I don't feel good, I can't stand in front of her and tell I am sorry, sorry and that it really hurt you but through cell phone, I can SMS her once or twice and if she says yes, then obviously everything is clear and we can meet and all. Yeah, cell phones help to build a relationship with girls. My friends in hostel also their bill comes to 2800 or 3000 [INR] because they do talk to girls at night. You can't be with a girl at 11 or 12 at night. In such a city like Bombay you can be if her parents are allowing her to go but if their parents are not allowing then. Yeah, girls have more restrictions.[29]

This pleasure of proximation, embedded in the very movement involved in the experience of bringing the object closer, is what Deleuze terms a 'durational affect', a certain intensive transition between states, and it forms a feedback loop with the force of proximation itself.[30] This drive, fed back towards proximity, would have its own gradient of intensity, from absolute integration or fantasized possession (buying airline tickets or new trainers through mobile Internet, or taking a mobile snapshot of someone you fancy on the train without their consent or knowledge, or sleeping with the mobile under one's pillow) to loose connectivity (occasional email, SMS or Facebook posting). For instance, and as we shall see in more detail below, when a camera phone is used to take pictures of an individual's experience

---

[28]   'With continual technological improvements in mobile devices and various MVAS [mobile value-added services] available to mobile subscribers, the mobile handset has gradually become an "Information Swiss Army Knife"' (IMAI, *Report on Mobile VAS In India: 2010*, p. 13); Nilabh Jha, 'Reliance 3G in 140 Cities by March', *The Mobile Indian*, 25 February 2011 <http://www.themobileindian.com/news/709_Reliance-3G-in-140-cities-by-March> (accessed 10 June 2012).

[29]   Quoted in Priyanka Matanhelia, 'Mobile Phone Use by Young Adults in India: A Case Study' (PhD dissertation, University of Maryland, 2010).

[30]   Deleuze, *Spinoza*, p. 49.

of the here and now, it becomes a tool for communicating intimate expressions instantly – the generation of the user in the movement of user-generated media. Photos can be sent to anyone (via email) or no one in particular (uploaded to Facebook), thus becoming a mechanism for 'intimate visual co-presence'. The machinic desire of the mobile is maximized in the force of proximation.[31]

If desire, then, is a force of habituated, passionate proximation, we can analyse the various forms of habituated 'closeness' that mobile networks legitimate, valorize and render sensible. Matanhelia summarizes some of her findings regarding mobile use among twenty-something Mumbaites in this way:

> Almost all the respondents in Mumbai commuted by local trains or buses every day to their colleges. During their commute, the participants used their cell phones to entertain themselves in a variety of ways. Listening to music, clicking pictures, playing games, sharing jokes via text messages (SMS) and videos through multi-media messages (MMS) were some of the ways in which participants used mobile phones for entertainment. At the same time, some participants also mentioned that mobile phones are also popular for showing pornographic material. Although the participants enjoyed clicking pictures and sharing them with friends, they also noted that clicking pictures of females without their permission is not an appropriate activity.[32]

The camera function available on almost all new mobiles over INR 1,000 (ca. USD 18.00) signals a shift not only in how photos are taken and shared, but also in how desire is expressed through new media photography. As media critic Dong-Hoo Lee notes in the context of Korea, mobile phones have contributed to the overall relativization of time and space by enabling communication en route to almost anywhere, and allowing accessibility almost everywhere, once again correlating the force of proximation with the experience of movement itself. Moreover, when mobile phones incorporate cameras within their multimedia functions, 'they provide us with a chance to explore the cameras' abilities to visually document and talk about our experience of the world as it unfolds around us. Camera phones have affected not only people's photographic practices but also their post-production mode of communication.'[33] For Lee, camera phones fundamentally obscure distinctions between public and private domains, the former characterized by its openness and visibility, the latter apparently 'secured by its invisibility against

[31] Dong-Hoo Lee, 'Mobile Snapshots and Private/Public Boundaries', *Knowledge, Technology & Policy*, 22/3 (2009): p. 163.

[32] Matanhelia, 'Mobile Phone Use by Young Adults in India', p. 106.

[33] Dong-Hoo Lee, 'Mobile Snapshots', p. 161. See also Kelsey Good and Steven Moulton, 'Consequences of Camera Phones in Today's Society', in Kay R. Larsen and Zoya A. Voronovich (eds), *Convenient or Invasive: The Information Age* (Boulder, CO, 2007), pp. 200–209. Available at: <http://www.ethicapublishing.com/ConvenientorInvasive.pdf> (accessed 10 June 2012).

the unwanted gaze of others'.[34] Through its capacity to capture a moment as it unfolds, as well as to share these 'displaced moments' via wireless communication networks, the mobile has 'complicated the dichotomy of the visible public domain with the invisible private domain'.[35] Moreover, the prevalence of camera phones has intensified the circuit of voyeurism–exhibitionism seemingly endemic to post-Internet cultures.

While the connectivity of new communication technologies has increased individuals' accessibility to the public domain, the growing uses of personal digital cameras, as well as surveillance cameras in public places, have made activities and events in every place more visible and have turned them into visually observable objects. While images captured by surveillance cameras can be utilized in strategies of social control, which then serve to strengthen the contemporary surveillance system, so-called home web-cams can reveal an individual's everyday life on the Internet and provide a resource for an individual's digital subjectivity. The ubiquitous cameras serve not only as instruments of surveillance, but also as those of countersurveillance. In particular, web-cams allow an individual to be both a subject and an object of surveillance, fulfilling his or her desire for self-exposure.[36]

In Mumbai, we should further note, it is strictly illegal to take photos anywhere near the stations, platforms or compartments of public trains. A friend was fined INR 5,000 (ca. USD 90) and had his camera seized by security authorities for taking photos of stations on Republic Day. Returning to the more general idea of the multifunctionality of the mobile 'Swiss Army knife', we can see not only how the mobile has come to be an anchor for emergent habituations, but also the sometimes anomalous position of sound in this emergence. Music, photos, games, jokes, porn: these are the habituated desires brought together in the ecology of sensation of mobile networks. Through them a certain proximate state or object is consumed and/or shared with others, suggesting that the mobile facilitates a wide range of desires between possession and connectivity. Below I pursue this diagram of desire further with another example from mobile advertising.

Let's turn to Bollywood 'wingman' Sharman Joshi, endorsing the Nokia 5233 in an ad titled 'Flirt'. In this ad, actress Adah Sharma plays Sharman's romantic partner, and they are doing what middle-class Indians often do today – shopping in a mall. In the first shot, through a partially obscured frame, Adah finds some outfits she wants to try on (we will conclude with some speculations concerning the repetition of this partially obscured, even voyeuristic shot below). The next segment is from Sharman's point of view, as he sits outside the changing room listening to songs on his 5233. Adah comes out, wearing a modest, almost traditional Indian *kurta*; without saying a word, Sharman scrolls his touch screen

---

[34] Lee, 'Mobile Snapshots', pp. 161–2.

[35] Ibid., p. 162.

[36] Ibid., pp. 162–3.

to play '*Tujh mein Rab dikta hai*' ('I see God in you').[37] As Adah returns to her changing cubicle, smiling flirtatiously, a blonde-wigged woman in tight leather-look shorts and a bright red form-fitting top walks out from an adjacent cubicle. She is overcoded as the stereotypical 'vixen' or, in Bollywood parlance, 'item girl'. Sharman looks around and frantically scrolls for the killer tune, 'Hey Sexy Lady' by Shaggy,[38] as his mobile blares out, 'Hey sexy lady, I like your flow / Your body's bangin', out of controoooooool!!! (Uh!).' She smiles and goes back to her cubicle.

Adah walks out next in a party sari, and Joshi finds the appropriate tune once again: 'My Desi Girl' ('My Indian Girl').[39] She does a little *bhangra* jig, swaying her hips, flashes a smile, and goes back in. Out walks the blonde again, this time in a tight, black mini-dress. Sharman does not miss a beat: 'Beware the Devil woman, she's got evil on her mind / Beware the devil woman, she's gonna catch you from behind'.[40] The blonde gives him a look as if she is absolutely smitten, just as Adah walks back out, ready to go. She looks at the two of them, glares down at his devilish mobile and storms off, with Sharman in guilty pursuit. Voiceover (in English): 'Get to your songs faster with Nokia 5233.' Cut to a digital image of a phone, spinning round, and as it stops … All is lost!? Not with Sharman and the 5233: he finds just the right song in '*Koi haseena jab rooth jaati hai to aur bhi haseen ho jaati hai*' ('When a beautiful woman gets angry she becomes even more beautiful').[41] Adah turns back to him, taps his face lightly and smiles. Voiceover (in Hindi): '*Ab dil ki baat ek touch se sunao*' ('Now express your heart's secret with a click of your mobile'). The final medium-range shot is of Sharman looking into the camera, touching his heart in relief, as the 'Nokia – Connecting People' logo flashes in white.

What is Nokia/Sharman selling here? Who could have known that the 'blonde' was in the next cubicle? With the Nokia 5233, says the ad, you, too, can flirt with chance! It is significant, given recent trends around only releasing song 'hooks' through Japanese mobile networks, that each time Sharman plays a song it only plays the chorus, as if every song is set to trigger a maximal, timely and appropriate force of expression (the mobile as Sharman's phallic extension, or maybe his orgasmic beat box). The oscillation between flirting with the 'desi girl' and the 'devil woman' is only a familiar cliché of heterosexual men's habituated fantasy of femininity. What grabs the attention in this commercial is the fact that

---

[37]   Featuring in *Rab Ne Bana Di Jodi* (*A Match Made by God*) (2008, India), dir. Aditya Chopra, lyrics Jaideep Sahni, vocals Roopkumar Rathod, Yash Raj Films.

[38]   Shaggy, featuring Brian and Tony Gold, 'Hey Sexy Lady', *Lucky Day* (MCA Records, 2002).

[39]   Featuring in *Dostana* (*Friendship*) (2008, India), dir. Tarun Mansukhani, lyrics Anvita Dutt Guptan and Kumaar Vishal Dadlani, vocals Shankar Mahadevan and Sunidhi Chauhan, Dharma Productions.

[40]   Cliff Richard, 'Devil Woman', *I'm Nearly Famous* (EMI, 1976).

[41]   Featuring in *Sholay* (*Flames*) (1976, India), dir. Ramesh Sippy, lyrics Anand Bakshi, vocals Kishore Kumar, Eros Entertainment.

Sharman demonstrates that he is equal to every unpredictable turn of life as long as his mobile is fully charged and fully networked. The ad further underscores another basic point in the branding of mobile networks: with mobile connectivity the expression of your desire ('*dil ki baat*') can be flexible, agile and immediate, like the ideal of youthfulness itself.

So, cultural expressions of sound, vibration and movement are important to the experience of the mobile – its everyday phenomenology.

One might even speculate further and say that, in India, sound is returning to its ontological tendencies in movement. As Helmholtz noted many years ago:

> In the inorganic world the kind of motion we see reveals the kind of moving force in action, and in the last resort the only method of recognizing and measuring the elementary powers of nature consists in determining the motions they generate, and this is also the case for the motions of bodies or of voices which take place under the influence of human feelings. Hence the properties of musical movements which possess a graceful, dallying, or a heavy, forced, a dull or a powerful, a quiet or excited character, and so on, evidently chiefly depend on psychological action.[42]

My sense is that my mother understood the properties of a movement – in her case, the particular movement of Hindi–Urdu cinema in the 1950s and 1960s. That movement she continued by becoming a pirate-parasite of image and sound in the diaspora. The piles and piles of VHS cassettes lining my parents' walls are a testament to that intensive affirmation.

If part of the experience of sound in mainstream Hindi cinema has gone from tinny stratospherics (for example, Lata Mangeshkar singing in *Guide*[43]) to deep bass meant for earphones (for example, Rahat Fateh Ali Khan singing '*Dil to Bachcha Hai*' in *Ishqiya*[44]), what does this suggest about the changing habituations of the new media assemblage in India?

If this shift to private headphones suggests an ominous turn towards an emergent neoliberal entrepreneur of the self in India – the *jugaadwallah*/trickster caught in her self-ironizing bubble – how does the user-generating parasitism of mobile technology harness the 'hacker phylum'[45] towards other assemblages of sound and sensation?

---

[42]   Hermann Helmholtz, *On the Sensations of Tone as the Physiological Basis for the Theory of Music*, trans. Alexander J. Ellis (London, 1912), p. 2.

[43]   *Guide* (1965, India), dir. Vijay Anand, lyrics Shailendra, music S.D. Burman, Navketan International Films.

[44]   *Ishqiya* (*Love*) (2010, India), dir. Abhishek Chaubey, music Vishal Bhardwaj, Shemaroo Entertainment and Vishal Bhardwaj Pictures.

[45]   Following on from the machinic becoming of mobile technologies necessitates engaging with practices of refusal of mobile media value, resistance to the network mode of power, while simultaneously affirming the autonomy of peer-to-peer sharing and open information tactics. Thus, 'hacker phylum' here suggests the co-evolution of hacking

How do operators, value-added service providers and the everyday user negotiate this new organization of sound? If value-processes (production, circulation, consumption) of sound in mobile ecologies are being harnessed to correlate sensations of tactility, vision and sound with brand equity, how are thresholds of practice and non-linear information self-organizing lines of flight from that branded horizon?

Neoliberal and autonomous ecologies of sensation both work on attention: how will sound be integrated into new media tactics of attention and modulation? This is both an ideological project and an ontological becoming.

Conclusion

At the outset of this essay I asked: 'How does sound, through the micro-speakers of the contemporary handset, feed back with the experience of embodied movement itself?' We can see that capitalist media assemblages accumulate speculative value on anticipated attention; this is the gambit of the value-added creative consultant. Its diagram is the abstract machine of the net-risk society. What is at stake in the disintegration of a regime of film-centred sound becoming intermedia? The app store is now available on the Indian iPad (one of the first apps my daughter and I started playing with was Soundrop).

Isabelle Stengers writes that prehension is a 'taking into account', and Whitehead intended to free the term from all subjective or intellectual connotations, as well as from everything else that such a connotation implies. Prehension makes the operation and production of reality coincide. 'What prehends realizes itself in the process of prehensive unification, my hesitation "here," my coat "there," the threatening sky up above, and so on'.[46] If prehension in India today has gone through a torsion of movement – of migrant populations across India, of women moving outside the home and contesting the specific structures of gender and sexual domination and unpaid domestic labour, of a new transnational pornography that brings huddled groups of urban men together on stoops and in rickshaws, the emergence of new aesthetic genres and their different modes and scales of consumption, of ongoing corruption in the auctioning of information bandwidth, of the Adarshification[47]

---

practices with copyrighted intellectual property regimes, both differently traversed by revolutionary becomings.

[46]   Isabelle Stengers, *Thinking with Whitehead: A Free and Wild Creation of Concepts* (Cambridge, MA, 2011), p. 147.

[47]   'Adarshification' alludes to the Adarsh Housing Society scam, a plot involving the violation of several rules and a series of criminal acts by politicians, bureaucrats and top military officers in order to have a high-rise constructed in the Colaba locality of Mumbai, India. The scam developed in a period of ten years, from February 2002 through the public break of the scandal in 2010, until a number of arrests were carried out by the Indian Central Bureau of Investigation in 2012.

of class and ecology in cities such as Bangalore and Gurgaon (for example, Palm Meadows in Whitefield, Bangalore) in the boom and bust cycle of the net-risk economy, of the molecularization of time and the modularity of space in mobile media – sound has become an intensive experience of transvaluing the regime of capture that tied the aural to the monumental and the dynastic (the era of legendary singers Lata, Asha, Rafi and Kishore), morphing new modes of capture through networked power-capacity/power-interpellation and risk management, as well as affirming, in its immanent movement, the autonomous becomings of the hacker phylum.

Chapter 5

Seen and Heard:
Visible Playback Technology in Film

Tim McNelis and Elena Boschi

Whether we think of film music as a prominent narrative element or 'inaudible'[1] score, movie soundtracks have long been an important element of people's everyday listening experiences. Although film soundtracks may not be the first thing that comes to mind when thinking of ubiquitous musics, parallels are often drawn between the combination of music and visuals in film and audiovisual perception during other listening experiences. As Tia DeNora states, '[music] works, within the scenes of "real life" as it works in the cinema, bestowing meaning upon the actions and settings that transpire within its sonic frame'.[2] Similarly, respondents in ethnographic studies often speak in cinematic terms of listening experiences involving mobile playback technology.[3] Just as playback technology affects various listening experiences in the real world, so too does visible playback technology in film influence different audiences' cinematic experiences. Music in films is not only aurally present, but is also often visible through its technological sources, which, as we shall argue, contributes to what music can signify in a film. The instances where sources of music in the film world are seen as well as heard are a straightforward way of foregrounding the music, but their narrative implications go beyond this somewhat apparent function.

Visible playback technology has had various functions through the history of film, and its presence has influenced constructions of identity, as well as agency, in a number of ways. According to Kathryn Kalinak, limitations of sound recording technology and aesthetic preferences for realism in the early Hollywood talkies often led filmmakers to include visible sources of music, whether human or mechanical, in the *mise-en-scène* to justify the presence of music.[4] Discussing 1960s Hollywood scores composed in popular idioms, Jeff Smith notes how Henry

---

[1]   Claudia Gorbman, *Unheard Melodies: Narrative Film Music* (Bloomington, IN, 1987).

[2]   Tia DeNora, *Music in Everyday Life* (Cambridge, 2000), p. 143.

[3]   See, for example, Michael Bull, *Sound Moves: iPod Culture and Urban Experience* (London and New York, 2007).

[4]   Kathryn Kalinak, *Settling the Score: Music and the Classical Hollywood Film* (Madison, WI, 1992), pp. 66–7.

Mancini, in his compositions for films such as *Breakfast at Tiffany's*,[5] included source music cues for visible radios and phonographs to insert catchy tunes that would later be re-recorded in fuller versions for a soundtrack album.[6]

Pamela Robertson Wojcik illustrates how 'the trope of the girl and the phonograph' articulates transgression, female desire and lack.[7] While not denying the music's obvious importance, she focuses on the meaning of women using playback technology as a signifying element in itself. Robynn J. Stilwell, however, suggests that Wojcik places too much emphasis on the masculine connotations of the phonograph.[8] She argues that, in girls' coming-of-age films, the bedroom becomes extremely important due to the traditional restriction of female characters to domestic space, and the phonograph is a key component of this refuge. In these films, records and the music they contain are 'central to the cinematic articulation of the girl's self-discovery'.[9] Finally, Tim Anderson discusses films in which records function as a site of nostalgia and collectors are in danger of fostering a regressive obsession with what they consider to be a more 'authentic' past.[10] This focus on the past, he argues, can inhibit the collector's ability to engage with the present. Anderson elaborates on the connections between the record, music, characters and audience:

> ... these films configure the recording and listener into a specific cinematic trope that allows the audience to sense and experience the appeal of this configuration as a source of palpable nostalgia. In other words, as the record is employed within the *mise-en-scène* of these films, this nostalgic temptation is often deployed through clever music supervision wherein recordings are selected to deliver specific mnemonic charges to the listening audience in a manner that permeates listening space by superseding the diegetic space of the film. Indeed, the record in these settings takes on a number of functions for both the characters in the film and the spectator. Or, to paraphrase Allen Zweig's documentary on record collecting, *Vinyl*, the record is often 'about more than the music' (2000).[11]

---

[5]   *Breakfast at Tiffany's* (1961, USA), dir. Blake Edwards, music Henry Mancini, Paramount Home Entertainment.

[6]   Jeff Smith, *The Sounds of Commerce: Marketing Popular Film Music* (New York, 1998), pp. 79–81.

[7]   Pamela Robertson Wojcik, 'The Girl and the Phonograph; or the Vamp and the Machine Revisited', in Pamela Robertson Wojcik and Arthur Knight (eds), *Soundtrack Available: Essays on Film and Popular Music* (Durham, NC, 2001), p. 440.

[8]   Robynn J. Stilwell, 'Vinyl Communication: The Record as Ritual Object in Girls' Rites-of-Passage Films', in Phil Powrie and Robynn Stilwell (eds), *Changing Tunes: The Use of Pre-existing Music in Film* (Aldershot, 2006), p. 157.

[9]   Ibid., pp. 153–8.

[10]   Tim Anderson, 'As if History was Merely a Record: The Pathology of Nostalgia and the Figure of the Recording in Contemporary Popular Cinema', *Music, Sound, and the Moving Image*, 2/1 (2008): pp. 51–76.

[11]   Ibid., p. 53.

It is this relationship between record, playback technology and audience – as mediated by music and characters – that we wish to expand on throughout this chapter, considering not only phonographs and records, but also cassettes and CDs, as well as their associated playing devices.

All of the above contributions offer fascinating perspectives on the sources of music present in the film world, but the way visible playback technology not only inflects film music's narrative meaning but also carries meaning independent of what music it is playing has yet to be fully explored. Phonographs, boomboxes and other devices can offer further meaning for different audiovisual constructions of a character, setting and other narrative aspects. In the following pages, we will draw on examples from *Ghost World, The Full Monty, Barrio, Do the Right Thing, Save the Last Dance* and *All Over Me* to argue that visible playback technology is a key signifying element in films that can influence how songs are perceived and bear meaning accrued through both its cinematic and real-life uses. We have chosen films from the late 1980s to the early 2000s in order to discuss a transitional period when multiple physical media and forms of playback technology were still in regular use.

Ghost World

In *Ghost World*,[12] recent high school graduate and non-conformist Enid (Thora Birch) obsessively explores her self-identity through various genres of music played on video cassette, audio cassette and vinyl. In this film, the medium from which music is played carries connotations as important as those of genre. *Ghost World* begins with the opening dance scene from the Bollywood film *Gumnaam*,[13] showing masked men and women in black suits and bright dresses dancing to 'Jaan Pehechaan Ho' – a twangy, surf-tinged rock 'n' roll song performed by Mohammad Rafi. The music bridges a cut to an average-looking neighbourhood and continues as the camera surveys the windows of several apartments showing the mundane yet slightly bizarre activities of the inhabitants. It is then revealed that Enid is playing the Bollywood film in her bedroom and imitating the actors' dance moves in her graduation gown. This short opening sequence establishes Enid as an intriguing character in contrast to her dull neighbours. Far from being the typical teen character who only listens to pop music while dressing for the prom, Enid actively seeks out different musical forms. According to Jason Sperb, this opening also establishes one of the film's key themes.[14] Sperb suggests that

---

12 *Ghost World* (2001, USA), dir. Terry Zwigoff, music David Kitay, music supervision Melissa Axelrod and Christine Bergen, Icon Home Entertainment.

13 *Gumnaam* (1965, India), dir. Raja Nawathe, music Jaikishan Dayabhai Pankal and Shankar Singh Raghuwanshi, Eros Entertainment.

14 Jason Sperb, '*Ghost* without a Machine: Enid's Anxiety of Depth(lessness) in Terry Zwigoff's *Ghost World*', *Quarterly Review of Film and Video*, 21/3 (2004): pp. 209–17.

'opening *Ghost World* with clips from *Gumnaam*, instead of images of Enid or of another one of the film's characters, emphasizes the film's pre-occupation with simulation, with facades that mask depth'.[15] In addition, this opening emphasizes the film's preoccupation with mediation, which plays an important role in Enid's construction of self-identity. By 2001 the video cassette recorder was a dying breed, but for a teenager it still provided access to various types of audiovisual content, from films to music videos. Video cassettes also served social functions such as enabling people to record and copy content, which could then be shared, swapped or even sold. The use of a VCR in this scene, then, brings a certain DIY aesthetic and agency to Enid's initial musical exploration. However, Enid does not return to any video cassettes in her search for a musical identity.

Later in the film, Enid uses punk rock to rebel against her best friend Rebecca's (Scarlett Johansson) move towards traditional adulthood as the two make plans to move in together. After Rebecca suggests they buy nice clothes and pretend to be yuppies to impress potential landlords, Enid glares at her suspiciously. With a cut to Enid's bedroom, 'What Do I Get' by 1970s English punk band The Buzzcocks blasts from her cassette deck as she dyes her hair green. Enid has decided to go for what she later describes as a '1977 original punk rock look' – complete with black leather jacket – and she uses this song to score her transformation. Fittingly, the song's lyrics reflect Enid's dissatisfaction with her current lifestyle and future prospects. Enid's musical rebirth is short-lived, however. Her new look upsets Rebecca because she's afraid it will hurt their chances of getting the ideal apartment, as well as Enid's likelihood of landing a job. Shortly thereafter, Enid is insulted by three young men in a comic book store. This cold reception and Rebecca's dissatisfaction result in her abandonment of the punk image. Rather than gaining respect from her peers, Enid's attempt to rebel is met with cynicism. Once again, the plastic, re-recordable medium – this time audio cassette, with similar promises of DIY youth cultural exchange – brings an unfulfilling experience, perhaps because it represents an identity in transition, an unfixed medium for a developing personality.

Enid tries on different musical personae throughout *Ghost World* in the hope of finding some meaningful form of self-expression. In her exploration of musical genres, she becomes obsessed with 40-something record collector Seymour's (Steve Buscemi) taste in old jazz and blues records, largely because of the 'authenticity' these artefacts seem to exude. This musical soul-searching proves hollow, however, and any attempts to gain agency through music are ultimately unsuccessful. Sperb argues that although Enid somewhat recognizes the emptiness of texts that are mere simulations of some mythical authentic experience, she 'embraces these texts because, as a teenager in America, simulation constitutes her only point of reference for history or authenticity …'[16] Despite her knowledge of the empty promise this authenticity contains, Enid continues to search for a

---

[15]   Ibid., p. 210.

[16]   Ibid., p. 210.

musical experience with some real depth throughout the film – 'to uncover depth beneath the cultural simulation, or to ascribe and impose depth on the world around her'.[17] Paradoxically, in this search for authenticity, Enid cycles through and abandons current media and playback technology, including audio cassettes, video cassettes and CDs (which she is never shown playing, but do appear on her floor), which could represent her failure to connect with a common generational experience. These media of the (then) modern youth culture, with their potential for re-recording and sharing content, are abandoned for the medium of a bygone youth culture – vinyl.

When Enid gets home from the comic book store, she starts playing 'What Do I Get' again, but the song, like the punk image, no longer fits. After rummaging through a pile of cassettes on her floor, she removes the tape from her stereo and dismissively throws it, along with a few other cassettes, back on to the pile. The sound of plastic cassette and CD cases crashing against each other emphasizes the connotations of disposability such media carry. On discarding the Buzzcocks tape, Enid decides to play an old country-blues record she has bought from Seymour. The slow, archaic, acoustic blues of 'Devil Got My Woman' by Skip James begins with a cut to a warped record spinning on a tiny phonograph. Enid's reflection is then shown in a mirror, once again with black hair but still wearing the jeans and T-shirt from her punk outfit. Her facial expression suggests an immediate and intense fascination with what she is hearing. After she has walked from the bathroom into her bedroom, Enid is shown from behind with the record spinning over her shoulder. A reverse shot then shows her from the front, contemplating the song. The shot-reverse shot is a technique typically used to naturalize a conversation between two characters. However, in this case it structures an interaction between Enid and the phonograph/record/song, as well as serving to personify the music and its source. This strategy turns the act of listening into a conversation between Enid and both the music on the record and the physical object itself. Next, the camera rotates nearly 180° around the front of Enid, emphasizing her enthralment with the song and mimicking the spinning of the phonograph, creating an analogy between Enid and the record. After another cut to a close-up of the needle on the record, there is a fade to Enid reclining in front of the phonograph, now wearing a black floral print robe, showing the passage of time. She has obviously been listening to the song repeatedly, and she moves the needle back yet again as the music ends.

In her discussion of records in girls' rites-of-passage films, Stilwell describes this scene in the following way:

> The circularity of the experience is emphasized, from the obviously repetitive motion of Enid placing the needle at the beginning of the track once again, to the spinning of the record accentuated by the warp, to the track of the needle in

---

[17]   Ibid., p. 211.

the groove, echoed by the camera's motion, spiralling in on Enid's moment of self-discovery.[18]

This circularity not only reflects Enid's repeated playing of the record, but is also symbolic of her quest for identity. Enid cycles through music and clothing styles, always returning to try on a new persona when the previous one fails to satisfy.

'Devil Got My Woman' strongly resonates with Enid's quest for a meaningful musical identity and helps her connect with Seymour's record listening and collecting practices. She seems to desire Seymour's stability of image and his separation from conventional society. Both Sperb and Anderson emphasize the bridge that this song (and the record that contains it) builds between Enid and Seymour. As Anderson asserts, 'the record suggests a mysterious depth that Enid does not initially ascribe to Seymour's sad-sack profile'.[19] For Sperb, Seymour 'also represents a part of the album's past', and his character 'symbolizes Enid's desired journey from surface to depth, from simulation to origin'.[20] While Enid may connect this song's perceived authenticity, mystery and depth to Seymour, she must also identify with some element of the song on a personal level since she plays the record many times throughout the film. Enid uses the song, just as she uses Seymour, as a brief escape from the boredom and superficiality she experiences in everyday life. However, this journey leads to a dead end. Seymour 'owns' this music in a way Enid never will because, despite her search for a musically-inflected identity, she ultimately has little interest in settling into Seymour's groove.

As previously mentioned, a few CDs are visible in a pile on Enid's floor, but she does not play any of them throughout the film. The conspicuous absence of CDs in Enid's listening practices puts her at odds with modern times. It is important, too, that she plays records on a small, portable phonograph. Enid's turntable is the size of a 45, so the LP she repeatedly plays hangs well over the edge and wobbles because of its severely warped condition. This results in an awkward visual impression suggesting that the record is too big for her phonograph to handle, and that this misshapen record is inferior to those in Seymour's pristine collection. However, this image could also reflect Enid's strong belief in the beauty of imperfection (or at least imperfect people), which is both explicitly stated and alluded to throughout the film. In combination with the previously discussed analogy between Enid and the record in the scene where she first hears 'Devil Got My Woman', this image of the warped record on the tiny phonograph further emphasizes her incongruous relationship with the modern world – what Stilwell refers to as 'a mark of otherness, retrograde technology and nostalgic authenticity in the plastic, conformist world she scorns'.[21]

---

[18]   Stilwell, 'Vinyl Communication', p. 159.

[19]   Anderson, 'As if History was Merely a Record', p. 68.

[20]   Sperb, '*Ghost* without a Machine', p. 215.

[21]   Stilwell, 'Vinyl Communication', p. 166. For an extended discussion of the infantilizing effects of the small phonograph, see Timothy McNelis, 'Popular Music,

Wojcik describes how female use of phonographs in films 'comes to signify transgressive female desire and lack'.[22] She also claims that, especially in youth films, 'the phonograph marks awakening sexual desire'.[23] However, Wojcik asserts, this potentially empowering representation is often accompanied by more transgressive behaviour for which the character is later punished. This is surely the case in *Ghost World*, since Enid sleeps with Seymour and is eventually punished with the loss of an art college scholarship. Seymour's confusion about the sexual encounter results in his moving back in with his mother and seeing a therapist. Finally, Enid decides that her only option is to escape her problems, and the film ends with her boarding an old bus on a discontinued line to some unknown location – an action that could be read literally or metaphorically, representing some life-altering action or suicide.

In the end, it is the process of identity construction that engages Enid. It's important that she is able to control this process and identify with songs to which she feels a strong connection. Interestingly, Enid's use of music takes on a more 'feminine' character when compared to Seymour's 'masculine' record collecting habits. This engagement with music both allows her to move forward (as opposed to stagnating like Seymour) and prohibits her from ever finding music that complements the person she wishes to become. Stilwell recognizes a trend in this type of identity journey for teenage girls in cinema and the role records play in it:

> ... when I look to fictional depictions of girls in a number of recent films, it is striking how often the record functions as a ritual object in the narrative, key in the girl's transformation into *herself*. The picture may not be as consistent as the lonely, object-and-system-oriented male collector, but there is a constellation of issues that are engaged with varying intensities. As a ritual object, the record is inscribed with power, but it is an ambivalent power. Since it is more than an item to possess or a weapon to wield, its use is individual to each girl. The importance of records, as artefacts to venerate and relics of sound and self with which to resonate, is central to the symbolic narratives of girls finding their voices.[24]

In the case of records, girls are finding their own voices through a medium traditionally associated with male collection.[25] Yet Stilwell suggests their connection to specific records is represented as more personal and emotional than

---

Identity, and Musical Agency in U.S. Youth Films' (PhD thesis University of Liverpool, 2010).

[22] Wojcik, 'The Girl and the Phonograph', p. 448.

[23] Ibid., p. 441.

[24] Stilwell, 'Vinyl Communication', p. 166.

[25] See, for example, Will Straw, 'Sizing Up Record Collections: Gender and Connoisseurship in Rock Music Culture', in Sheila Whiteley (ed.), *Sexing the Groove: Popular Music and Gender* (London, 1997), pp. 3–16. Stilwell argues that this association is partly due to the exclusion of females from the discourse of records.

that of the stereotypical male hoarder. This is not to claim that all males who collect records lack emotional connections to particular records or songs, or that there are no female record hoarders. Rather, this type of representation is important because it provides a fresh and empowering tool for teenage girls' constructions of self-identities, even if they have always used records for this purpose in the real world. However, the depiction of the record as authentic and the cassette as disposable is contradicted by other cinematic representations of cassettes and portable players as tools of sonic empowerment and agency.

The Full Monty

In *The Full Monty*,[26] working and jobless men are set apart through music-related practices involving musical instruments and playback technology respectively. A brass band marches outside the abandoned factory where ex-workers Dave and Gaz, and the latter's son Nathan, are attempting to steal a girder. Lomper, who plays in the brass band as well as working as a security guard in the disused factory, notices an open door and locks it, thus locking Gaz and Dave in their empty former workplace.

The British brass band movement's resonance for working-class culture[27] makes its audiovisual placement significant. In the opening sequence, the brass band becomes a surviving aural vestige of a working-class male community shattered by prolonged joblessness. Hence, Dave and Gaz getting locked in really seems to be a reverse representation of their getting locked out of public space, excluded by their community, here embodied by the brass band and its sound.[28] Later, the jobless men's reappropriation of their abandoned workplace and renegotiation of their roles as males take place through music and dance. While the instruments the brass band members use for their affirmation as a working-class community are a visible and often discussed component of their musical practices, scholarly writing about *The Full Monty* does not address the technological devices through which Gaz and his friends reconstruct bonds among members of a jobless community.

Early on in the film, all three men participate in the playing of Hot Chocolate's 'You Sexy Thing' – Lomper brings the record, Dave and Gaz choose it and Dave plays it using a turntable and the factory PA. The piece accompanies Gaz's first awkward striptease attempt and audibly stops after a loud scratch on the record

---

[26]   *The Full Monty* (1997, UK), dir. Peter Cattaneo, music Anne Dudley, music supervision Liz Gallacher, 20th Century Fox.

[27]   For a comprehensive account, see Susan J. Smith, 'Beyond Geography's Visible Worlds: A Cultural Politics of Music', *Progress in Human Geography*, 21/4 (1997): pp. 502–29.

[28]   For an extensive discussion of the brass band's significance, see: Elena Boschi, '"Playing" Cultural Identities in and out of the Cinematic Nation: Popular Songs in British, Spanish, and Italian Cinema of the Late 1990s' (PhD thesis, University of Liverpool, 2010).

when Dave lifts the arm, which works as a damning sonic comment on a clumsy performance. Their rehearsal music fills job-related locations, which becomes a recurrent trope, but, later, cassettes and boombox largely replace records and turntable. The oversized 1980s-style boombox that becomes visible for the first time at the auditions accompanies every group rehearsal and has a Rolling Stones Hot Licks logo sticker on the middle and two green eyes stickers on the top corners, which foregrounds its quasi-humanized presence. While the boombox becomes significant in its own right, who controls it also matters. Nathan's regular involvement as the boombox operator is a signifier of his support for his father's unusual pursuit, which remains otherwise unexpressed until the end. The boombox not only becomes a means through which the men aurally reclaim their factory, but also comes to symbolize Nathan's involvement in his father's project below his initial surface disapproval.

Through its first appearance the connection between the boombox and blackness emerges. In the first productive audition, a sparkling performance by Horse, the older black man dancing to Wilson Pickett's 'Land Of 1,000 Dances', follows a hapless attempt by an older white guy who awkwardly undresses as he hardly dances to 'Je t'aime ... moi non plus' by Serge Gainsbourg and Jane Birkin. The alignment between a black man who can dance, a recording of a black man singing soul and a piece of playback technology often associated with urban black youth and their music marks the point where Gaz's plans start to look plausible, potentially foregrounding the boombox's connotation as a signifier not only of black musical culture in general, but also of aural reclamation of urban space through portable playback technology.

Interestingly, while the boombox always accompanies a group rehearsal, a turntable is audible/visible only when Gaz is dancing alone, first in the factory and later at home, and the music is stopped after he makes a mistake. Records' connotation as a potentially regressive technology[29] seems to match Gaz's inconclusive solo performances, whereas the boombox helps the group to improve and aurally occupy their empty factory via its connotation as a vehicle through which a marginalized group can reclaim urban space. A different piece of playback technology would bring different meaning, therefore substantially modifying the rehearsal sequences. While a turntable and records might stand for regressive individualism and failure, a boombox and cassettes symbolize affirmative community sense and fulfilled aspirations. Halfway through the story, a radio playing Donna Summer's 'Hot Stuff' (heard earlier at the first group rehearsal) accompanies the legendary dole queue scene. Being outside the men's control, the radio becomes a Greek chorus-like technology, bringing aural reassurance into a location related to their joblessness. A few minutes later, the boombox makes its final appearance at a costume rehearsal. After a policeman finds the thong-clad men dancing to Gary Glitter's 'Rock and Roll, Part 2' in the empty factory, there are other occurrences of source music, but playback technology is not seen again.

---

[29]   Anderson, 'As if History was Merely a Record', pp. 51–78.

The boombox is a signifier of the men's collective struggle to reclaim pride after their marginalization through chronic joblessness and fills the factory with the sound of other marginalities. Its early disappearance could be taken as a warning about failure after the film's happy ending and a hint that their success in the fight to reconstruct their lives as working men is a temporary fix.

Barrio

While a boombox and cassettes acquire a hopeful meaning in *The Full Monty*, cassette players stand for something quite different in *Barrio*.[30] The story follows Javi (Timy Benito), Manu (Eloi Yebra) and Rai (Críspulo Cabezas) on the high-rise housing estates outside Madrid where, despite the impending summer holidays, nothing changes and the three friends can only dream of getting away from their neighbourhood. If Latin American music becomes a vehicle for a group attempt at 'distributed tourism',[31] the rickety playback technology through which it is aurally projected in the film world conveys the chronic impossibility of a getaway – however virtual – alongside other aspects of music's audiovisual mediation.

In her essay about world music in coffee shops and retail stores, Anahid Kassabian addresses questions about how listeners are located in the world by world music, putting forward interesting reflections about those listening practices she terms 'distributed tourism'.[32] Built on ideas of distributed subjectivity[33] that she discusses elsewhere, the concept she calls 'distributed tourism' expresses 'the presence of a network, many places at once'. She continues, 'Sitting in my office, listening to Putumayo CDs, I am a distributed tourist. I move from space to space without changing places.'[34] Although Kassabian applies these ideas about listening to ubiquitous musics, the concept can offer a new perspective on source songs' ability to evoke another place, which, we argue, depends heavily on their visible sources. A discrepancy between music's visible sources and the place/ideas that

---

[30]   *Barrio* (1998, Spain), dir. Fernando Léon de Aranoa, music Hechos contra el decoro, music supervision Lucía Cárdenes, Warner Sogefilms SA.

[31]   Anahid Kassabian, 'Would You Like Some World Music with your Latte? Starbucks, Putumayo, and Distributed Tourism', *Twentieth-Century Music*, 1/2 (2004): pp. 209–23.

[32]   Ibid.

[33]   Kassabian chooses to call subjectivity 'distributed' to apply the concept of distributed computing to listening practices. 'Desktop computing takes the computer as a discrete entity, like the Enlightenment subject; it relies solely on the processing power contained in the desktop unit. Distributed computing, however, links smaller units together so that they can share processing power in a pool of sorts ... Each computer, then, is a dense node in a network, neither discrete nor flattened. Such a perspective on computing power offers a powerful model for subjectivity; each subject is a dense node in an enormous network that is addressed by various participants in various ways and with varying degrees of power.' (ibid., p. 213).

[34]   Ibid., p. 218.

the music might evoke can influence – and sometimes spoil – the evocative power a given piece/genre can possess.

An example is a scene in *Barrio* where the well-known Latin American piece 'Moliendo Café' by Venezuelan José Manzo Perroni is performed by gypsies in the liminal space between housing estates and railway lines. Their performance features mariachi trumpets accompanied by a synthesized rhythmic base, and a goat turning on a tiny pedestal, which is typical of these increasingly unusual urban shows. The discrepancy between the music's discernible Latin American origins and its underclass Spanish performers potentially damages the effectiveness and reveals the emptiness of the other place that Latin American music has offered throughout the first half of the film.[35] Similarly, playback technology becomes a visual reminder of a dimension still inescapable for its inhabitants, despite their attempt to evade it through another world's music. The smaller portable cassette players owned by *Barrio*'s youth are not boomboxes, but range from medium twin-deck cassette players to Walkmans with headphones. However, as a scene set in a music store makes clear, the countless CDs on display on the shelves are the current medium, not cassettes, which establishes the surpassed playback technology owned by the three friends as a further signifier of their marginalization. The vehicle through which Latin American music reaches the film world undercuts the potential for cinematic distributed tourism. Cassette players are a constant reminder of a severed dimension from where all musical tourism fails, drawing attention towards the other place's simulatedness and therefore revealing its unreality.

The order in which visible playback technology appears bears further consideration, as it follows a decreasing pattern from large and clearly audible to small and aurally contained. Playback technology first appears in the opening sequence of *Barrio*. A young man carries a large boombox, which, while unheard because of dramatic music, clearly implies the potential to claim space aurally through music in the film world. Later, a salsa piece playing on the twin-deck cassette player in the bedroom of Javi's sister, Susana (Marieta Orozco), draws Rai's attention and leads him towards her own private space, where she keeps dancing for him until Javi arrives to interrupt. Javi, on the other hand, owns nothing but a single-deck cassette player, which he is shown operating twice. After a row between his parents, he plays 'Jesucristo García' by Spanish rock band Extremoduro in the small bedroom he is made to share with his deaf grandfather, who continues to nap while Javi and Rai hang out and play music. Later, Javi's single-deck cassette player reappears at the tropical party thrown by the three friends under the motorway bridge where they have been shown hanging out earlier. Javi, Manu and Rai turn their rundown gathering place into a Caribbean

---

[35] For an extensive discussion of the gypsies' performance, see Boschi, '"Playing" Cultural Identities'; and Elena Boschi, '"Canción prohibida": Simulacros musicales y otros mundos en *Barrio* de Fernando León de Aranoa', in Eduardo Viñuela Suárez and Teresa Fraile Prieto (eds), *La música en el lenguaje audiovisual* (Seville, 2012), pp. 399–406.

set using items burgled from the neighbourhood travel agency. Rai dances to 'Virgen del Cobre' by Cuban singer Celina González, holding a cardboard cut-out Caribbean woman shown earlier in the travel agency's window. The fantasy dissolves abruptly after Manu and Rai break the cardboard woman's head in a fight about who has the right to dance with her, and Javi stops the music, which aurally seals the rupture between simulation and the other dimension they believed each simulacrum could deliver to their rundown neighbourhood. Finally, Javi plays 'Confessions' by Mexican-American rap duo Tha Mexakinz on the Walkman to drown out his parents' umpteenth fight in the next room, and his point of audition takes over. Earlier, the three friends mention dubbing cassettes using Susana's twin-deck cassette player and selling them as a potential initiative to raise money to go on holiday, therefore identifying playback technology as a way out. However, various factors undermine the possibility of a getaway – however virtual – through music. The sound-projecting power of these visible devices gradually decreases – from Susana's twin-deck cassette player filling the whole apartment at the beginning to Javi's Walkman and headphones combination at the end – and rock and hip-hop songs replace Latin American music,[36] undermining music's power to deliver another place. Although their looks are racially unmarked and their accents quite average, Javi, Manu and Rai represent the socially different – a trait clearly expressed through the setting, conversations and the old rickety playback technology that surrounds them, reminding audiences that average leisure goods are still unattainable for the neighbourhood's residents.

Finally, playback technology reminds us of the three friends' chronic failure to inhabit a dominant gaze. After narrowly missing the last train on Manu's birthday, the three friends start walking along empty tunnels and finally come across the disused underground station known as the ghost station, which some say is inhabited. As they approach it, the Arabic-language song 'Douha Alia' by Algerian rai artist Cheb Mami gradually increases in volume and, as the boys walk along the railway, its source – a medium single-deck cassette player – is shown providing music for a small subterranean immigrant community of African origins. Instead of empowering them, the friends' attempt at temporarily inhabiting a dominant gaze makes them the subjects of an essentializing gaze, similar to that inflicted on them by news reports about juvenile delinquency in the outskirts; it also shows parallels between their invisible lives and those of their lower Other. Earlier, the ghost station's existence becomes a topic for a few conversations where ignorance about, and fascination for, a totally unknown Other are clearly expressed. Alongside perhaps the gypsies, the African immigrants who inhabit the ghost station are considered as a lower class, even by Javi, Manu and Rai. Playback technology becomes a vehicle to evoke faraway homelands for those

---

[36] *Barrio* shows a startlingly close audiovisual correlation between Latin American songs and escapist sequences, on the one hand, and the urban rhythms of hip hop and rock, and inescapable reality, on the other, which is discussed extensively in Boschi, '"Playing" Cultural Identities' and Boschi, '"Canción prohibida"'.

men and women, but the similar devices owned by Javi and the ghost station's inhabitants are reminders of their similarly marginal condition.

Do the Right Thing

In *Barrio*, visible devices playing music outside Javi's house aurally claim uncontested space and therefore do not involve any substantial changes in the power relations among the neighbourhood's inhabitants. In other films, however, portable playback technology serves as a weapon to contest territory. Agency and general mobility are enhanced with the ability to project one's music outside of the home. One famous example of portable music's ability to facilitate agency and political expression and to assert power within public space can be found in *Do the Right Thing*.[37] Throughout the film, Radio Raheem (Bill Nunn), a young African-American man, obsessively blasts Public Enemy's 'Fight the Power' from the cassette in his oversized boombox. During one scene, Radio Raheem engages in a music duel with a group of young Puerto Rican men. The scene begins after a cut from local DJ Mister Señor Love Daddy (Samuel L. Jackson) putting a needle on the record featuring 'Tú y Yo' ('You and I') by politically-engaged Panamanian singer Rubén Blades. The song then bridges a cut to the Puerto Rican men sitting on the steps in front of a house and drinking beer. After Stevie (Luis Antonio Ramos) reads aloud a passage he has written in Spanish about salsa music being the sound of his beautiful island, Puerto Rico, the camera pans over to show the source of the music – a beat-up boombox sitting on top of a car, with a sticker on the front that appears to depict the head of Jesus Christ. Within seconds, however, we hear an instrumental passage of 'Fight the Power' enter the sonic space. This cues a pan over to Radio Raheem's boombox and then a tilt up to show the owner's defiant face. After some angry words from the Puerto Rican men, Stevie takes up the challenge. He walks over to the radio on top of the car and raises the volume, exposing the Puerto Rican flag sticker on the side. Another pan shows Radio Raheem turning up the volume on his modern, shiny, much larger boombox. Finally, Stevie accepts defeat, lowers his volume to zero and says 'You got it, bro', leaving the sound of 'Fight the Power' hanging in the air as a final pan shows Radio Raheem walking away, celebrating his victory through reciprocal high-fives with a young boy.

The scene described above illustrates not only the ubiquity of music in the lives of urban youths, but also how music can be used to express identity and claim territory, as well as how playback technology can influence the perceiver's understanding of power and race relations. Although the salsa music is actually broadcast over the radio and is therefore not a completely active choice by Stevie and his friends, it nevertheless serves as an expression of their ethnic pride and

---

[37]   *Do the Right Thing* (1989, USA), dir. Spike Lee, music Bill Lee, Universal Studios Home Entertainment.

is used to lay claim to their territory during the duel. The Puerto Rican flag and Jesus stickers on the radio serve to further situate the music as a tool of the Puerto Rican characters. Since the racial/ethnic tensions bubbling beneath the surface of this Brooklyn neighbourhood are central to the film's narrative, playing music is just one of many ways through which characters struggle to claim space and assert power. Radio Raheem eventually wins this battle not only because his boombox is bigger and louder, but also possibly because he has chosen the music he plays, and he continues to play it with conviction throughout the film.

Throughout *Do the Right Thing*, Radio Raheem wears a 'Bed-Stuy' T-shirt referring to Bedford-Stuyvesant, the Brooklyn neighbourhood where the film is set. This, in addition to his music, contributes to Raheem's territorial claim. His two confrontations with white, Italian-American pizzeria owner Sal (Danny Aiello) both end in defeat, however. In the first instance, Raheem is persuaded to turn off his music after Sal yells and refuses to serve him pizza. When he finally submits, we hear the distinctive click of the stop button, connecting us tactilely to the cassette deck. Later in the film, Radio Raheem once again enters Sal's Famous Pizzeria, this time insisting, with two other characters, that some photos of famous African-Americans be put up on the 'wall of fame', where Sal hangs photos of famous Italian-Americans. On this occasion Raheem refuses to turn off his music, which leads Sal to smash his radio with a baseball bat. Once again the materiality of the playback technology is sonically foregrounded – a cacophony of shattering plastic and metal, as well as the final movements of the cassette deck, is heard each time the bat hits the boombox. Events escalate from here: Raheem pulls Sal over the counter, and the two fight until separated by police officers who eventually kill Radio Raheem while restraining him with excessive force. In the end, no one wins the musical turf war. Raheem ends up dead and Sal's pizzeria is set alight and burnt beyond repair. But these consequences serve to further emphasize the power of portable playback technology as a tool for protest and a site over which power is contested.

Save the Last Dance

Boomboxes and cassettes are also used to enable agency and signify African-American street culture in *Save the Last Dance*.[38] In this film, Sara (Julia Stiles), a white teenager from the suburbs who moves into her father's Chicago apartment following her mother's death, learns hip-hop dance from Derek (Sean Patrick Thomas), an African-American student at her new high school. Sara, classically trained in ballet, uses hip-hop dance to fit in with her new social group and eventually fuses hip hop with ballet at an audition for entry to the prestigious Juilliard performing arts conservatory.

---

[38] *Save the Last Dance* (2001, USA), dir. Thomas Carter, music Mark Isham, music supervision Michael McQuarn, Paramount Home Video.

Portable music-playing devices are first made prominent when Sara's father drops her off at her new high school: the rap song 'You Don't Really Want Some' by Blaqout is playing outside as she opens the car door. The volume jumps with a cut to some of the students and continues at that level over several shots of various students wearing headphones, dancing, talking, smoking and hanging out in front of the school. Finally, the volume lowers again as Sara enters the school and fades out shortly after. Thus, the music is heard from Sara's point of audition, although the level is too continuous throughout most of the scene to reflect this realistically.

As Sara walks through the crowd, she passes a boy with a boombox – the obvious source of the music. Although this music emanates from a source belonging to a student and is not simply dramatic score, it still carries some of the stereotypical implication of threat in relation to the white, female protagonist due to the prevalence of this type of scene in urban high school films. The lyrics of the song, which include the lines 'Leave that thing on fire / 'Til you're ready to retire' and 'You don't wanna see me / The black Ron Jeremy', carry obvious sexual meaning,[39] and as Sara passes the student with the boombox, he says to her, 'Oh, what's up baby?' In the context of the rest of the film, 'You Don't Really Want Some' also serves as a challenge to Sara, both lyrically and through its cultural context. Although different from the intended lyrical meaning, in this scene the 'some' in the title could refer to urban African-American culture more generally and hip-hop culture more specifically (despite the obvious sexual connotations). Sara may not have chosen to move to this neighbourhood and attend this school, but she is here now. She has to stand up for herself and adapt to her new cultural surroundings. Thus, on a larger scale, the song asks if Sara is willing to accept, and indeed participate in, the musical and cultural world of the student body.

In this scene, the student with the boombox is in control of the sonic environment – he both plays music and speaks. While it is not clear whether the music comes from a cassette or a radio station, he nonetheless musically asserts his authority over the space. There are also three students with personal cassette players and headphones shown throughout the scene. Although these students do not project their own musical identities and are therefore silenced in a way, they are nonetheless participants in a portable musical culture that affirms their belonging both as individual agents and within the larger social group. Portable playback technology continues to accompany agency throughout the rest of the film.

As the plot progresses, Sara moves away from her position on the margins of hip-hop culture, thanks initially to her friendship with Derek's sister Chenille (Kerry Washington) and, later, through Derek's teaching. In a montage cut to 'U Know What's Up' by Donell Jones, Derek teaches Sara not only how to dance, but also how to show hip-hop attitude in the way she walks, sits and interacts with others. Although the cuts make the onscreen source of the music, Derek's radio, temporally impossible (thus positioning the cue as source scoring), one accepts that this is his music and that he is sharing his musical agency with Sara. Although

---

[39] Ron Jeremy is a famous US pornographic film star.

the music is Sara's gateway to hip-hop culture, her transformation involves more than just a change in musical taste. The fact that the music plays from a cassette becomes obvious after the song has finished. The cassette is not actually visible when Derek removes it, but his hand motions, as well as the sounds of the cassette sliding into the plastic case and the case being closed, make the medium obvious. These sounds amount to more than nods to a realistic soundscape, however. The feel of recorded media and their various sleeves and cases are integral to our relationships with recorded music. The crunches and snaps of plastic can trigger tactile memories not only of the physical act of listening to cassettes but also of exchanging dubbed and mix tapes with friends and siblings.

Derek's boombox is shown again in a few other dance montages in what appears to be an abandoned warehouse. In the second of these scenes, the rap music playing from the boombox continues over cuts between the couple dancing in the warehouse and Sara rehearsing ballet in a studio. The source of this music is visible in the warehouse, and its music sonically dominates the ballet studio, where no visible source of music is shown. Once again, the boombox/cassette is equated with amateur street culture which, despite lacking the implied professionalism and legitimacy of ballet, has a greater influence on agency and culturally dominates the sequence. Later in the film, Sara is shown practising alone under a railway bridge, with a barely visible boombox as the implied musical source, despite the song having started in the warehouse with Derek's boombox visible before the cut. Thus, Sara now demonstrates her own musical agency and lays sonic claim to public space.

All Over Me

Since the historical situation of recorded media is crucial to the meaning that different types of playback technology bring to films, modern media also serve a function beyond signifying the absence of history or lack of nostalgia. One example of a recorded medium's implication of certain aspects of the present can be found in *All Over Me*.[40] This film centres on teenage protagonist Claude's (Alison Folland) unrequited love for her best friend Ellen (Tara Subkoff) and the dangers her sexuality brings to her life in the Hell's Kitchen neighbourhood of Manhattan, New York. Claude is temporarily distracted from her exploits with Ellen when she meets Lucy (Leisha Hailey), a musician whose band, Coochie Pop, has just finished a gig. Lucy later invites Claude back to her house, where they bond over their common love of music and play CDs for one another. After playing a few songs on her stereo, Lucy invites Claude to pick some music. Claude chooses 'Pissing in a River' by Patti Smith, although she is aware of the feelings the song will betray – she even says 'I'd better not' before playing it. As she sways

---

[40]   *All Over Me* (1997, USA), dir. Alex Sichel, music Miki Navazio, music supervision Bill Coleman, Alliance.

to the moody music, Claude mouths the words that reflect her ambivalence about the present situation with Lucy and her feelings about Ellen: 'Should I pursue a path so twisted? / Should I crawl defeated and gifted? / Should I go the length of a river?' Claude's emotional contemplation climaxes with the line 'Everything I've done I've done for you', as she obviously reappropriates the song's lyrics to describe her relationship with Ellen.

'Pissing in a River' provides continuity on the soundtrack from its position as source scoring – it plays throughout the sequence, which cross-cuts between Claude and Lucy in Lucy's bedroom, and Ellen and her abusive boyfriend Mark (Cole Hauser) in Claude's bedroom. Tensions boil between Ellen and Mark as Ellen snorts several lines of cocaine and Mark repeatedly tells her she has had enough. Mark eventually picks Ellen up and throws her out of Claude's room. The connection between the two locations is strengthened by the presence of the Patti Smith poster on the wall of Claude's bedroom. As Claude's distress mounts, she breaks into tears and sways mournfully. It is as if Claude can see and hear Ellen and Mark in her bedroom through the eyes and ears of the vigilant Patti Smith – who is present both visually and aurally. Claude becomes almost omniscient through the song's inexplicable presence in her bedroom, where Ellen and Mark are at the time. With cuts to Claude's bedroom, the level of the music drops as if it were coming from a nearby source, even though Claude's bedroom is nowhere near Lucy's.

This scene clearly demonstrates Claude's intimate relationship with music. She uses the Patti Smith song to express her own emotions and work through her confusion. The explicit connection to a strong female musician and use of music to express identity are not often available to teenage girls in films. However, in her discussion of female friendship and adolescent empowerment in youth films, Mary Celeste Kearney confirms this as a trend in some independent films of the 1990s:

> The use of feminist music and the portrayal of female musicians in films focusing on teenage girls are notable attempts to move beyond the formula of studio-produced female teenpics, which continue to rely predominantly on male-created music for their soundtracks and portray male figures as girls' primary role models and objects of desire.[41]

In addition, the medium that Claude and Lucy use to share songs is also important. As discussed earlier in this chapter, record collecting is usually considered a masculine practice, even though some women are avid collectors. In *All Over Me*, however, the often nostalgic, male-centred practice of record collecting does not connect with what is ultimately a female-dominated musical

---

[41] Mary Celeste Kearney, 'Girlfriends and Girl Power: Female Adolescence in Contemporary U.S. Cinema', in Frances Gateward and Murray Pomerance (eds), *Sugar, Spice, and Everything Nice: Cinemas of Girlhood* (Detroit, MI, 2002), pp. 138–9.

atmosphere of the film – the soundtrack is full of Riot Grrrl music, Lucy's band plays to an audience almost exclusively made up of young women, Claude plays the electric guitar and Patti Smith is both visually and aurally foregrounded. The fact that Patti Smith is played from a CD rather than a record connects her music with the modern world. Rather than showing the young women bonding through a musical practice long seen as traditionally masculine, this film portrays Claude and Lucy as agents in their own current musical culture. After all, despite the homophobic violence shown in the film, Claude and Lucy are likely to be in a better position to reveal their sexuality in the modern world than they would have been in the past. For them, the nostalgia associated with record collecting offers a past that would have no doubt been more complicated than the present.

Conclusion

The films discussed throughout this chapter place similar playback technology in a different network of meaning where songs, the character controlling the music, different devices' power to project sound, their histories and their relation to other visible playback technology in the film world can enter audiences' understanding of film soundtracks. As we hope to have demonstrated, Wojcik's argument that 'the trope of the girl and the phonograph' can produce meaning despite the music[42] also applies to other devices. The boombox's known history as a visible element in the aural occupation of urban space follows it into the film world, where character appropriation, relations between visible devices and these devices' cinematic appearances can signify without music. While music clearly matters, songs' visible sources are not only ads for the music, but also bearers of added meaning.

The examples we have discussed show that, in addition to helping characters attempt to commune with an idealized past as in Anderson's discussion,[43] playback technology also enables characters to engage with the present in ways influenced by their particular social/cultural/historical situations. For audiences, such technology can be seen as a source of agency or a sign of limitations. The devices that characters use to play music, whether based on preference or availability, are always closely related to identity. The narrative becomes the crossroad where different connections between music, its visible sources and other non-musical aspects combine, producing different audiovisual scenarios depending on the items one unpacks from the baggage songs carry and the visible devices that make music audible. As we hope to have demonstrated, where sources of music in the film world are visible as well as audible, the meaning that different devices can bring to the narrative calls for as much attention as the music itself.

---

42   Wojcik, 'The Girl and the Phonograph', pp. 433–54.
43   Anderson, 'As if History was Merely a Record'.

Chapter 6

Body and Context in Mobile Listening to Digital Players

Marta García Quiñones

While the use of music as background in public spaces could be considered as the prototype for ubiquitous musics, the concept is also applicable to other listening situations that are no less common in contemporary urban settings, and where music listening takes place also '"alongside" or simultaneously with other activities'.[1] Particularly interesting instances are the 'mobile listening' situations made possible by portable digital players or mp3 players which provide users with a continuous self-selected musical background to their everyday activities. Users of portable digital players listen to music mostly through earphones or headphones: despite the fact that their listening often takes place in public, it is commonly conceived as a private activity, and it is sometimes portrayed as a contextless, disembodied and self-absorbed occupation. Contrarily, in this essay I focus on how the mobile listener negotiates the relationship between her body, the shifting context and the music. To explore it, I draw on Michael Bull's research into the experiences of iPod users,[2] but I also supplement – and occasionally object to – his analysis and theorization of users' testimonies on the basis of my personal experience as an iPod user and as an observer of the behaviour of iPod users in everyday life. I also bring to the discussion some concepts concerning human perception and emotions that are currently being explored by neurobiologists and have already been adopted by a few music scholars, although they have not so far been applied to the comprehension of mobile listening. These concepts point to an understanding of mobile listening – and music listening altogether – as an activity engaging the body at many levels, from physical gestures to brain processing.

---

[1] Anahid Kassabian, 'Ubiquitous Listening', in David Hesmondhalgh and Keith Negus (eds), *Popular Music Studies* (London, 2002), p. 137.

[2] See Michael Bull, 'No Dead Air! The iPod and the Culture of Mobile Listening', *Leisure Studies*, 24/4 (2005): pp. 343–55; and Michael Bull, *Sound Moves: iPod Culture and Urban Experience* (London and New York, 2007).

On Mobile Listening: Some Historical Glimpses

Even if mobile audio technologies are intrinsically linked to the question of portability – in fact, in this essay I will constantly refer to '*portable* digital players' – perhaps it would be useful to begin by distinguishing between properly 'portable' and 'mobile' (or 'personal') music players. Portable audio technologies are designed to be easily transported from place to place, but they are neither normally listened to during transportation nor are they conceived specifically for individual users, although they can occasionally be connected to headphones. While they can be listened to in private, either attentively or with different levels of distraction, sitting close to the player or moving around while doing something else, they are more frequently listened to in company and may also serve to create party atmospheres. In contrast, mobile audio technologies combine two main aspects: miniaturization, which makes them wearable, and earphones (or, less frequently, headphones), which transform portability into an individual experience. The experience of consuming mobile technologies is often called 'mobile listening', although this denomination is slightly equivocal, as it refers to devices designed to be worn while on the move even when they are used – as they sometimes are – for stationary listening. In this essay I will focus particularly on mobile listening outdoors – that is, on mobile listening in public spaces.[3]

The first portable audio technologies were portable valve radios, invented in the 1920s. Portable gramophones were introduced later, in the 1930s, and portable stereo record players were developed at the beginning of the 1960s as an evolution of the portable gramophone. In the mid-1970s these functionalities were transferred to portable cassette players or boomboxes, which took advantage of magnetic tape's greater durability and ease of copying. Even though they were portable, they were often used as mobile technologies, accompanying users on their strolls through the city. However, they were rarely listened to through headphones – or at least users wouldn't listen through them while moving around. Portability later took the form of CD boomboxes, and of smaller and smaller hi-fi equipment. Today a portable audio device can be just a pair of capsule speakers connected to a digital player – generally speaking, ever-shrinking technologies tend to blur the line between portability and mobility, although it is still visible.

---

[3]   A further concern would be whether the term 'listening' adequately describes what happens in these situations. This essay suggests it may not, although it may probably be also inaccurate to refer to more conventional listening situations, if we analyse them deeply. However, 'listening' is certainly a socially accepted term to describe a socially recognizable way of interacting/reacting to music – it is in this sense that I feel entitled to use it here. Yet, it is significant that nowadays music psychologists seem more and more inclined to employ other denominations, such as 'responses to music', instead; see, for instance, Susan Hallam, Ian Cross and Michael Thaut (eds), *The Oxford Handbook of Music Psychology* (Oxford, 2009).

On the other hand, mobile audio technologies can be traced back to the mid-1950s, when the first portable transistor radios were commercialized.[4] Portable transistor radios could be quite compact and were often listened to through earphones – a characteristic that was also typical of the first stationary radio receivers, although these were connected to a pair of earphones or headphones whereas portable transistor radios were normally connected to single earphones. An important step was taken in 1979, when Sony launched the Walkman. Only slightly bigger than a cassette tape, this mobile cassette player combined the mobility of a portable transistor radio with the possibility of listening to one's favourite music, including the custom-made compilations that were so typical of the cassette era. Basically, the Walkman defined what a portable player would henceforth be: a tiny, wearable audio player connected to a pair of headphones or earphones. In the case of the Walkman, the headphones were often supra-aural (over the ear) – a new design that was introduced in the 1980s. Unlike traditional circumaural headphones, supra-aural headphones do not cover the ear completely and hence are not only lighter, more comfortable, but also more appropriate to situations in which the user should not totally detach herself from what is happening around her.

The big success of the Sony Walkman posed some questions that would influence the public reception of subsequent mobile players. Thus, although they could occasionally be shared (with one user listening through the right earphone and the other through the left earphone), personal cassette players were primarily associated with a desire for isolation, or rather with a desire for privacy in the open. Walkman users were repeatedly accused of inhibiting interpersonal interaction, and their apparently oblivious attitude – fully absorbed, staring at the void – was bitterly criticized. Needless to say, these concerns were not related to mobility *per se*, but to the use of headphones. Apparently, they were a reaction against the public exposure of the – until then – private practice of listening through headphones, which was mainly associated with hi-fi culture and the immersive listening sessions of domestic audiophiles. As Jean-Paul Thibaud has observed, personal cassette players implied a movement 'from private listening to public secret':[5] by introducing a new element in social life that others found difficult to read, they revealed at the same time the tacit codes that regulated the body's expressiveness in public. This movement from private to public was particularly controversial because the Walkman's earliest adopters were youngsters, and the controversy was also aggravated by the faulty isolation of headphones at the time, which often made the music perfectly audible to everyone in the user's vicinity. In

---

[4]   On mobile audio technologies, see Michael Bull, 'Investigating the Culture of Mobile Listening: from Walkman to iPod', in Kenton O'Hara (ed.), *Consuming Music Together: Social and Collaborative Aspects of Music Consumption Technologies* (New York, 2006), pp. 131–49.

[5]   Jean-Paul Thibaud, 'The Sonic Composition of the City', in Michael Bull and Les Back (eds), *The Auditory Culture Reader* (Oxford, 2003), p. 331.

2000 an ethnographical investigation into the use of personal cassette players – or 'personal stereos', as the author chose to call them – conducted by Michael Bull analysed some of the intentions and strategies of their users.[6] On the one hand, Bull presented the Walkman as a tool through which users exerted, or tried to exert, control over their surroundings or over specific elements of their surroundings: blocking external noise, detaching themselves from other people, feeling more protected in hostile environments, appropriating the monotonous time invested in everyday routines and so on. On the other hand, the narratives of some users revealed a notion of the Walkman as an instrument for managing moods and inner sensations, and ultimately as a possibility for inhabiting a different space.[7] Ultimately, these users expressed a longing for something like a 'sonic bubble' – an image that, under different names, came to identify mobile listeners in the popular imagination.

In 1984, while cassette tapes were gradually being replaced by the new digital technology of CDs,[8] Sony commercialized the first portable CD player, called the Discman, which adopted the features of the Walkman but was not so technically reliable on the move. In fact, at the beginning of the 1990s various attempts were made to introduce various digital alternatives to the CD player – Sony's MiniDisc and Philips' Digital Compact Cassette were the most popular ones – but none of these attained mass-market popularity. Personal CD players – like stationary ones – featured for the first time a 'random' button, which allowed users to listen to the tracks of a CD in random order, and which set a precedent for digital players' 'shuffle mode'.

Portable Digital Players: Continuities and Discontinuities

At the end of the 1980s an international team of researchers developed an audio compression format called 'mp3', which was adopted as a standard in 1991. However, the first portable device that took advantage of the new format was

---

[6]   Michael Bull, *Sounding Out the City: Personal Stereos and the Management of Everyday Life* (Oxford, 2000); for a later ethnographic research based in Germany, see Heike Weber, 'Taking Your Favorite Sound Along: Portable Audio Technologies for Mobile Music Listening', in Karin Bijsterveld and José van Dijck (eds), *Sound Souvenirs: Audio Technologies, Memory and Cultural Practices* (Amsterdam, 2009), pp. 69–82. Two other relevant, more theoretically-oriented studies on Walkman culture are: Shuhei Hosokawa, 'The Walkman Effect', *Popular Music*, 4 (1984): pp. 171–3; and Paul Du Gay, Stuart Hall, Linda Janes, Hugh Mackay and Keith Negus, *Doing Cultural Studies: The Story of the Sony Walkman* (London, 1997).

[7]   For a summary of the many situations described in Bull's study, see the 'typology of personal-stereo use' included in the last chapter of his *Sounding Out the City*, pp. 186–90.

[8]   On the history of digitalization in music, see Franco Fabbri, 'La musica nell'era digitale', in T. Gregory (ed.), *XXI secolo. Comunicare e rappresentare* (Rome, 2009), pp. 625–34.

introduced only in 1997 by SaeHan Information Systems; it was a model called MPMan F10. As a result of the new compression techniques of digital audio data, digital players (or mp3 players) are able to store thousands and thousands of music files. Indeed, some portable digital players – particularly those models that offer more storage, such as Apple's iPod Classic, which can store up to 160 GB, equivalent to 40,000 songs – are employed as repositories in which users keep their whole music libraries. Although they are mostly listened to through earphones, mp3 players can also be connected to a pair of loudspeakers and function as stationary stereos.

Even if many companies have commercialized different mp3 players since their invention, they are frequently identified with Apple's iPod,[9] which, from its launch in November 2001, has sold over 300,000,000 units of its different models worldwide and holds a dominant position in the market.[10] Thanks to its design and marketing, the iPod has acquired the status of a fashionable upmarket product, invested with meanings that go far beyond its functionality.[11] Mobile listening has gained thus social prestige, and iPods have been given access to some environments – offices, for instance – where Walkmans and Discmans were admitted only reluctantly. On the other hand, iPods, and portable digital players generally, are also increasingly used to store other kinds of files, mainly visual and audiovisual – a trend that grows in parallel with the possibility of storing and playing compressed audio files in portable devices other than digital players or laptop computers, such as mobile phones, smartphones or personal tablets.

The whole point of the mp3 – and of newer compression formats, such as the AAC – is precisely to facilitate the storage and exchange of audio files. Therefore, it is not surprising that its adoption as a standard resulted in an exponential increase of the universal stock of compressed digital musical files and in a rise in their exchange – both person-to-person and on the Internet, by legal or illegal means – to an unprecedented scale. But the mp3 has had many other consequences. For instance, it has helped to establish the status of individual audio files as primary musical units: mp3 files (usually called 'songs'), organized in music libraries and

---

[9]   Although iPods can reproduce mp3 files, they are linked to the iTunes software and the iTunes online store, which sells music codified in AAC (Advanced Audio Coding), the probable successor of the mp3 format.

[10]   Sherilynn Macale, 'Apple has Sold 300M iPods, Currently Holds 78% of the Music Player Market', *TNW: The Next Web – Apple Channel*, 4 October 2011 <http://thenextweb. com/apple/2011/10/04/apple-has-sold-300m-ipods-currently-holds-78-of-the-music-player-market7> (accessed 30 May 2012). In 2012 Apple reported sales of 35.2 million iPods; see Darrell Etherington, 'Apple Hardware Sales in FY 2012: 125.04M iPhones, 58.23M iPads, 18.1M Macs and 35.2M iPods', *TechCrunch*, 25 October 2012 <http:// techcrunch.com/2012/10/25/apple-hardware-sales-in-fy-2012-125-04m-iphones-58-23m-ipads-18-1m-macs-and-35-2m-ipods/> (accessed 11 February 2013).

[11]   See, for instance, Leander Kahney, *The Cult of iPod* (San Francisco, CA, 2005); and Steven Levy, *The Perfect Thing: How the iPod Shuffles Commerce, Culture, and Coolness* (New York, 2006).

lists of reproduction (called 'playlists') have now become the basic elements of musical consumption. It has also raised many issues of copyright, authorship and the right of public access to culture that are still at the centre of international debate. Nevertheless, as Jonathan Sterne has explained, the most fascinating aspect of the mp3 is probably the nature of the coding itself: known as 'perceptual coding', it is a process that relies on some principles of human psychoacoustics to 'get rid of the sounds that we would not hear anyway'.[12] While the loss caused by the compression can sometimes be perceived if the mp3 is compared to a CD recording of the same song, 'it is much more difficult – and sometimes impossible – to tell the difference between a CD recording and an mp3 if someone is listening to mp3s in noisy environments, through poor quality speakers or earbuds'[13] – that is, if mp3s are listened to in conditions that are fairly common among mobile listeners. Apparently, mp3 files 'are meant for casual listening, moments when listeners may or may not attend directly to the music'.[14] Therefore, we could say that in portable digital players not only the psychophysical mechanisms of perception, but also the social situation is present at the level of the format.

Regarding the headphones of portable digital players, there is a clear 'perceived miniaturization of headphone culture', as Sean Nye has called it,[15] which has run parallel to the progressive miniaturization of the audio players themselves. Thus, headphones have evolved from circumaural to supra-aural, and later to earphones or earbuds (in-ear) and IEMs (in-ear monitors that send the sound directly into the user's ear canal). Today portable digital players are often listened to through earbuds or IEMs – for instance, all iPod models come with a characteristic pair of white earbuds.[16] At the same time, earphone designers have tested and adopted different technologies to reduce or block contextual noises. These technologies are basically of two kinds: noise-cancellation technologies and noise-isolation ones. Noise-cancellation technologies identify unwanted ambient sounds and emit other sounds to counterbalance them. They can be quite effective against continuous mechanical noise but are not designed to cancel other more variable noises, like human talk. Noise-isolation technologies are represented basically by IEMs, which physically obstruct the ear canal to block incoming noise. These

---

[12]   Jonathan Sterne, 'The mp3 as Cultural Artifact', *New Media & Society*, 8 (2006): p. 834; for a more extensive treatment of mp3's 'perceptual technics', see Jonathan Sterne's recent book, *MP3: The Meaning of a Format* (Durham, NC, 2012).

[13]   Jonathan Sterne, 'The Death and Life of Digital Audio', *Interdisciplinary Science Reviews*, 31/4 (2006): p. 339.

[14]   Sterne, 'The mp3 as Cultural Artifact', p. 835.

[15]   Sean Nye, 'Headphone-Headset-Jetset: DJ Culture, Mobility and Science Fictions of Listening', *Dancecult: Journal of Electronic Dance Music Culture*, 3/1 (2011): p. 73. Available at: <http://dj.dancecult.net/index.php/journal/article/view/90> (accessed 30 May 2012).

[16]   Yet this process of miniaturization can occasionally be contradicted by fashion trends, which may dictate the convenience of showing off bigger headphones of a certain kind or by a certain producer.

technological developments also bear witness to the centrality of the surrounding context to the experience of mobile listeners – an aspect that, as I will try to show hereafter, has not always been recognized in analysing the meaning and impact of mobile listening to portable digital players.

In addition, it is important to mention a third technological element that, while not limited to mp3 players (it has to do with the recording process and therefore has effects on all music-playing devices), seems to be connected to the rapid diffusion of mobile listening thanks to the new compression formats. I am referring to the increasing use of hypercompression techniques (not to be confused with compressed digital formats, such as mp3) for boosting the dynamics of recordings: that is, for making them louder while necessarily decreasing their total dynamic range – the controversial subject at the centre of the so-called 'loudness war'.[17] Even if this tendency towards loudness is normally justified by users' supposed preference for louder sounds, it is undeniably true that louder, hypercompressed recordings work better than recordings with a wider dynamic range when they have to compete against ambient noise – for instance, when they are listened to through earphones while exercising in a busy gym. Therefore, the current upsurge in hypercompressed recordings gives significant evidence to the role of noisy environments as catalysts to the evolution of digital audio production. This should incline us to analyse mobile listening situations as complex interactions of audio technologies, human perception and sensations, and contextual factors.

Mobile Listening out of Context: Sonic Bubbles and Dancing Silhouettes

Yet, in contrast to what I have just argued, context seems to occupy an ambiguous place in the discourse of iPod users, as it can be deduced from Michael Bull's pioneering study, based on online qualitative questionnaires and personal interviews.[18] According to Bull, the functions described by iPod users show a marked continuity with those of personal stereos: like Walkmans, iPods are generally considered as personal tools for controlling time, reappropriating urban spaces, managing emotions, avoiding social interaction and aestheticizing daily routines. However, Bull emphasizes that iPods' greater capacity has 'empowered' their users further: the fact of being able to carry their whole music libraries with them gives users a sensation of unprecedented control while in public.[19] Users can, for instance, distance themselves from their surroundings to listen to

---

[17]   On the 'loudness war', cf. Earl Vickers, 'The Loudness War: Background, Speculation and Recommendations', paper presented at the AES 129th Convention, San Francisco, CA, 4–7 November 2010 <http://www.sfxmachine.com/docs/loudnesswar/> (accessed 30 May 2012).

[18]   See Bull, 'No Dead Air!' and Bull, *Sound Moves*. For more interview-based research into iPod use, see Andrew Williams, *Portable Music and its Functions* (New York, 2007).

[19]   See Bull, *Sound Moves*, pp. 127–30.

a song or artist befitting their current mood or instantly select a song that feels particularly appropriate to a certain scene. They can try to speed up commuting time by listening to a particular playlist and can continuously adapt their song selection to their energy level. As a consequence – Bull contends – iPod users embrace the image of the 'sonic bubble' in a very decided way. Many of them evoke the desire for a private space for listening that allows them to choose the music they deem most appropriate to the moment, to detach themselves from their surroundings, and even to impose a personal narrative based on their musical taste upon the everyday. As summarized by Bull, iPod users 'live within a mediated and perpetual sound matrix, each user inhabiting a different auditory world'.[20]

In addition, advertising campaigns for portable digital players often resort to the image of the 'sonic bubble' – that is, to the ability of their products to create a personal music space for users regardless of the surrounding context.[21] Probably the most successful attempt to date to deliver this message has been the iPod 'silhouette campaign', launched by Apple in October 2003, which combined images of private, mostly solitary enjoyment with very powerful images of bodily engagement to the music.[22] Thus, the printed ads for the iPod silhouette campaign showed various black silhouettes wearing iPods and dancing, running, skating or just gesturing against a monochromatic (or sometimes psychedelic) background; the television commercials also presented black silhouettes, dressed in different youthful urban styles, wearing iPods and dancing or moving around frenetically to the rhythm of the most diverse musical styles.[23] In all cases, the situations depicted

---

[20]   Ibid., p. 7.

[21]   Sometimes – as in the television campaign for the Samsung YP-K5, released in 2006 – commercials have even played explicitly with that image; see 'Samsung MP3 Player Dance to the Music Cool Ads', uploaded by amyloer, 2 June 2008 <http://www. youtube.com/watch?v=8LgfnQmi7VQ> (accessed 30 May 2012); and 'Samsung MP3 Player K5 Commercial "Bubble"', uploaded by princetongolfer, 5 September 2006 <http:// www.youtube.com/watch?v=BKSmW6TI5kU&feature=related> (accessed 30 May 2012). Nevertheless, these television commercials were ambiguous in their representation of the 'sonic bubble', which was – somewhat contradictorily – conceived instead as a possible space for personal interaction.

[22]   The black silhouettes have not been employed to promote the most recent iPod models, the marketing of which seems to be more focused on visual functionalities. See, for instance, a television commercial for the iPod Touch: 'Apple – iPod touch – TV Ad – Share The Fun', uploaded by Apple, 23 November 2011 <http://www.youtube.com/ watch?v=gGrDMVk2isc> (accessed 30 May 2012]) and for the new iPod Nano: 'OFFICIAL Apple iPod Nano-chromatic Commercial', uploaded by AppleInc, 8 October 2008 <http:// www.youtube.com/watch?v=lEwYjF2Igjg&feature=related> (accessed 30 May 2012).

[23]   A list of television commercials for the iPod silhouette campaign can be found on this anonymous webpage: 'iPod Advertising', *iPod History – The Complete History of the iPod* (n.d.) <http://www.ipodhistory.com/ipod-advertising/> (accessed 30 May 2012). For other reflections on the iPod silhouette campaign, see Joshua Gunn and Mirko M. Hall, 'Stick it in Your Ear: The Psychodynamics of iPod Enjoyment', *Communication and*

were abstract: the setting was just a background colour, or changing background colours, and so it did not represent any public or private space. Whereas the printed silhouettes danced mainly alone, connected to their iPods, in the television commercials sometimes the silhouettes appeared to interact choreographically with one another, although they also remained connected to their devices. Besides, the soundtrack of the television ads – songs by already famous performers like U2 or The Black Eyed Peas, and by more or less 'indie' bands like The Prototypes or The Fratellis – created the illusion that it was the same music the silhouettes were listening to through their iPods' earbuds, except that there was no intrusion of possible contextual noise, just loud music in the foreground.

On the one hand, the Apple silhouette campaign intended to communicate the passion of eventual iPod users for engaging with the music, and it did so by choosing to ignore the possible surrounding contexts. In this sense, it resonated with the notion of a 'sonic bubble' – namely, with iPod users' desire for 'privatised sound atmospheres'[24] and with the personal pleasure they reportedly obtain from their devices. On the other hand, the Apple campaign displayed images of an activity (dancing with the iPod) that is practically absent not only from the streets of our cities,[25] but also from the narratives of iPod users examined by Bull. Instead of facilitating physical engagement to the music, the bubbles that some iPod users inhabit seem to be filled mostly with feelings, thoughts and fantasies, while users themselves are often involved in various degrees of self-absorption and detached observation. In other words, while the bodily aspect of mobile listening is presented in commercials in a passionately exaggerated way, iPod users often leave their bodies and the bodily aspects involved in the question of mobility out of their stories.

Mobility and Bodily Engagement in Mobile Listening

In fact, mobile listening – that is, the practice of moving around while listening to music – involves at least two different movements or mobilities: the movement of the subject (understood not only as actual movement, but also as a general state of alertness to the context) and the movement of the music (namely, the rhythmic and melodic movements that are inherent in it). With regard to the mobility of the subject, it is easy to observe that – except maybe in pauses during travels, waiting

---

Critical/Cultural Studies, 5/2 (2008): pp. 147–8; and Nye, 'Headphone-Headset-Jetset', p. 73.

[24]   Bull, *Sound Moves*, p. 11.

[25]   This is proved by the huge popularity and the comments raised by videos posted online where different people do just so: dancing with an iPod. The most recent worldwide success of this kind is probably 'Dancing with an iPod in Public – Christmas Edition', uploaded by Preston Leatherman, 28 November 2011 <http://www.youtube.com/watch?v=VlZ8DXRnM-0> (accessed 30 May 2012).

time, or other (mostly provisory) situations in which attention to the environment can be kept at a minimum – mobile listeners can only seldom abstract themselves from their context, either acoustically or visually. Thus, while being psychically and physically connected to the music, they are simultaneously social actors in shared spaces. As such, they routinely perform the actions dictated by the social situations they are in, like holding an umbrella, stopping and waiting in front of traffic lights and so on. Moreover, mobile users may be forced to keep vigilant even during daily routines, as they might anyway face many competing stimuli – not only auditory stimuli, but also visual and tactile ones, which may even interrupt their listening. In fact, sometimes their condition of mobile listening may prompt them to pay more attention to other external stimuli than they would otherwise – listening to an iPod is more of a multisensory experience than just an auditory one.

However, this does not mean that users are always physically disconnected to their iPod music. They may not sing along, dance, jump or move to the music openly, but they can respond to it in other, less evident ways – for example, lip-synching, synchronizing their walk to the rhythm of the music, tapping their feet or fingers, shaking their head and so on. In other words, although there may be no clear, outward, physical response to music, the users' bodies can make continuous adjustments to rhythm changes in both their surroundings and their music. Thus, iPod users may decide to 'move to their own rhythm' – that is, to synchronize their attention to the rhythm of their selected music, to 'entrain' to it[26] – and they can do this either in tune with or in opposition to the rhythms they perceive in their environment.[27] Although these adjustments would conventionally be interpreted in terms of cognitive engagement, recent neurobiological research has demonstrated that they are regulated instead by the neurological mechanisms that control our bodily movement.[28] To put it quite bluntly, iPod users do not tap because they are mentally following a rhythm, but their following a rhythm might best be described as a form of 'mentally tapping' to it.

Yet, the bodily dimension of mobile listening is not restricted to rhythmical attention and entrainment; it is also part of the emotional episodes that are so often associated with iPod usage. Indeed, a keyword for understanding these self-centred episodes is 'mood' – a term that keeps coming up in the testimonies gathered by Bull and in his own reflections. As it is employed by users – and as it is generally conceived – 'mood' would be a synonym for 'feeling' or 'state of mind' (where 'mind', however, would not be understood as exclusively intellectual), or for a complex of inner sensations, including also physical sensations. Thus,

---

[26]   On the importance of the concept of 'entrainment' for music studies, and specifically for ethnomusicology, see Martin Clayton, Rebecca Sager and Udo Will, 'In Time with the Music: The Concept of Entrainment and its Significance for Ethnomusicology', *European Meetings in Ethnomusicology*, 11 (ESEM-CounterPoint, 1) (2005): pp. 1–82.

[27]   Bull, *Sound Moves*, pp. 28–9.

[28]   Ian Cross, 'Listening as Covert Performance', *Journal of the Royal Musical Association*, 135/sup. 1 (2010): pp. 73–4.

users sometimes describe themselves as being overwhelmed by emotions and memories elicited by specific songs and recount how they use music to boost or counterbalance certain moods.[29] Mobile listeners associate moods not only with the music of their iPods, but also with their surrounding circumstances, like weather conditions or the overall impression they get from the places they pass through.[30] Besides, moods do not seem to be necessarily conscious: users can notice them and talk about it, but they can also discover them suddenly, sometimes precisely through music – a circumstance that is often associated with the practice of listening in random or 'shuffle mode'.[31]

To understand how these episodes might be possible, I propose to resort to the notion of 'mood' elaborated by neurologist Antonio Damasio in his *The Feeling of What Happens*. According to Damasio, moods are just emotions or feelings sustained in time, but they can be either primary emotions (the core types defined by Darwin, which are usually at the foreground of our minds) or what he calls 'background emotions' (or 'feelings'). 'Background feelings' (like fatigue, wellness, relaxation, instability and so on) are 'feelings that are not in the foreground of our mind' and are probably 'a faithful index of momentary parameters of inner organism state'.[32] They may be caused either by certain internal conditions engendered by ongoing physiological processes or by the organism's interactions with the environment, or by both.[33] Thus, thinking in terms of background feelings allows us to address moods not as a sort of second level, superimposed on bodily sensations, but as being continuous with them. In that sense, music can act as a catalyst to, or a sedative for, particular moods at a conscious or non-conscious level, but it always implies a connection to inner, bodily sensations.

Moreover, signs of motor response to music may exist even at the neuronal level, involving the so-called 'mirror neurons' or 'echo neurons'.[34] Mirror or echo neurons are a type of neurons found in the human brain that were initially identified as discharging both when the individual performs an action and when she sees somebody else performing the same action.[35] However, they are now

---

[29]   See Bull, *Sound Moves*, pp. 125–7.

[30]   Ibid., pp. 44–7.

[31]   Ibid., p. 126, and specifically on the shuffle mode, see Marta García Quiñones, 'Listening in Shuffle Mode', *Lied und populäre Kultur/Song and Popular Culture. Jahrbuch des Deutschen Volksliedarchivs*, 52 (2007): pp. 11–22, and Tuck Leong, Frank Vetere, and Steve Howard, 'Abdicating Choice: the Rewards of Letting Go', *Digital Creativity*, 19/4 (2008): pp. 233–43.

[32]   See Antonio Damasio, *The Feeling of What Happens: Body, Emotion and the Making of Consciousness* (London, 2000), pp. 285–6.

[33]   Ibid., p. 52.

[34]   See Robert J. Zatorre, Joyce L. Chen and Virginia B. Penhune, 'When the Brain Plays Music: Auditory–Motor Interactions in Music Perception and Production', *Nature Reviews/Neuroscience*, 8 July 2007: pp. 547–58.

[35]   See Giacomo Rizzolatti and Laila Craighero, 'The Mirror-Neuron System', *Annual Review of Neuroscience*, 27 (2004): pp. 169–92.

also being investigated for reacting in the same way to the sound produced by an action.[36] Even if it is too early to draw any conclusions from these incipient investigations, they also appear to support the notion that listening is intrinsically linked to action – a notion that it would be interesting to test in mobile listening conditions, to see how mirror neurons deal with both actual movements and the movements implied in the music.

Mobile Listening and Ubiquitous Subjectivity

As I have explained above, the image of the 'sonic bubble' evoked by many iPod users suggests the possibility of an almost disembodied, aesthetic absorption in mobile listening – a possibility apparently reinforced by the lack of a clear, outward, physical response to music. Instead, I have tried to show that while listening to their portable digital players, mobile users fluctuate between different ways of exercising attention and memory and different forms of interaction with the surrounding context, but also between different levels of bodily engagement. Therefore, although some iPod users consider their devices as a tool to protect themselves from the music contexts that others try to impose on them,[37] and while agency is undoubtedly a key aspect of the iPod experience – at least when it is not played in shuffle mode – mobile listening and listening to background music are not so fundamentally different. In fact, both listening situations are similar at least in the important sense that users may be simultaneously listening and moving around.

In fact, the issue of bodily engagement is as central to mobile listening as it is to dancing, running, doing aerobic exercises or any other 'peak experiences' that come more quickly to mind when thinking of bodily interaction to music.[38] Therefore, beyond their marketing scopes, the dancing black silhouettes of the iPod campaign may be read as an iconic image of the kind of covert motor participation that portable digital players trigger in their users, or as emblem of the promise of physical interaction that is tacitly expected from human relationships to music. In that sense, their frenetic movements sublimate the complex position of the human body and bodily sensations in mobile listening. Exploring this complexity would require a better understanding of the physical and neural mechanisms that both link perception to action and regulate the fluctuation between different locations and levels of attention typical of mobile listening and of ubiquitous musics generally.

---

[36]   See Istvan Molnar-Szakacs, and Katie Overy, 'Music and Mirror Neurons: From Motion to "E"motion', *SCAN*, 1 (2006): p. 236.

[37]   Bull, 'No Dead Air!', p. 347.

[38]   On ubiquitous listening during aerobic exercises, see Serena Facci's contribution to this collection, pp. 139–60; and also Tia DeNora, *Music in Everyday Life* (Cambridge, 2000), especially ch. 4: 'Music and the Body', pp. 75–108.

PART III
Spaces

Chapter 7

The Non-aggressive Music Deterrent

Jonathan Sterne

I had a nightmare that the man who invented Muzak invented something else.

Lily Tomlin[1]

In the early 1990s a curious phenomenon appeared on the English-language press's radar screen. Convenience stores and even whole shopping districts began to blast programmed music – best known by its brand name, Muzak – outdoors in parking lots, walkways, doorways and parks. For decades, the characteristic easy-listening 'background' sounds of Mantovani and a legion of imitators had been an easily recognized interior feature of elevators, supermarkets, convenience stores and telephone-hold systems. Now, as a new population management strategy, they flowed outdoors as well. The earliest reports depict a group of retail managers and owners, in different places, who turned to music in an attempt to chase away youths who loitered near their stores:

> According to one account, the store owners originally intended to use classical music to drive away the kids, but they couldn't find any canned Beethoven. So they turned to easy listening as what one of them called a 'nonaggressive music deterrent' and blasted them with stringed versions of Rolling Stones hits and other rock songs. Elevator music. Background music. The teen-age hangers-about found the sounds so offensive they fled to another part of town.[2]

Soon after the success of a 7-Eleven convenience store in Edmonton, other downtown businesses joined together to blast Muzak in a city park to drive away 'drug dealers and their clients. Police say drug activity has dropped dramatically.'[3] By the end of the year *The New York Times* hailed this new use of programmed music as one of the major events of 1990.[4] Following trial runs in western Canada, the Pacific Northwest and Los Angeles suburbs, in 1990 and 1991 Southland Corporation installed Muzak speakers in the parking lots of its 7-Eleven stores all over Canada and the United States. Soon after, the New York Port Authority

---

[1]   Quoted in Steven Mazey, 'Messiah Beats Muzak for Sounds of the Season', *Ottawa Citizen*, 28 November 1998, p. 5e.

[2]   Diane White, 'Mantovani Clears the Mall', *Boston Globe*, 1 September 1990, p. 9.

[3]   Ned and Lucy Howard Zemen, 'Let's Split', *Newsweek*, 20 August 1990, p. 2.

[4]   Jan Benzel and Alessandra Stanley Benzel, '1990: The Agony and the Ecstasy', *The New York Times*, 30 December 1990, p. 1.

Bus Terminal began to use programmed music to deter loitering.[5] By 1992 it had become a familiar tactic:

> A group of Cincinnati merchants is among the newest clients piping Muzak into the streets to repel teenagers and vagrants. 'We're trying to cut the crowds of young kids', says Robert Howard, president of the Corryville Community Council. High-school students, skateboarders, and vagrants flock to the urban college neighborhood in droves, he says. Summertime crowds are so thick that cars sometimes can't get through. So Corryville merchants installed stereo speakers along the three block shopping area, filling the streets with Muzak as well as Mozart. The music seems to be an effective deterrent so far, though cold weather may be helping the re-recorded Barry Manilow drive the loiterers elsewhere. At the same time, the music appears to be encouraging prospective customers. Scott Snow, owner of Bearcat Bob's sports bar, says 'there's a 97% to 98% positive acceptance rate among shoppers.'[6]

The 'Muzak Attack' story saw several recurrent bursts of coverage throughout the 1990s. This may have been due to the growing popularity of the technique; realistically, it may also be a result of press interest. After all, the 'Muzak Attack' story has a certain 'man bites dog' flavour to it.

Each case is somewhat different, but the stories all have similar features. Some store, street corner or open section of a town attracts a large group of people. Businesses in the area find these groups undesirable because they are thought to chase away customers. They install a programmed music service of either easy-listening selections or light classical music, and the group dissipates – ostensibly because the Muzak renders the space inhospitable to them.

The unpopularity of so-called elevator music is perhaps its most widely noted feature. Scholars have long attacked Muzak in its various forms, and indeed it has proven an easy target: Muzak 'slips into the growing spaces of activity void of meaning and relations'; it is 'a treatment akin to castration'; it is 'the most extreme case' of music as 'scientifically engineered propaganda'. Muzak populates the spaces where 'the value-demolishing errands of high technology capitalism are being run'. Or to put it in stark, elegant terms, Muzak is 'the honeyed antidote to hell on earth'.[7] Countless journalists have expressed the same disdain for Muzak over the second half of the twentieth century, and this case was no different. Even

---

[5] Psyche Pascual, 'This 7-Eleven is Alive with the Sound of Muzak', *Los Angeles Times*, 17 November 1991, p. 1b.

[6] Valerie Reitman, 'Muzak Once Again Calls the Tune in Retailers' War on the Unwanted', *Wall Street Journal*, 14 December 1992, p. B1.

[7] Jacques Attali, *Noise: The Political Economy of Music*, trans. Brian Massumi (Minneapolis, 1985), pp. 111–12; Michael Chanan, *Repeated Takes: A Short History of Recording and its Effects on Music* (London and New York, 1995), pp. 15–17; Jerry Herron, 'Muzak: A Personal View; or, a Superstructural Mystery in Five Pieces', *Journal*

newspaper reports, clearly sympathetic to the store owners and managers, could not resist taking a dig at the means used to achieve the desired end: 'the news that convenience store owners in Washington State and British Columbia have been using easy listening music to discourage teenage loiterers shouldn't surprise anyone who's ever fled a public place rather than be subjected to the stuff'.[8]

While the almost universal distaste for Mantovaniesque programmed music is hard to deny (unless you are Andy Warhol), the question of taste takes on a different valence in this essay. I examine how stores and municipalities use programmed music outdoors to regulate the movement of populations such as teenagers and homeless people who they deem to be outside the domain of normal production and consumption. Rather than lambast elevator music as a sonic pox on our aesthetic health, I start from a simple and extremely important assumption: some people do not like background music, and other people are aware of, and make instrumental use of, this fact.

Programmed music services like Muzak have always been part of a second-order media economy. They use already-familiar music – music that has already circulated through our culture as a commodity – to engineer the acoustic dimensions of spaces and experiences for listeners. Programmed music requires an earlier, 'first' moment of circulation, prior to its own. Whether we talk about the clichéd example of a 101-strings cover of The Beatles on an elevator speaker, or more common and up-to-date examples such as Natalie Imbruglia in Starbucks (or Nat King Cole near Christmas), programmed music operates on the assumption that people are already familiar with the song. The first part of this essay examines the use of programmed music to chase people away. I will call this new use 'the non-aggressive music deterrent' (following the unnamed executive in one of the quotes above) and will examine it in the schematic context of the political economy of culture and the wider field of programmed music. I argue that the second-order economy that programmed music inhabits requires media scholars to rethink our schemes of 'production' and 'consumption'. Having established the parameters of the second-order consumption that subtends programmed music, I then use my analysis of programmed music to recast some key questions about the control and design of public spaces, especially as acoustic spaces.

Programmed Music, or the Political Economy of Music in Reverse

Throughout its remarkable history, programmed music has been a form of environmental design, but not until the last 23 years or so has it become a deliberate form of aesthetic aggression, aimed at alienating groups of potential listeners. Programmed music has been in wide use since the 1940s, first in factories and later

---

of American Culture, 4/4 (1981): p. 125; R. Murray Schafer, The Soundscape: Our Sonic Environment and the Tuning of the World (Rochester, VT, 1994), p. 96.

    8   White, 'Mantovani Clears the Mall'.

in other commercial spaces, and it now comes in two varieties: background music and foreground music. Background music is what we conventionally describe as elevator music: syrupy or jazzed-down versions of already popular songs. It is what normally comes to mind when the word 'Muzak' is uttered and it is the form of music most frequently used as the non-aggressive music deterrent. It is also an increasingly small segment of the programmed music market.

In contrast, foreground music takes existing recordings and places them in a programme or flow of some sort. Foreground music sounds like radio, but differs from radio in a few important respects. Because of copyright law, it is technically illegal to play radio in business establishments for customers unless the business pays royalties to the proper publishers. Programmed music services are therefore especially attractive to large, national chains that are concerned about legal liability for copyright infringement and are less likely to ignore the law. In addition to covering legalities, the purchase of a programmed music service helps businesses shape their corporate personalities. Most programmed music providers offer many genres and channels to choose from, each carefully programmed to a set of specifications. In addition to the range of standard genres (classical, rock, country, urban, top 40, light jazz and so on), most providers also offer more expensive, customized programming. Different providers offer different rationales for their programming, but all guarantee their corporate customers that nothing offensive will come over the network, and that both style and sequence will offer maximum consistency.[9]

One possible reading of the non-aggressive music deterrent is that it simply represents a new market for background music, a product that had been in decline for more than a decade. Since the early 1970s Muzak's competitors (most notably Audio Environments Inc., which began the practice) have offered foreground music as a more appealing version of programmed music. Their reasoning follows the logic of the popular distaste for background music: why listen to a cheesy remake when you can hear the original? Whether or not this makes a difference to listeners' perceptions, the market share of background music has steadily declined. Muzak itself started offering foreground music services in 1983. Since then, the vast majority of its new service contracts have been for foreground music.[10] Even markets that have been traditional strongholds of background music have moved over to foreground music: for instance, many companies now play 'classical' selections, instead of background music, for their telephonic customers waiting on hold.[11]

---

[9]   Simon Jones and Thomas Schumacher, 'Muzak: On Functional Music and Power', *Critical Studies in Mass Communication*, 9 (1992): pp. 156–69; Jonathan Sterne, 'Sounds Like the Mall of America: Programmed Music and the Architectonics of Commercial Space', *Ethnomusicology*, 41/1 (1997): pp. 22–50.

[10]   Sterne, 'Sounds Like the Mall of America'.

[11]   Bryan Hay, 'The 90s Has Muzak Customers Whistling to a Different Tune', *The Morning Call*, 12 May 1996, p. 3b.

One might therefore reasonably conclude that retailers that want to chase away unwanted people constitute a new market for background music. Yet most of these retailers already used some kind of programmed music service. In the case of 7-Eleven, the Muzak outside was simply an extension of the Muzak available inside. As a result, it is doubtful that 'Muzak Attacks' have accounted for a major increase in programmed music providers' profitability. Moreover, the non-aggressive music deterrent was originally an innovative use of the product by Southland Corporation, a client. Only after Southland Corporation's success at the 7-Eleven stores did Muzak begin marketing it as one possible use of their background service.

> A bemused representative of Muzak Inc., the corporation with perhaps the best handle on how to tailor one's piped-in music to attract a specific audience, calls this the perfect reverse of normal music-customer relations: 'Usually you choose your music with an eye to the sort of customers you want to attract; why not for the sort of customers you want to repel?'[12]

When Muzak executives call the non-aggressive music deterrent the reversal of their service, they index a reversal of affect: prior to the 1990s programmed music was meant to encourage, comfort, familiarize and domesticate spaces. In fact, almost all previous academic analyses of programmed music start from this 'domestication of public space' premise.[13] The non-aggressive music deterrent reverses the logic by targeting a population to chase away from commercial spaces. Economically and mechanically, it is simply a new application of the principle on which programmed music is based.

Plausible as the new-market-for-old-product explanation seems, there is also a deeper answer that portends a slight theoretical shift for media scholars in how we usually discuss the consumption of culture. As I have already suggested, the economy and social organization of programmed music presumes and exists on top of a whole culture and economy of recorded music. In other words, programmed music presumes that music has already become a commodity and that the recording has already been around the commodity circuit several times. Put simply, programmed music makes use not only of existing recordings, but

---

[12] 'Easy Listening', *Washington Post*, 27 August 1990, p. A10.

[13] Tia DeNora, *Music in Everyday Life* (Cambridge, 2000); Alex Greene, 'The Tyranny of Melody', *Etc.*, 43/3 (1986): pp. 285–90; Herron, 'Muzak'; Jane Hulting, 'Muzak: A Study in Sonic Ideology' (MA thesis, University of Pennsylvania, 1988); Jerri Husch, 'Music of the Workplace: A Study of Muzak Culture' (PhD dissertation, University of Massachusetts, 1984); Jones and Schumacher, 'Muzak'; Joseph Lanza, *Elevator Music: A Surreal History of Muzak, Easy-Listening, and Other Moodsong* (New York, 1994); Ronald Radano, 'Interpreting Muzak: Speculations of the Musical Experience in Everyday Life', *American Music*, 7/4 (1989): pp. 448–60; Sterne, 'Sounds Like the Mall of America'.

also of what market researchers know about people's existing listening habits. Soundtracks for stores and factories alike are programmed on the basis of what they expect their desired visitors to have already heard and the reactions they expect of their listeners.

But 'reaction' can mean two very different things here. Muzak's 'stimulus progression' scheme, originally developed for its background music programming in factories, treated 'reaction' as more mechanical than aesthetic: faster music would be played in the late morning and mid-afternoon when workers might be dragging a little; slower music would be used in the morning and right after lunch to get people to slow down. In this model, it did not matter whether factory workers liked the music or not: 'in some cases, it is possible to achieve a direct production increase which completely ignores employee preferences and concentrates on the functional aspects only'.[14]

Foreground music, meanwhile, attends to aesthetic preferences by instrumentalizing taste for use towards another end: the creation of an environmental 'feel'. The use of certain kinds of classical music can give a 'classy' feeling to lingerie in a Victoria's Secret store, while 1950s rock 'n' roll hits in a hamburger joint can provide an 'all-American' feel.[15] As these examples suggest, the desired 'messages' are always designed to be semantically simple and (at least potentially) affectively powerful. Stores want listeners to feel a certain way about the store and its wares: programmed music helps to convey a mood. Of course, they can no more guarantee listeners' responses to the music than the producer of any cultural text can guarantee its meaning in advance. So they hedge their bets, use familiar formulas based on the already-extant circulation of recordings, and hope to succeed more often than they fail. Essentially, the corporate use of programmed music is about the purchase of an environment conducive to certain cultural dispositions. Retailers and factory managers alike invest in programmed music in the hopes that, by properly tailoring (and sometimes Taylorizing) their acoustic environments, they will achieve desired results in increased production or consumption. Pick your explanation: through behavioural–psychological processes (*à la* Skinner – the preferred explanation of Muzak), ideological machinations (the preferred explanation of most Muzak critics) or through regimes of practice (*à la* Foucault – the preferred explanation of Jones and Schumacher), stores and organizations buy programmed music in an effort to elicit a subjective response in listeners. Although each of these explanations may be compelling to different audiences, none of them actually has to be true. Just like any other product, its purchasers buy it on its promise. Programmed music does not have to work in order for its customers to buy it.[16]

---

[14]   Lanza, *Elevator Music*, pp. 48–9.

[15]   DeNora, *Music in Everyday Life*, pp. 109–50; Sterne, 'Sounds Like the Mall of America', pp. 36–41.

[16]   Please note that I leave aside the question of whether, as a programming technique, stimulus progression is based on sound psychological principles. My point is simply that both Muzak and their clients believed that it worked.

As Adorno famously argued about the varieties of 'culture' subsumed under the many cultural industries, the only thing they have in common is that they all are forms of cultural 'administration' for profit.[17] For its part, programmed music combines two forms of administration: the administration of recordings and the administration of social space. Whether in elevators or stores in shopping malls, programmed music is a form of architecture. People purchase and install programmed music to give spaces an acoustic shape, flavour or rhythm. As a form of sonic architecture, programmed music can also mark the borders of physical spaces. It can create an interior and exterior space through thresholds of audibility. For all who hear it, programmed music territorializes physical spaces. It codes them with meaning and, like brick-and-mortar architecture, it gives spaces a shape and consistency.[18] This is important because, as we will see, the non-aggressive music deterrent extends this territorializing function outdoors.

Programmed music is a distant cousin of another medium that administers recordings and social space: radio.[19] Just as stores are the real consumers of programmed music (to shape a space and achieve a desired effect in listeners), advertisers are the real consumers of programming (to achieve a desired audience for their ads); broadcasters sell audiences to advertisers through programming and ratings.[20] However, the analogy does not follow all the way: programmed music presupposes the circulation of music through both radio and album purchases (for that matter, downloaded mp3s – authorized or not – would work just as well). Through its repetitive playlists, commercial radio helps to render music familiar, and while programmed music may also assist in that project, it requires that the music has already circulated through radio and, quite possibly, television. For instance, another economic function of radio is to advertise recorded music for purchase, thereby serving the needs of the music industry directly. Programmed music, on the other hand, pays royalties to musicians' unions because it then sells the music as a service to clients. In the past, while programmed music could occasionally result in increased sales of recordings, this would be a purely accidental outcome. In an age of increased attention to branding and corporate consciousness, programmed music has become more of a marketing tool. Victoria's Secret is now the world's most successful dealer of classical music. It sells soundtracks to the programmed music it plays in its stores. These CDs combine relatively well-known selections from the so-called classical repertoire that fits with the company's desired corporate image. Similarly, Starbucks, Pottery

---

[17]   Theodor Adorno, 'Culture and Administration', *Telos*, 37 (1978): pp. 93–111.

[18]   DeNora, *Music in Everyday Life*; Sterne, 'Sounds Like the Mall of America'.

[19]   Jody Berland, 'Contradicting Media: Toward a Political Phenomenology of Listening', in Neil Strauss (ed.), *Radiotext(E)* (New York, 1993), pp. 209–17.

[20]   Eileen Meehan, 'Why We Don't Count: The Commodity Audience', in Patricia Mellencamp (ed.), *Logics of Television* (Bloomington, IN, 1990), pp. 117–37.

Barn and several other major chains have started to sell anthologies of music that can be heard in their coffee shops.[21]

The distinctive commodity status of programmed music calls into question some of our cherished habits of describing the production–consumption circuit. Most often, production is considered to be a large, structural process. Most of the major works of the political economy of communication thrive on structural explanations of production processes.[22] Even in famous ethnographies of cultural production – for instance, Todd Gitlin's classic *Inside Prime Time* – individual response is cast in a larger institutional context.[23] Consumption, meanwhile, is often analysed as a more atomized, personal, almost individual and inherently unpredictable practice. No doubt this is partly a result of the popularity of texts like de Certeau's first volume of *The Practice of Everyday Life*, the 'from the bottom up' turn in cultural history following E.P. Thompson and a desire to recover and respect those individual-level dimensions of everyday experience lost in structural explanation.[24] And, indeed, the model can work very well. Consider another iteration: Stuart Hall's 'encoding/decoding' model.[25] Many writers still find its rudiments quite compelling; they argue that meaning is produced and reshaped through the practice of consumption. Hall's case study considered television news, but, on its face, Hall's model might seem applicable to almost any communication context. For instance, John Durham Peters cites Hall next to Søren Kierkegaard to argue that:

> ... the moments of encoding and decoding (production and consumption, roughly) are relatively autonomous, allowing audiences to find meanings wildly divergent from those intended by the producers. But this gap between encoding and decoding, I suggest, may well be the mark of all forms of communication.[26]

---

[21]   Anahid Kassabian, 'Would You Like Some World Music with your Latte?: Starbucks, Putumayo, and Distributed Tourism', *Twentieth-Century Music*, 1/2 (2004): pp. 209–23.

[22]   Robert McChesney, *Rich Media, Poor Democracy: Communication Politics in Dubious Times* (Urbana, IL, 1993); Vincent Mosco, *The Political Economy of Communication: Rethinking and Renewal* (Thousand Oaks, CA, 1996); Dan Schiller, *Digital Capitalism: Networking the Global Market System* (Cambridge, MA, 1999); Herbert Schiller, *Culture, Inc.: The Corporate Takeover of Public Expression* (New York, 1989); Dallas Smythe, *Counterclockwise: Perspectives on Communication* (Boulder, CO, 1994).

[23]   Todd Gitlin, *Inside Prime Time* (New York, 1985).

[24]   Michel de Certeau, *The Practice of Everyday Life*, trans. Steven Rendall (Berkeley, CA, 1984); E.P. Thompson, *The Making of the English Working Class* (New York, 1966).

[25]   Stuart Hall, 'Encoding/Decoding', in Stuart Hall, Dorothy Hobson, Andrew Lowe and Paul Willis (eds), *Culture, Media, Language: Working Papers in Cultural Studies 1972–9* (London, 1980), pp. 128–38; David Morley, *Television, Audiences, and Cultural Studies* (New York, 1993).

[26]   John Durham Peters, *Speaking into the Air: A History of the Idea of Communication* (Chicago, IL, 1999), p. 52.

This principle holds true for the non-aggressive music deterrent as well: while Southland Corporation executives initially described the music as 'teen-age repellant' and claimed that it was 'working' to keep teenagers away, Thousand Oaks police took an interest in Muzak as a form of crime prevention during the non-aggressive music deterrent's trial run outside Los Angeles. Patrol cars would be summoned almost every weekend to break up groups of over 100 teenagers hanging out in mall parking lots. Although police said that they did not notice a decline in complaints, they were 'keeping an open mind'.[27] In 1998 the city of Toronto undertook a $2,000 experiment in piping programmed classical music through its subways, but found that the teenagers it hoped to chase away could listen to their own music with a $15 headset. According to a reporter, other teenagers seemed unaffected by the music. While most other commuters interviewed found the experiment amusing, some complained bitterly; meanwhile, subway employees tuned in to other music in their kiosks.[28] It would be easy to concoct an entire 'resistance theory' scenario here, with the 'poaching' teenagers resisting the Toronto transit authority's 'hegemonic' moves. Although there is some truth to such a reading, it also leaves out an important political dimension of the non-aggressive music deterrent.

If we really want to understand programmed music as a practice of consumption, we need to look beyond the responses of individual listeners and at stores instead. It is the stores that consume the programmed music service insofar as they purchase it, install it and use it. This is why it is so important to think of programmed music as a second-order economy of music; it does not follow the production (big institutions)–circulation (big institutions)–consumption (individuals) circuit that we have become so accustomed to describing. The scale of production and consumption is fundamentally different when cultural commodities are recirculated as part of a service, as in the case of programmed music.

If stores and organizations consume the non-aggressive music deterrent, then we need to re-ask the standard questions of consumption studies. Why are they consuming it? To what end and with what effect? Above, I briefly explained how programmed music serves an architectonic function, how it works as a form of acoustic design. But what is at stake when it moves outside? Who has the right to design the acoustic dimensions of the outdoor urban and suburban spaces? And by what means?

Programmed Music and the Politics of Public Space

On its face, the non-aggressive music deterrent seems like an ultimately benign response to populations that stores or municipal authorities do not want hanging

---

[27]   Pascual, 'This 7-Eleven is Alive with the Sound of Muzak'.
[28]   Rosie Dimanno, 'Headsets Drown out the Maestros', *Toronto Star*, 25 March 1998, p. 1b.

around – essentially, the stores or authorities chase people away by making the space they occupy less pleasing. This is a simple enough tactic, and it is in fact part of a much longer tradition of crime prevention through environmental design (CPTED). CPTED (pronounced 'sep-ted' and also known as 'defensible space') is a movement in urban design. According to CPTED, one can make an outdoor environment less hospitable to crimes of opportunity by controlling aspects such as lighting, signage, landscaping and adopting other measures. CPTED also aims to make the people an institution *wants* in an environment feel safer and make others feel unwelcome. Textbook examples of CPTED include: the removal of shrubbery around parking lots and the addition of bright lighting so that people feel safer returning to their cars at night; increased signage in and around a university to increase the sense that one is in a powerful institution; or even the bars one sees across the middle of benches on bus stops, so that it is impossible to lay down (and sleep) on them.[29] The non-aggressive music deterrent extends the premises of CPTED into the acoustic realm. It manages urban space to promote a sense of safety and control for its preferred occupants.

If we are to believe the existing literature on programmed music, the non-aggressive music deterrent accomplishes its goal because it assumes that some people will find Mantovani-in-the-convenience-store-parking-lot a pleasing and welcoming gesture, while others will find it offensive and hostile. Obviously, the assumption is that the people disposed to shop in the store will be welcomed and loitering teenagers or other unwanted persons will be deterred. Obviously, this is not always going to be the case. As with the lighting of parking lots, the construction of outdoor benches and the placement of foliage, the non-aggressive music deterrent plays against a law of averages. All these strategies require the assumption that they will work well enough for most people most of the time to be worth the trouble.

The very term 'crime prevention through environmental design' begs a crucial question: are people who loiter in convenience store parking lots, skateboarders at public fountains or homeless people in front of fast-food stores best thought of as criminals or potential criminals? They are not doing anything illegal by being there. Yet the articles that describe the non-aggressive music deterrent do not really distinguish between teenagers with lots of time (but not much money) on their hands and other forms of activity that are actually criminal. Rather, teenagers, drug dealers, the homeless, sex workers and low-income non-white populations are all lumped together as targets of the new Muzak.

Teenagers, for instance, are not sufficiently valuable as potential customers to keep them around. An article that compares Corryville's use of programmed music to an Indianapolis ordinance banning skateboarding in a hip retail section of town describes the target groups as 'teen-agers with orange hair and pierced noses,

---

[29]   For more on CPTED, see Carrie Rentschler, 'Designing Fear: Environmental Security and Violence against Women', *Cultural Studies: A Research Annual*, 5 (2000): pp. 281–310.

many on skateboards and few spending any money'.[30] Similarly, city authorities described large groups of youth in the E Block of Minneapolis as creating 'some uncomfortable meetings' with adult consumers on their way to downtown events: 'they don't feel safe if they have to pass through a crowd of 50 to 60 loitering kids'.[31] Race is also an unspoken context here. One wonders whether the crowds of loitering adults, a block or two away, would provoke the same reaction. At least in the Minneapolis E Block example, the kids were often African-American and the adults were often white.

In contrast, only a few news stories directly mention crime as a problem. The use of Muzak in Toronto followed a wave of subway violence. In Dallas, a McDonald's that began piping in classics had previously been the site of over 115 arrests a year (which, strictly speaking, is not evidence of crime but of police activity). In Minneapolis, a local mall serenaded a parking lot across the street that had been the site of some car vandalism. One Houston store reported being the site of gang graffiti until it installed a CD player and some speakers outside its front door.[32] Even there, the legality of the loiterers' presence is far from clear-cut. One report on Dallas referred vaguely to 'street toughs' and 'troublemakers'.[33] Another account of the same event does explicitly mention crack dealing, incitement to riot and the shooting of a police officer; it is also clear about the blame for the problem. While the author describes the McDonald's as 'Exhibit A in the average person's case against ever setting foot in downtown again', he is careful about placing blame: 'Not that McDonald's was to blame for any of this chaotic, even deadly, street life, what with dozens of bus lines converging within blocks of its glass doors, and a nearby Greyhound serving as a pipeline for trouble.'[34] Class and race are slippery slopes towards crime here: 'average' people in Dallas apparently own cars and can avoid downtown bus hubs. Fast food is innocent while public transport is to blame for middle-class fears about the area.

Behind these discussions is a latent theory of neighbourhoods, most famously put forward by Wesley Skogan: signs of 'decay' or 'blight' in a neighbourhood help contribute to its further decline.[35] Skogan had in mind things like graffiti and

---

[30]   Will Higgins, 'Ohio Merchants Aim Muzak at Skateboarders', *Indianapolis News*, 19 July 1995, p. 2a.

[31]   Doug Grow, 'City Turns to Classical Tunes to Keep Tunes off Block E', *Minneapolis Star Tribune*, 3 March 1995, p. 3b.

[32]   Dimanno, 'Headsets Drown out the Maestros'; John Flinn, 'Stores Turn on Classics to Turn Away Teens', *Houston Chronicle*, 27 June 1993, p. 4a; Doug Grow, 'City Turns to Classical Tunes to Keep Tunes off Block E'; Thomas Korosec, 'Mcfugue, No Cheese: Beethoven and the Dead European Males Clean up a Notorious Street Corner', *Dallas Observer*, 24 April 1997, p. 1b.

[33]   Janine Zuniga, 'McDonald's in Dallas Gives Thugs the Bach', *Austin American Statesman*, 25 April 1996, p. 1c.

[34]   Korosec, 'Mcfugue, No Cheese'.

[35]   Wesley Skogan, *Disorder and Decline: Crime and the Spiral of Decay in American Neighborhoods* (New York, 1990).

broken windows. If the graffiti is allowed to stand or the broken windows are not fixed, he argued, then it is likely that more serious forms of criminal activity will soon manifest themselves in a neighbourhood. While Skogan's argument is not directly aimed at loitering youth or homeless people, the same logic is at work in retailers' use of the non-aggressive music deterrent: 'respectable' people are less likely to move through a space filled with pink-haired teenagers and street people. Or to put it even more bluntly, the non-aggressive music deterrent is built on the belief that people – especially upper-middle-class people – should not have to encounter people of lower social classes in their daily or leisure travels. The non-aggressive music deterrent is designed to discourage people from perceiving outdoor environments in terms of shared, multiple meanings and uses. In this way, programmed music used outdoors is an attempt to code space and, specifically, to code it in terms of social class, race and age.

Many writers, ranging from theorists of 'the public' to critical geographers, have criticized this class-polarization of public space. All these writers make a similar set of points. The standard story of American public space is that it more or less disappeared with the increasing importance of suburbanization, first in the 1920s and then in earnest in the 1950s (although this is not to say that American suburbanization began in the 1920s – it is a much older process).[36] However, in recent years the American middle class has sought to reclaim some lost dimensions of the urban experience. One approach has been to create 'simulacra' of urban experience in suburban downtowns, shopping malls and other spaces of the 'middle landscape'.[37] A second approach has been to reconstruct urban space through gentrification, which essentially re-creates some dimensions of the urban experience while importing the class and race segregation of suburban living back

---

[36] The classic statement in communication studies is Jürgen Habermas's *Structural Transformation of the Public Sphere*, although Habermas draws heavily on the work of American sociologists like David Reisman, William Whyte and C. Wright Mills. See Jürgen Habermas, *The Structural Transformation of the Public Sphere: An Inquiry into a Category of Bourgeois Society*, trans. Thomas Burger with the assistance of Frederick Lawrence (Cambridge, MA, 1989). For other classic takes on the matter, see Richard Sennett, *The Fall of Public Man* (New York, 1977); and Jane Jacobs, *The Death and Life of Great American Cities* (New York, 1961). For a long view on the history of suburbs in America, see W. John Archer, 'Ideology and Aspiration: Individualism, the Middle Class, and the Genesis of the Anglo-American Suburb', *Journal of Urban History*, 14/2 (1988): pp. 214–53; and Robert Fishmann, *Bourgeois Utopias: The Rise and Fall of Suburbia* (New York, 1989).

[37] Edward Soja, *Postmodern Geographies: The Reassertion of Space in Critical Social Theory* (New York, 1989); Edward Soja, *Thirdspace: Journeys to Los Angeles and Other Real-and-Imagined Places* (Oxford, 1996); Michael Sorkin (ed.), *Variations on a Theme Park: The New American City and the End of Public Space* (New York, 1992); Peter Rowe, *Making a Middle Landscape* (Cambridge, MA, 1991); Sharon Zukin, *Landscapes of Power: From Detroit to Disney World* (Berkeley, CA, 1991).

into city space.[38] A third approach has been the new urbanism, which seeks to create vital, mixed-use neighbourhoods and offers a 'softer' version of gentrification.[39] As a spatial strategy, the non-aggressive music deterrent fits within both the second and third camps: outdoors, the non-aggressive music deterrent is about organizing urban space in a way that, as far as possible, reduces the chances of cross-class encounters – especially those encounters where people out shopping might interact with people who cannot afford to be out shopping. While CPTED is directly about law enforcement and the perception of safety, the non-aggressive music deterrent is more about a comfort zone for a certain set of middle-class visitors to a space. Ultimately, stores and cities use the non-aggressive music deterrent to help reduce cross-class encounters in parking lots, on sidewalks and in downtowns. It is about turning mixed-use spaces into single-use spaces.

One could even go so far as to read the non-aggressive music deterrent as a kind of low-intensity psychological warfare against urban populations that stores or cities wish to disperse. As in the remarkably inflammatory Dallas story quoted above, the rhetoric of warfare and the subtext of class warfare lay just beneath the surface of several reports of the non-aggressive music deterrent. Retailers' use of Muzak drew repeated comparisons to the United States' use of loud rock music in its siege against Manuel Noriega and, later, the use of the same tactic against David Koresh and the Branch Davidian compound outside Waco, Texas. 'Noise warfare' has become one of a set of psychological strategies used by the US military.[40] Alongside the more famous Noriega and Koresh examples, US forces also blasted loud rock music at Iraqi troops prior to attacks in both Gulf Wars. The parallel is hard to miss.

The non-aggressive music deterrent exists somewhere on a continuum between CPTED and psychological operations. To refer to the non-aggressive music deterrent as psychological warfare is 'too much', because it is simply about moving people around. But to refer to it as CPTED is 'too little', because the use of Muzak outdoors signals a kind of social struggle that does not only exist on the plane of crime. The non-aggressive music deterrent is an attempt by stores and municipalities to subtly organize the conduct of two groups of people who pass through their spaces. Here, we return to the various mechanistic analyses of the 'effects' of Muzak I discussed above. The non-aggressive music deterrent can be

---

[38] Sharon Zukin, *Loft Living: Culture and Capital in Urban Change* (Baltimore, MD, 1982); Mike Davis, *City of Quartz: Excavating the Future in Los Angeles* (New York, 1992); Neil Smith, *The New Urban Frontier: Gentrification and the Revanchist City* (New York, 1996).

[39] James Hay, 'Unaided Virtues: The (Neo)Liberalization of the Domestic Sphere and the New Architecture of Community', in Jack Z. Bratich, Jeremy Packer and Cameron McCarthy (eds), *Foucault, Cultural Studies, and Governmentality* (Albany, NY, 2003), pp. 165–206; Andrew Ross, *The Celebration Chronicles: Life, Liberty and the Pursuit of Property in Disney's New Town* (New York, 1999).

[40] Higgins, 'Ohio Merchants Aim Muzak at Skateboarders'.

seen as a form of behaviourism or conditioning – the music says 'come here' or 'stay away'. It can be analysed as a form of ideological manipulation: it literally 'hails' people within earshot, to use Althusser's famous formulation. It can also be analysed in a Foucauldian framework: indeed, the attempt to use Muzak to organize movement is very evocative of his concept of governmentality, which he defined as 'the conduct of conduct'.[41]

As a new use for one of the oldest forms of Muzak, the non-aggressive music deterrent marks a particular moment in the history of urban design. This moment is characterized by a deep ambivalence. On the one side there is a strongly felt longing for varieties of urban experience, especially a nostalgia for walking in the city, for 'flaneurship', for all those metaphors of movement through urban space that have populated cultural theory for the last 30 years. On the other side lies a deep anxiety about the widening barriers between affluent and poor, between young and old, between consumerist leisure and other public forms of leisure. The non-aggressive music deterrent helps facilitate a form of urban experience adorned with the nostalgic trappings of an earlier period. But like all nostalgias, it corrects the past to fit a consumerist fantasy in which the only meaningful social distinctions are those of consumer taste. It is, above all else, an attempt to mask the very real social differences that currently rock our cities and suburbs, and suffuse our social spaces. Behind the non-aggressive music deterrent is a real aggression towards the poor, the young and all other 'non-consumers'. It is about moving these people out of the 'front' spaces of consumerism.

Epilogue

Whatever its political valence, programmed music does not always work and even if it did, it would be very hard to know for sure without devising a novel strategy for isolating music from other environmental variables. In some cases, reports of Muzak's success have been somewhat exaggerated. In Dallas, for instance, police were quick to credit a rerouting of bus lines, along with other environmental factors, such as a fence erected around the parking lot facing the McDonald's outlet and landscaping that prevented people from crossing the street mid-block.[42] The Muzak in the Toronto subway accompanied other more conventional security measures such as video cameras and a regular subway patrol. But the point is not whether Muzak ultimately 'works' but, rather, why it is there at all. This essay has argued that the non-aggressive music deterrent is a form of second-order consumption – an attempt to manage outdoor, urban and other

---

[41]   Louis Althusser, *Lenin and Philosophy*, trans. Ben Brewster (New York, 1978 [1971]), pp. 127–86; Michel Foucault, 'Governmentality', in Graham Burchell, Colin Gordon and Peter Miller (eds), *The Foucault Effect: Studies in Governmentality* (Chicago, IL, 1991), pp. 87–104.

[42]   Korosec, 'Mcfugue, No Cheese'.

public spaces to make them hospitable to the kinds of consumers that stores and cities hope to attract. In the process, the non-aggressive music deterrent has also become a weapon in an ongoing, low-intensity form of social warfare that aims to reproduce some semblance of a cosmopolitan urban experience while limiting social interactions among strangers of different social strata – at least outdoors. Muzak is a form of sonic architecture or design and, like all forms of design, it is created and used with a specific aesthetic and social purpose in mind.

So what is to be done? It would be easy to end this essay by decrying the invasion of programmed music into public spaces and argue for more authentic forms of social interaction. I could imagine riffing on Jean Baudrillard's concept of 'mediatization', in which mediated forms of experience take over so-called 'live' forms of interaction, or borrowing Todd Gitlin's very seductive critique of the encroachment of media into all dimensions of everyday life.[43] Yet there is something disingenuous about that move. If the non-aggressive music deterrent is a spatial strategy, then it needs to be considered alongside other such strategies. We would never expect a critique of urban design that helps maintain social inequality to conclude with an attack on urban design or architecture *as such*. Rather, we would expect such a critique to call for better and more egalitarian design. As it is in architecture and urban planning, so it should be in media: technology and design are defining aspects of the human landscape. We need better, more egalitarian forms of urban media design. As Emily Thompson has written, acoustic design is one of the forgotten dimensions of architectural history, yet architectural acoustics have proven essential not only to the experience of twentieth-century music, but also to the experience of middle-class work and leisure.[44] Indeed, there is a long line of scholars, most notably R. Murray Schafer and Barry Truax, who call for more attention to the acoustic design of our lived environments.[45] If this essay has demonstrated anything, it is that such calls for better acoustic design are not simply aesthetic calls; they also have an irreducible political and ethical dimension. The design of sound space, like the design of urban space, is at once a question of sensuous experience *and* a question of justice. To understand the stakes, let us return to the Muzak Corporation.

Now that it is older and sports a different 'look', Muzak now seems to be aligning itself with some of the 'orange-haired' youth it helped chase around in the 1990s:

---

[43]   See Jean Baudrillard, *For a Critique of the Political Economy of the Sign*, trans. Charles Levin (St Louis, MO, 1981), pp. 175–6; Philip Auslander, *Liveness: Performance in a Mediatized Culture* (New York, 1999); Todd Gitlin, *Media Unlimited: How the Torrent of Images and Sounds Overwhelms Our Lives* (New York, 2001).

[44]   Emily Thompson, *The Soundscape of Modernity: Architectural Acoustics and the Culture of Listening in America 1900–1930* (Cambridge, MA, and London, 2002).

[45]   While I diverge from these authors on the nature of good design (they are naturalist in orientation, and I am not), we are in agreement about its importance. See Schafer, *The Soundscape*; Barry Truax, *Acoustic Communication* (Norwood, NJ, 1984).

> Graphic designer Murray Dameron, 28, knew Muzak was for him when he saw a company ad featuring an 'audio architect' – one of the folks who programme play lists. The guy in the ad sported a shaved head and patterned shirt, and was listening to headphones.[46]

Muzak, like many other companies, has cultivated a hipper, younger image to attract its employees. Like many other music companies, it seeks to create and sustain a unique 'corporate culture' through norms of behaviour, dress and attitude.[47] Indeed, we might even hear echoes of Tom Frank's 'conquest of cool' thesis: corporations have adopted the stances of the counterculture in order to sell more products and, as in Muzak's case, to make their corporate culture more enticing to younger employees.[48] Although they both sport hairstyles that might have a little countercultural flavour, the difference between an orange-haired youth in front of a convenience store and a twenty-something employee with a shaved head is not simply a difference of ten years. It is, most importantly, a difference of utility. Whereas the orange-haired teenager is a marketing point for the non-aggressive music deterrent (or its inverse within a mall's confines), his older self is an 'acoustic architect'.

Glimpses of Muzak's own putative corporate culture offer a microcosm of the social form its products help to create. It is a study in contrasts between indoors and outdoors. Indoors, in Fort Mill, South Carolina (just outside Charlotte), Muzak's new corporate headquarters offers a pseudo-egalitarian feel through its interior design:

> ... from the CEO to the rank-and-file, staffers have the same amount of work space for the same desks, chairs and laptops, and none are enclosed by office walls. Piped-in background noise creates enough of a hum to keep nearby conversations from becoming interruptions. Boyd says that allows him to discuss everything from personnel to planning with any employee at a desk anyone can see. 'Unless the employee is going to cry,' he says, grinning, while passing a private conference room.[49]

For a corporate office, the space appears unusually egalitarian – until the company fires you – and has attracted the attention of business professors from a number of universities. But, of course, that is inside.

---

[46]   Peter Smolowitz, 'Muzak's Offbeat Approach Appeals to York County, S.C., Businessmen', *Charlotte Observer*, 31 January 2001, p. 1b.

[47]   Keith Negus, *Music Genres and Corporate Cultures* (New York, 1998).

[48]   Thomas Frank, *The Conquest of Cool: Business Culture, Counterculture, and the Rise of Hip Consumerism* (Chicago, IL, 1998).

[49]   Smolowitz, 'Muzak's Offbeat Approach Appeals to York County, S.C., Businessmen'.

Outside, the Muzak building blares upbeat music, to be sure, but the corporate office building and parking lot are no more cosmopolitan than any other such structure. The inviting music in Muzak's parking lot may only restate the tune played in countless other outdoor spaces throughout the 1990s and into this decade: 'Employees and consumers, the world is your playground.' For everyone else, the music has a different message: 'go away'.

Chapter 8

An Anthropology of Soundtracks in Gym Centres

Serena Facci, translated by Elena Boschi

My aim is to help my clients to burn fat and improve their cardiovascular and respiratory function. I can achieve the same results with individual exercises and a treadmill, but it's not the same. My discipline is effective also because we're together and there's music. This gives a boost and motivation.

Tony[1]

Tony is a step-aerobics and Total Body instructor and personal trainer. He trained in fitness dance choreography, an aerobic discipline that, in addition to music, uses some dance principles. In gyms, music is used extensively, and the motivations expressed by Tony, as well as by other instructors, are very articulate and denote remarkable awareness.

In this chapter I will report and comment on the results of research I undertook in a number of sport centres and gyms in Italy.[2] Right from the outset, it was interesting to note that music was present both in the disciplines that have been placed between gymnastics and dance (such as aerobics) since the 1980s and in activities that had nothing to do with dance, such as spinning, running, work-out machines, Pilates, postural gymnastics and so on.

Physical Response as Musical Function

For all animals, including *Homo sapiens*, sounds are one of the guides through which they relate to the world, and motor reaction to sounds is biologically important. For prey, it is vital to perceive motion produced by a predator and vice versa. Moreover, sounds not only produce motor reactions, but are themselves the product of motion. Psychologically, we are used to associating sounds with ideas

---

[1]   Interview with Antonio (Tony), instructor at the Centro Sportivo Forum in Rome, January 2012.

[2]   Part of the results of this research have been published in Serena Facci, '"Funziona?" Valori e usi della musica nella contemporaneità', in Serena Facci and Francesco Giannattasio (eds), *L'Etnomusicologia e le musiche contemporanee* (Venice, 2009) <http://www.cini. it/publications/letnomusicologia-e-le-musiche-contemporanee-it> (accessed 20 January 2013).

of motion and therefore vitality, excitation and sometimes danger. Conversely, silence evokes lull, tranquillity and, taken to the extreme, absence of life. 'Silence worries', said one of the gymnastics instructors I interviewed when summing up the complex of reasons that pushed her to use music in various ways in many gymnastic disciplines.[3]

In an attempt to understand the relationship between music and sporting activities, it is appropriate, first, to remind ourselves of this atavistic universal background. The next step, however, is to understand how sounds that are specifically musical (that is, organized according to rhythmic, melodic and timbral criteria combined in various ways) induce and organize motion.

In his fundamental book *The Anthropology of Music*, Alan Merriam places physical response in the list of music's functions intended in the socio-cultural sense, but observes how

> … it is questionable whether physical response can or should be listed in what is essentially a group of social functions. However, the fact that music elicits physical response is counted in its use in human society, though the responses may be shaped by cultural conventions. Possession, for example is clearly elicited in part at least by music functioning in a total situation, and without possession certain religious ceremonials in certain cultures are considered unsuccessful … Music also elicits, excites, and channels crowd behaviour; it encourages physical reactions of the warrior and the hunter; it calls forth the physical response of the dance, which may be of prime necessity to the occasion at hand. The production of physical response seems to be an important function of music; the question of whether this is primarily a biological response is probably overridden by the fact that it is culturally shaped.[4]

The 'biological' motor response to sound and musical stimuli that Merriam talks about is very common. Just watch how our legs instinctively keep time while we are listening to a song, the ease with which even small children spontaneously move in the presence of singing or music, and, as recently observed, the spontaneous propensity to move shown by Alzheimer patients – even in advanced stages of the illness – if stimulated by music.[5] The phenomenon of entrainment (whereby two oscillators moving at different rhythms tend to synchronize if put in contact) is probably also at the basis of rhythmic interaction at a biological level. Various research studies in the neurosciences, biomusicology, music therapy

---

[3]   Interview with Alessandra, spinning and holistic disciplines instructor at the Centro Sportivo Venice Gym in Rome, May 2006.

[4]   Alan Merriam, *The Anthropology of Music* (Evanston, IL, 1964), pp. 223–4.

[5]   Emmanuel Bigand, 'Ethnomusicology, Evolutionary Musicology and the Neurosciences', paper presented at the 17th International Seminar in Ethnomusicology, Fondazione Cini, Venice, January 2012.

and ethnomusicology, use entrainment to explain how musicians converge on a common tempo and interact in various ways during performances.[6]

However, as Merriam stated, a physical response to musical sounds (which acquire different and less basic aims than simple signals) often occurs within complex events and is therefore intertwined, in individual as well as in group experience, with other aesthetic, emotional, communicative, affective and relational reactions, which are largely regulated by culturally shared codes. In his book *Il concetto di musica*, Italian ethnomusicologist Francesco Giannattasio proposes categorizing music's functions into three groups: (1) expressive functions, (2) organization and support of social activities, (3) induction and coordination of sensorimotor functions.[7] It is not difficult to recognize all three categories – albeit with different weights – in any musical experience. Giannattasio, for example, describes the wealth of functions in work chants.[8] In eurhythmic chants, in which music and work gestures share the same beat or rhythmic model, sensorimotor reactions are often accompanied by the chants' ability to facilitate social organization – evident in group work – and to communicate information and considerations not necessarily tied to work activities. Moreover, chants help make time pass more pleasantly.

In the matching of music and gymnastic activities the situation is not very different: the stimulus to react and organize motion is intertwined, as I will illustrate, with many other effects that make the presence of music significant on various levels, improving performance and distracting from the sensation of fatigue.

Music and Sport

In the last few decades, experimental research has been carried out on the relationship between music and sport,[9] which has highlighted music's different effects:

> *Psychological* effects refer to how music influences mood, emotion, affect (feelings of pleasure or displeasure), cognition (thought processes) and

[6]   Martin Clayton, Rebecca Sager and Udo Will, 'In Time with the Music: The Concept of Entrainment and Its Significance for Ethnomusicology', *European Meetings in Ethnomusicology*, 11 (ESEM-CounterPoint, 1) (2005): pp. 1–82. As far as ethnomusicology is concerned, the intuitions and influence on subsequent studies of John Blacking must be mentioned, as he positions the potential and limitations of the human body at the centre of his articulated reflections on music–making. See John Blacking, *How Musical is Man?* (Seattle and London, 1974); and John Blacking (ed.), *The Anthropology of the Body* (London, 1977).

[7]   Francesco Giannattasio, *Il concetto di musica* (Rome, 1992), p. 210.

[8]   Ibid., pp. 218–28.

[9]   Anthony Bateman and John Bale (eds), *Sporting Sounds: Relationships between Sport and Music* (London, 2009).

behaviour. The *psychophysical* effects of music refer to the psychological perception of physical effort as measured by ratings of perceived exertion (RPE) ... Music engenders an *ergogenic* effect when it enhances work output or yields higher than expected levels of endurance, power, productivity or strength.[10]

Such effects have been registered in all stages of aerobic activities involving prolonged effort, whereas the effects of music seem to be indifferent in maximum-effort anaerobic stages (for example, during sprinting): 'The aspect of the model most relevant to this phenomenon is known as the *load-dependent* hypothesis; when work intensity increases beyond anaerobic threshold, external cues such as music do not have any significant impact on perceived exertion.'[11] In this chapter, I will deal with some non-competitive aerobic disciplines carried out in sport centres, such as step, spinning and Pilates. In these disciplines, music is an integral part of the protocol.

However, it is worth remembering that there are also experimental studies on professional athletes and team sports. Music listening is a psychological aid for the training of athletes, too, and the support of chanting fans and music played over the stadium's PA system conditions team performance. In this case, music acts asynchronously.[12]

Equally significant is the function of music in individual sporting activities such as athletics and running. The debate within sport, in this case, is about which musics or even which songs are the most effective, and it involves technical motivations (for example, the importance of choosing pieces with a beat with the right tempo to run to or for aesthetic motivations, taking into account the pleasure of running and training while listening to one's favourite music. The Web is full of sites that give advice on and offer selections of music to run to, sorted by bpm (beats per minute). In particular, I would like to point out the website Run2Rhythm, where an article extolling the benefits of running in synch with the music's tempo analyses 'Eye of the Tiger' by Survivor (1982). According to the author and founder of the website, Gary Blake, the song's bpm is too slow for the right running rhythm – despite the extramusical reference to the soundtrack of the film *Rocky III* (Sylvester Stallone, 1982) and the routine use of the song at the openings of big sporting events in the United States.[13]

---

[10]   Costas I. Karageorghis and Peter C. Terry, 'The Psychological, Psychophysical, and Ergogenic Effects of Music in Sport. A Review and Synthesis', in Bateman and Bale, *Sporting Sounds*, p. 15 (italics in original).

[11]   Ibid., p. 18.

[12]   Karageorghis and Perry have identified three different ways music can be associated with sport: asynchronously, synchronously and pre-task.

[13]   Gary Blake, 'Running Music – Rhythm and Beat', in *Run2Rhythm* <http://www.run2r.com/rhythm-n-beat.aspx> (accessed 31 May 2012).

The complexity of musical language works on multiple levels. In this chapter, I will consider the list of music's motivational qualities in sport identified by Costas Karageorghis and Peter Terry:

> Rhythm response relates to natural responses to the rhythmical and temporal elements of music, especially tempo. Musicality refers to pitch-related (as opposed to rhythm-related) elements of music such as melody and harmony. Cultural impact draws upon the pervasiveness of music within society or a particular sub-cultural group, whereby frequent exposure to music increases its familiarity which has an important role in determining preference. Finally, association pertains to the extra-musical associations that music may evoke.[14]

This is not very far from what Giannattasio states in relation to work chants. However, unlike what used to take place in pre-sound-recording societies, in gyms we mainly make use of reproduced music – that is, music composed for other purposes and chosen or adapted for the occasion.

Musicalization

The pervasiveness of reproduced music in gyms falls within a broader phenomenon that I would define as 'musicalization' of the soundscape.[15] According to studies on the anthropology of sound as conceived by Steven Feld in his research in the rainforest or in Europe, the sounds that characterize an environment (be they natural such as birdsong or produced by humans such as bells) carry essential value for affective relationships as well as relationships of cohabitation between people and the space they inhabit. These relationships obviously end up involving music as well.[16]

Various studies, including this book, deal with urban realities like the Italian ones that I am discussing, where reproduced music is increasingly taking the place of ambient sounds and becoming a constituent part of the soundscape.[17] Its status as

---

[14]   Karageorghis and Terry, *Psychological, Psychophysical, and Ergogenic Effects of Music in Sport*, p. 17.

[15]   The term 'musicalization' is used above all in theatre and literature to define the musical quality of texts and plays. Personally, I have already used it with regard to phone ringtones, the evolution of which, both by producers and by users, has seen musical features being given to the sound signal; see Serena Facci, 'Musicalizzazioni: le suonerie', *AAA TAC: Acoustical, Art and Artifacts. Technology, Aesthetics, Communication*, 2 (2005): pp. 179–94.

[16]   Steven Feld, *Sound and Sentiment: Birds, Weeping, Poetics, and Song in Kaluli Expression* (Philadelphia, PA, 1990 [1982]); Giovanni Giuriati and Laura Tedeschini Lalli (eds), *Spazi sonori della musica* (Palermo, 2010).

[17]   Tia DeNora, *Music in Everyday Life* (Cambridge, 2000); Michael Bull and Les Back (eds), *The Auditory Culture Reader* (Oxford, 2003); Michael Bull, *Sound Moves: iPod Culture and Urban Experience* (London and New York, 2006).

aesthetic product certainly qualifies music as 'pleasant', its evocative abilities give it a familiar character and its ancient history alongside men makes it reassuring and human, beyond the differences between various genres. Music is thus a useful system to humanize and render the sonic environment familiar, and deliver it not only from the cacophony of machine noise, but also from the vacuum of silence.

The 'musicalization' of the sonic space means that a status similar to that of events traditionally connected to music (dance, meditation, celebration) is also attributed to activities carried out in the gym. In the words of step instructor Valentina Ziliani: 'Sometimes, near the entrance on the street there's a speaker blasting dance music at full volume, as if to say that inside there's a party.'[18] As we will see later, functional music for gymnastics is often an aesthetic choice and experience.

Music has different roles. First, to use Merriam's words again, it adds the dimension of 'aesthetic pleasure' to physical activities through 'musicalization'.[19] Through a process similar to that of designing for the figurative arts, a bit of art is added to events that started with a completely different aim. It is a phenomenon similar to the one I studied in Burundi, where, in some situations, women use sung (that is, musicalized) greeting formulas. They do it to give the encounter a more solemn value, but also with the declared purpose of having fun and doing something beautiful (*akahibongozo*).[20]

To be truly effective, this process of 'musicalization' requires certain competences. Managers and instructors in sport centres must know how to choose and apportion the music to offer. As far as I was able to observe, the best ones achieve remarkable levels of sensitivity and creativity in evaluating and reusing musical pieces.

Sport Centres

Since the 1980s, in Italy, being active has been one of the most widely shared pleasures and duties. In cities, as well as in small towns, there are both large and small sport centres where one can practise different activities, ranging from sports like football and tennis, to swimming and other aquatic disciplines, to various kinds of gymnastics.

The term 'fitness' is often used to refer to a set of gymnastic disciplines that can be practised individually (such as muscle strengthening and slimming

---

18   Interview with Valentina, musicologist and step instructor at the Centro Sportivo Toto Modo in Cremona, October 2006.

19   Merriam, *The Anthropology of Music*, p. 223.

20   Serena Facci, 'Akazehe del Burundi. Saluti a incastro polifonico e cerimonialità femminili', in Maurizio Agamennone (ed.), *Polifonie. Procedimenti, tassonomie e forme: una riflessione 'a più voci'* (Venice, 1996), pp. 123–61.

programmes involving specific machines) or in a group (aerobic disciplines such as step or holistic ones like Pilates, and so on). To best pursue the objective of fitness, larger sport centres are sometimes combined with beauty centres offering massages and other beauty treatments, as well as medical assistance.

In her socio-anthropological study of gyms in Italy, Roberta Sassatelli defines fitness as an obsession of our society, which is centred on caring for one's body in the medical and aesthetic sense.[21] Those who join a specialized centre generally do it to feel better and to take care of themselves, and go there alone. So, in contrast to what takes place on a tennis court or football pitch, in fitness centres people are in the company of strangers, and ephemeral and heterogeneous groups are formed to meet the requirements imposed by the various disciplines.

Those who work in these centres claim that music helps clients overcome the unease of finding themselves alone doing demanding work among strangers with whom they have to share even intimate spaces like the showers. As the manager of a sport centre in Rome has pointed out:

> Here people are all together, sometimes they socialize, but it's not easy. We need to make sure they're at ease. In the fitness suites where everybody does their own programme by themselves, we have the radio and sometimes the TV on, so those who want can watch it to kill time, but also so they don't have to look at others. Some clients though prefer bringing their iPod, so they can listen to their own music. (Stefania)[22]

Filling our ears with music from an iPod while doing an individual programme in the fitness suite next to another client whom we do not know or even letting the music piped into the changing rooms envelope us are sufficient techniques to maintain our privacy. Through music we build a familiar space in a place we have to share with a mix of strangers, a fictitious environment of isolation – whatever the musical genre might be. This is why individual solutions that help a client feel at ease, such as listening to a favourite playlist (that is, iPods), are tolerated. Individual playlists are also used to measure the duration of an exercise (i.e. I ran on treadmill for five songs) in a more pleasant way than with a stopwatch.

Some centres play what is being broadcast by easy-listening and current chart hits radio stations in the reception area and in the changing rooms. Others choose the music on the basis of the time of day and type of clientele, as Valentina points out:

> In the morning it's Italian songs, because the clientele is mostly older women who love that kind of repertoire; at lunchtime, for clients who take advantage of

---

[21]   Roberta Sassatelli, *Anatomia della palestra: Cultura commerciale e disciplina del corpo* (Bologna, 2000).

[22]   Interview with Stefania, manager of the Centro Sportivo Venice Gym in Rome, May 2006.

the break from work, it's more dynamic music like commercial dance; after 6 pm it's all a party with disco and techno music. (Valentina)

Step – in Synch and in Tune

Group disciplines require many people to share the same space. Music is carefully chosen by the instructor who, among other things, aims to create – however temporarily – forms of solidarity and identity, including gender identity. Alessandra notes how '[i]n masculine disciplines such as Fitbox the music is always very strong; they mostly use hip hop'. The disciplines that are traditionally more intrinsically tied with music are the aerobic ones. In *Music in Everyday Life*, Tia DeNora devotes a significant part of her chapter on 'Music and the Body' to aerobics.[23] She points out how every class is rigidly governed by musical tempo, whose function is to produce a controlled acceleration of physical work and therefore of cardiac rhythm, followed by an equally gradual and controlled deceleration. Referring to research undertaken with Sophie Belcher, DeNora reconstructs the three essential phases of a class (warm-up, core, cool-down), identifying a precise grammar (aerobic grammar), shared and pursued both by instructors and participants. Music is an integral part of this grammar. However, it works on different levels, facilitating motor coordination, but also constructing motivational emotional reactions:

> On the one hand, music is a prosthetic technology of the body because it provides a resource for configuring motivation and entrainment, enabling the body to do what, without music, it could not do. On the other hand, the bodily movements that music profiles may lead actors to identify, work-up and modulate emotional and motivational states.[24]

My experience in Italy confirms much of DeNora's conclusion. Step, which I have dealt with in particular, has reached very high levels of 'musicalization'. For example, one of the varieties of this discipline, known as 'choreography', consists of preparing in every class a sequence of exercises that are combined, memorized and repeated by the group as if they were dancing. The instructor uses combinations of steps and choral motifs borrowed directly from dance styles like mambo, *chassé* and so on.

Instructor training, which takes place in specialized schools, therefore includes a musical component:

> In step, like in all aerobic disciplines, the session is based on prepared sequences of routines. The first thing we instructors learn is to recognize the master

---

[23]   DeNora, *Music in Everyday Life*, pp. 89–108.

[24]   Ibid., p. 107.

beat. Each routine consists of eight movements that correspond to eight beats recognizable in the musical accompaniment. Between the eighth beat of a routine and the first of the following (master beat) there's a signal (for example, a drum roll or a cymbal) that indicates the beginning of the new cycle. (Valentina)

Music forces us to count. Keeping count is important for an instructor, who is then sure that all the participants in the group are doing the necessary repetitions of the movement. Experience has helped me to increase my musical sensibility. In the end you're so in tune with the music that you no longer need to count the beats. I listen to the piece and I know when and how to organize the steps. (Tony)

The music used in step must have clearly demarcated sections:

1. regular and very evident beat and controlled variation of bpm;
2. no odd-numbered metric or formal structure;
3. varied musical genres (although pop and dance music are the most used), but the pieces are reduced to samples and are always remixed;
4. *forte* or *fortissimo* dynamics.

Controlled Beats

We have seen how Karageorghis and Terry, in their list of musical features that have 'motivational' effects on sport, distinguish between musicality, by which they mean melody and harmony, and rhythm.[25] For a musician or a musicologist, the splitting of rhythmic parameters from the concept of musicality may sound strange, as temporal organization and rhythmic figures are integral parts of musical language. But, for sports experts, rhythm is primarily a regulator of the human body's motor patterns, starting from the basic ones like heartbeat, breathing and steps.

So even if music works on various levels, tempo and rhythm remain a priority in both step and other kinds of gymnastics. Tony is persuaded of the wealth of stimuli that music brings to his choreography classes, which seem to cross into dance, but have clearly distinct aims, especially with regard to the management of tempo:

There is, however, a substantial difference between our classes and dance classes: we can't stop. Music always goes on, because we can never lose the right timing of breathing and cardiac rhythm. In dance classes teachers demonstrate the new step. Then they turn off the music and everybody learns it. They can slow down and stop, because the aim is to learn it well to then perform it again with the

---

[25]   Karageorghis and Terry, *Psychological, Psychophysical, and Ergogenic Effects of Music in Sport*, p. 17.

music. For us what counts is training. I gradually propose new steps, making the figure more and more complex, but the participants learn them by constantly continuing to move. (Tony)

It is principally the beat that synchronizes and regulates movements. Valentina notes how '[e]ach session is based on four phases: warm up, aerobic, cool down and relax. For each of these phases the bpm have to change. We start slower and reach a maximum speed of 140 bpm in the aerobic phase. Then we begin to slow down again.' According to Tony (whom I interviewed in 2011, a few years after Valentina) exceeding 136 bpm can be dangerous. His 'interval training' and 'step and tone' classes alternate step and strengthening exercises. As a general rule, however, the phases described by Valentina and identified by DeNora and Belcher are observed.

The ability to synchronize movements to sound stimuli is variously studied and connected to the above-mentioned phenomenon of entrainment, which, in this case, would guide all participants in a step class to move simultaneously, following the music's tempo. The perception of musical tempo and our ability to move to an external metre is due to neural circuits, located particularly in the cerebellum.[26] Studies in biomusicology have examined this phenomenon in some animal species and have traced evolutionary hypotheses that document how widespread this ability is in *Homo sapiens*.[27]

Obviously, when the movement performed is externally imposed, instead of being spontaneous, and the metric impulse is included in the music, synchronization is not at all mechanical, but rather an aim to achieve.[28] DeNora and Belcher have noted how, for example, 'bad music' (that is, music that did not produce the desired effects on the participants) was stopped by the instructor to avoid compromising

---

[26]   The cerebellum is one of the most ancient parts of the brain. Further studies are demonstrating that there are connections between the various areas of the brain dedicated to decoding musical parameters, which allows us to reconstruct the musical message in its entirety. Moreover, these studies are examining the relations between musical perception and emotional reactions. See Isabelle Peretz, 'La musica e il cervello', in Jean Jacques Nattiez with Margaret Bent, Mario Baroni and Rossana Dalmonte (eds), *Enciclopedia della musica: Il sapere musicale*, vol. 2 (Turin, 2002), pp. 260–64; Isabelle Peretz, 'Musical Emotions: Brain Organization', in Patrik N. Juslin and John Sloboda (eds), *Handbook of Music and Emotion: Theory, Research, Applications* (Oxford, 2010), pp. 104–26; Daniel J. Levitin, *This is Your Brain on Music: The Science of a Human Obsession* (London, 2007).

[27]   Bjorn H. Merker, Guy S. Madison and Patricia Eckerdal, 'On the Role and the Origin of Isochrony in Human Rhythmic Entrainment', *Cortex – Elsevier*, 45 (2009): pp. 4–17.

[28]   As some ethnomusicological studies have shown, the very perception of the beat is culturally conditioned, but even among individuals belonging to the same culture it can happen that the beat is perceived differently within the same musical piece – for example, by privileging the offbeat. See Clayton, Sager and Will, 'In Time with the Music'.

the outcome of the class.[29] Hence, for instructors it is fundamental that the beat is very clear: 'Musics must be remixed. Bass must be heard clearly, to guide the steps.' (Tony).

That said, my impression after observing his classes is that the phenomenon of entrainment in step is not exhausted by the synchronization of movements and basic pulse – however important this may be. For example, the way Tony – like others – communicates while teaching the exercises is essentially based on bodily communication: the instructor proposes a figure and the participants have to repeat it until they have learned it well. This teaching/learning mode, very widespread in oral musical traditions, is based on partly spontaneous imitative processes that fall within the field of proxemics and seem to descend from automatisms whereby bodies interact among them.[30]

Dance patterns that are transmitted this way are needed to move the various parts of the body in harmony and do not only respond to rhythmic musical stimuli, but also to melodic, timbral and dynamic ones. To choose 'good music' for a step session, instructors take into account the fact that music is a complex sound event, in which pitches, melodies, timbres and harmonies are rhythmically organized in time.

Square CDs

Music must be prepared ad hoc. First of all, its duration must match that of the class, if possible without pauses. Each instructor owns a set of CDs that have the same duration as the class, follow tempo acceleration and deceleration, have a powerful groove to guide movements and a formal structure following that of the routine:

> We call these 'square discs' because they are based on 4/4 bars and cycles of 8 beats marked by the master beat. If you look on the internet it is full of sites where DJs advertise their discs, good for every type of fitness discipline. Sometimes they sell them to us at training courses. (Valentina)

There is indeed a broad range of materials sold through the Web, and those working in the field note that there are commercial interests behind the whole world of fitness and therefore also in the specific sector of dedicated musical production. An example of this is the website Power Music that sells selections of hits divided by decade (starting from the 1940s), artist (Sinatra, Beatles, Madonna and so on), genre (dance, hip hop, classical, Broadway) and also specific typologies such as Christian and Christmas.[31]

---

[29]   DeNora, *Music in Everyday Life*, p. 96.
[30]   Clayton, Sager and Will, 'In Time with the Music'.
[31]   <http://uk.powermusic.com/> (accessed 31 May 2012).

However, many instructors, including Valentina and Tony, prefer to organize their own material, choosing musical pieces that they deem appropriate for the participants in their classes and relying on friends who are DJs to remix them. The division of the beats is binary, the bars are generally 4/4 and the form of the pieces is organized on combinations of cycles of eight beats that can originate combinations of 16 or 32 beats. Binary formulas (for example, a melody that is repeated identically twice) are useful for exercises because motor patterns must be repeated identically for the right and left side of the body:

> The basic cycle that ends with a marker is eight beats, but my choreographies are based on blocks of 32 beats. The steps are first orientated from right to left then from left to right. Everything I do towards the right, I then have to do towards the left. (Tony)

However, I do not think that it is purely functional reasons that guide the compositional procedures of DJs, which are significantly conditioned by cultural models. Four-four time signatures and melodic forms based on binary patterns are very widespread in Western music. Let us consider the eight-bar themes in the classical period, divided in phrases of four and strophes of two, or the 32-bar structure of Tin Pan Alley songs. These also prevail in pop and dance music, which are the most familiar genres for gym clients.

Fortissimo Dynamics

> Music is loud because it has to 'be there'. (Alessandra)

This quote by Alessandra makes us think of a saturating and almost tangible presence in the gym, due not only to high volume, but also to the use of a very wide spectrum of frequencies. We can observe in Figure 8.1 the sonogram of a fragment taken from a CD expressly created for a step session by DJ Marco Manara.[32] The harmonics of the sounds of the groove reach beyond 20,000 Hz (the conventional limit for human hearing). Images like this characterize electronic dance music and are definitely unusual in non-remixed music.

I attended one of Tony's interval training classes. It is a class in which the step routines are interspersed with rather demanding strengthening exercises (in this case with weights). The atmosphere of the gym was vibrant with very high-volume music, and Tony kept proposing exercises following the beat, but various participants preferred to move more slowly, depending on their abilities, and therefore fell out of synch with the tempo. The group that earlier looked compact, as in line dancing, seemed to break up. At the end of the class, I asked some participants who seemed among the most experienced whether music is necessary:

---

[32]   Telephone interview with Marco Manara, guitarist, composer and DJ, May 2007.

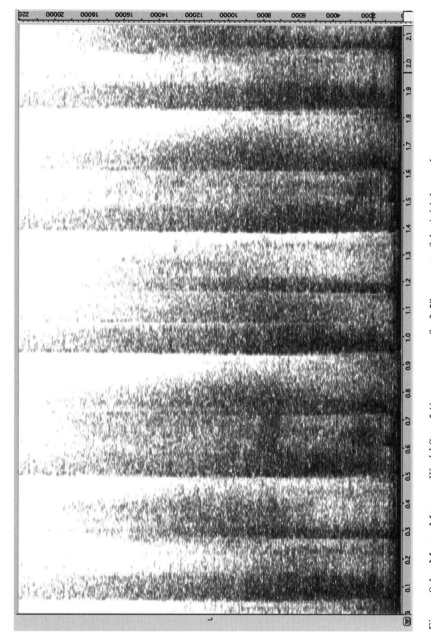

Figure 8.1   Marco Manara, *World Step 54'*, sonogram of a 3.5" excerpt of the initial sample.

'Music is essential in step. Without music we couldn't do anything.' I asked whether this was also true during exercises with weights, when not everybody managed to stay in synch, and a participant in the interval training class said: 'With weights everybody needs to find their own tempo, not everybody manages to follow that of the song. But music is still important, because it gives energy.'[33] So music gives energy even when it does not command a synchronized response. Exercises with weights would seem to escape the norms of step and, instead, fall within one of the cases of asynchronous use that Karageorghis and Terry talk about. The research presented in their article principally deals with tempo speed, and they have shown how a slow tempo (below 100 bpm) reduces the quality of the performance, whereas a fast tempo or – better still – an acceleration offers a better performance, even without synchronization.[34]

These studies do not address the role of dynamics. I spoke to Björn Merker about the evolutionary reconstruction of entrainment. My question was: 'Why is music, especially if very loud, perceived as useful to gather the necessary energy for demanding movements, even in an asynchronous situation?' According to the Swedish scientist, the answer lies in the level of excitement that is reached – for example, in collective party situations when many people find themselves in a loud and lively situation. Some phenomena observed among primates, like 'carnival display'[35] in chimpanzees, offer evidence of this among animals.[36] It is not difficult to find examples, both in our personal experiences and in the anthropological literature, of frenzy during parties or rituals, in music-saturated environments that help us stay active and awake for hours, even during night-time, without feeling tired. As an example, Merker mentioned rave parties. But we can also think of how children become hyperkinetic during school parties with music. We may have inherited a propensity for emotional excitement accompanied by loud vocalization and vigorous physical movement in a group setting from the common ancestor we share with chimpanzees, along the lines of what occurs today in the chaotic and unsynchronized chimpanzee carnival display. To this general background humans have, of course, added synchrony of both voices and movement to a common beat,

---

[33]   Interview with Sara, participant in the interval training course at Centro Sportivo Forum in Rome, January 2012.

[34]   Karageorghis and Terry, *Psychological, Psychophysical, and Ergogenic Effects of Music in Sport*, p. 27.

[35]   'On irregular occasions, typically when a foraging subgroup discovers a ripe fruit tree or when two subgroups of the same territory meet after a period of separation, the animals launch an excited bout of loud calling, stomping, bursts of running, slapping of tree buttresses, and other means of chaotic noise-making. There are no indications that any kind of inter-individual co-ordination, let alone rhythmic synchrony, forms part of these chimpanzee group displays.' See Merker, Madison and Eckerdal, 'On the Role and the Origin of Isochrony', p. 6.

[36]   See Merker, Madison and Eckerdal, 'On the Role and the Origin of Isochrony'. The discussion with Björn Merker occurred in Venice during the 17th Seminar in Ethnomusicology, January 2012.

but apparently, even in us, social and physical excitement can take place without it. Francesco Giannattasio, who has researched the difference between real time and musical time in possession rituals in Somalia and Nepal,[37] has commented that formal or even just rhythmic cyclical patterns of music push us to keep going upon hearing them. In other words, music 'pulls' us into its dimension where everything could proceed *ad infinitum* even if we cannot follow its tempo rigorously. To conclude, we can say that even when we are not in synch, we tune in with music and with others.

A fitness class is obviously not a party, and the physical work is often burdensome and boring, but sport centres offer a place of well-being where people can allow themselves a pleasant break from everyday stress, as if they were in a play situation or on holiday. Valentina, Tony and his instructor, Gil Lopes,[38] have clearly said that many elements of an aerobics class are reminiscent of the euphoria of a party, a club or entertainment activities in holiday resorts. In particular, Gil used this comparison to define aerobics conventions. These are events that take place annually in various parts of the world. Instructors meet for a few days to update and exchange experiences. Many motivated participants join very crowded classes attended by hundreds of people in a full immersion of aerobics, which is lived as a holiday. This is also one of the many aspects of 'musicalization'. I would add that the use of music is not aimed at entertaining or putting on shows, but at improving the exercises. However, sometimes sport centres do put on aerobic choreography shows.

Tastes, Contexts and Associations

Among the motivational values of music in sport, Karageorghis and Terry also include 'cultural impact' (that is, sport enthusiasts conforming to specific cultural models of behaviour and musical experience).[39] First, music has an effect on socialization. Synchronized motion is an expedient used in many contexts to create cohesion within a group and, if necessary, make enemies fear that group. Tia DeNora, in fact, looks at the comparison between synchrony in aerobics and among soldiers.[40]

Formalized choreographies in step use a formation that Curt Sachs was first to define 'frontal' in his *Eine Weltgeschichte des Tanzes* to differentiate it from

---

[37]   Giannattasio, *Il concetto di musica*, pp. 231–63. The discussion with Francesco Giannattasio occurred in Rome during his lectures in Ethnomusicology at Università La Sapienza, April 2012.

[38]   Interview with Gil, competitive aerobics instructor, multiple international champion, January 2012.

[39]   Karageorghis and Terry, *Psychological, Psychophysical, and Ergogenic Effects of Music in Sport*, p. 17.

[40]   DeNora, *Music in Everyday Life*, pp. 196–7.

a circular formation. Frontal line choreographies, unlike circular ones, generally have representational aims: one dances in front of, and for, someone. Participants in an aerobics group, whether they like it or not, project images of their bodies in motion and offer seductive messages.[41] Among the dances that use frontal formations Sachs mentions those very widespread courtship dances in which groups of men and women arrange themselves specularly in front of one another. In aerobics, the specular relationship is between the group and the instructor who performs the exercises, sometimes even on a stage in order to be visible by everybody. This formation recalls that of a show in which an artist performs in front of a participating audience. The instructor's charisma and the complicity established between them and the members of the group can produce affective reactions, esteem, trust and admiration. Both Tony and Gil have said that a good instructor must be able to galvanize the group, also by creating pleasant social moments outside the classes. According to Gil, '[m]usic puts us in communication with the others: we're all doing the same thing and we feel like a group. There isn't competitiveness like in sport.' This relationship also involves the instructor being sensitive to, and having respect for, the musical tastes of the participants:

> The genre most commonly used is American dance music, but you can use everything, as long as it's remixed. Generally I choose the pieces based on their current popularity, the type of mood they can transmit, but also based on the ages and tastes of the participants. You always need to mediate with other people's tastes and try not to displease anybody, even if it's not easy. (Tony)

Again, to make the class pleasant, instructors often change compilations in order not to bore participants:

> For the end of the class sometimes I ask my friend the DJ to prepare a section that's called 'show'. I choose a song that I know the group particularly likes (perhaps because it's the hit of the moment) and use the whole piece. For the group it's a surprise: being able to perform the exercises to a song they like, when they know the choreography well, gives them a lot of satisfaction. (Tony)

The last motivational quality that Karageorghis and Terry identify is the ability to create emotional and symbolic associations.

Valentina introduced me to the CD mentioned in Figure 8.1, entitled *World Step 54'*. The author of the remix, Marco Manara, used samples of musics and chants from various parts of the world, suitably edited and remixed on a base of electronic loops. The overall duration is 54 minutes, like a step class. It goes from Latin American examples, to North Africa, India, Australia, Spain, the United States and Ireland.

---

[41]   Curt Sachs, *Eine Weltgeschichte des Tanzes* (Berlin, 1933).

Musical genres are interchangeable, but it depends on the choreography you want to do. For the Irish step we use Irish music and movements with props. With Latin music we use 'Latino' steps with pelvic movements. Indian music: we do more movements with our hands. With *World Step 54'* it's like going around the world in step. (Valentina)

Although they respect the rigid organization of bpm and eight-beat cycles, the compositional criteria are those typical of electronic dance music: the cycles are concatenated, alternating denser and more rarefied parts, and the passages from one sample to the other happen with groove sections featuring variants from one to the next. Moreover, samples are dismembered in sections of four, two or even one single beat and solicit a more refined level of perception than just surrendering to the groove.[42] These expedients make the obsessive repetitiveness of the beat less boring and stimulate the creation of new choreographed motifs, as Valentina said. In Table 8.1 we can see a brief analysis of how the sample of what looks like an African-Caribbean piece, based on the alternation between a female chorus (section A, C, E) and a soloist (sections B, D, F-G), is dealt with. Each line corresponds to an eight-beat cycle. Each cell corresponds to one beat.

Table 8.1   Marco Manara, *World Step 54'*, segmentation analysis of the first sample.

Samples: dialogue between a women's choir (A, C, E) and a male soloist (sections B, D, F, G) in an African-Caribbean song								
...	Groove							
1	A		A		A		A	
2	A	B	A	B'	A	B	A	B
3	A	B	A	B'	A	B	A	B
4	Groove							
5	G				G			
6	G		G		G		G	
7	C	D	C	D	C	D	C	D
8	C	D	C	D	C	D	C	D
9	E		F		E		F	
10	E		F		E		F	

---

[42]   Philip Tagg, in 'From Refrain to Rave. The Decline of Figure and the Rise of Ground', *Popular Music*, 13/2 (1994), pp. 209–22, offered a first contribution on the relationship between form in electronic dance music and the psychological responses of listeners. See also Mark J. Butler, *Unlocking the Groove. Rhythm, Meter, and Musical Design in Electronic Dance Music* (Bloomington, IN), 2006.

11	E		F		E		G	
12	Groove							
13	A		A		A		A	
14	A	B	A	B'	A	B	A	B
15	A	B	A	B'	A	B	A	B
16	G				G			
17	G		G		G		G	
18	E		F		E		F	
19	E		F		E		F	
20	E		F		E		G	
21	E		F		E		G	
22	E		F		E		G	
...	Groove, change							

The musical evocation of faraway places and the gymnastic stylization of the 'trip' around the world contrast with the somewhat claustrophobic environment of a gym.

Representing another place is almost institutional in spinning, which, as Valentina told me, 'is a whole other thing' with respect to aerobics. A spinning instructor must guide the group of spin-bike users through an alternation of fast, dynamic pedalling with an aerobic function and harder, slower pedalling, useful for muscle strengthening, by imagining an itinerary now on a plain, now up a hill. 'The instructor talks to us, she tells us what we're doing, where we are, if on the mountains or by a river. The class becomes more fun this way', said a participant in a spinning class.[43] According to Alessandra:

> There isn't a speed curve, like in step, but rather alternate phases. For the plain we use specially prepared musics [remixed ad hoc], for the climb I choose them, slower, but also different according to the group or the situation I want to construct. (Alessandra)

Alessandra, too, takes the type of participants into account when choosing the pieces to add to her compilation:

> I choose the music according to the participants' tastes: for groups of over-45s I use Italian songs that can be sung along to. Once we used that song by Petrolini

---

[43]   Interview with Cristina, member of the Centro Sportivo Venice Gym in Rome, May 2007.

that Manfredi covered, 'Tanto pe' canta'' … We were playing about. It was a bit like going for an outing. (Alessandra)[44]

Spinning websites offer compilations and CDs of the duration of a class with so-called 'pedallable' musics. These are chosen from electronic repertoires with New Age references built around the imitation of natural sounds, with sounds that create the idea of open space and not too fast rhythmic parts, but at a tempo that, in this case, it is pertinent to define as *andante*.[45] For instructors, these websites offer tracklists appropriate for each phase of the class (warm-up, climb, sprints, cool-down). On the Spinning Music website each of these lists is preceded by a brief description of the musical features. For example:

> The key to a good climbing song is the beat: it's got to have a beat suitable for matching your cadence. Once you find it, the music will push you to keep going even when your legs are telling you to dial it back. These are my favourites. [46]

Or:

> There's no mistaking a good sprinting tune: whether it's seated or standing, it's got a beat that pushes you toward your own best race day pace. Many of these songs naturally move into a sprinting pace for each chorus, with the verses allowing for recovery in between sprints. Go![47]

Therefore, in spinning, the speed and energy of the pieces must be carefully dosed. Moreover, music offers infinite nuances in this sense, and the sensitivity of instructors is particularly important.

The Other Face of Music: Holistic Disciplines

Step and spinning share the need to organize a group. Other disciplines, like Pilates, stretching, yoga, gentle and postural gymnastics, require a strong individualization of physical work.

---

[44] 'Tanto pe' canta'', Italian song with Roman dialect influences composed by Ettore Petrolini and Natale Alberto Simeoni in 1932. It was recorded by Petrolini himself a few years later. The famous Italian actor, Nino Manfredi, covered it during a TV show in 1970, which made it very popular.

[45] Translator's note: While in English the Italian term '*andante*' is just a musical term, in Italian it is also the present participle of the verb *andare* (broadly meaning 'to go', often by various means of transportation including bikes) – hence its pertinence in this case.

[46] <http://spinningmusic.wordpress.com/climbs/> (accessed 31 May 2012).

[47] <http://spinningmusic.wordpress.com/sprints/> (accessed 31 May 2012).

The fruition of music is more individual. Music must favour isolation and concentration. As Alessandra puts it, '[m]usic must be background, like soft lighting, create an atmosphere'. The idea of 'background' can be confused with the idea of sonic wallpaper, of discreet and continuous presence, totally contrasting with the hammering presence of aerobics music. Valentina notes how '[n]on-pulsating musics are used in yoga'. But the use of the term 'background' must not lead us to think that the role of music is only ambient. Physiotherapist and gentle gymnastics instructor Monica Carcano clearly states that in her discipline music is a tool, not a background. For this reason, with participants/patients who start their training it would be better not to use it, as it may distract them from self-perception. In particular, rhythmical musics that impose their tempo, instead of allowing the patient complete freedom of movement, are not recommended. Past the initial stage there are several arguments in favour of using music:

> It adds auditory stimulation to other stimuli; it facilitates harmonization between bodily rhythms and motor coordination; it helps to memorize brief motor sequences without perceptive errors; it can stimulate the neurovegetative system by varying the tempo from slow to fast; it helps to automate postural correction by facilitating the attention and harmonization of the whole body. (Monica)[48]

Monica has introduced new, important reasons. In particular, help in 'memorizing' and 'automating' motor sequences. The support of musical coding to the memorization of verbal formulae is known to all those who study orality. Studies on ethnochoreology have also revealed a strict correlation between musical and motor memory. Indeed, in oral tradition contexts, quite often there is no sharp difference between dancers and instrumentalists in the first stages of their learning processes. They all experiment with both dancing and playing the music they dance to (sometimes going through singing) to better understand, memorize and internalize the whole complex of musical language in dance.[49]

Another reason introduced by Monica is 'harmonization'. In music, harmony is one of the binding elements that allows for the coordination of single parts into a whole. In holistic disciplines, the principal aim is precisely to work on the whole body thanks to the simultaneous perception of the various parts of themselves that participants/patients have.

Another instructor of holistic disciplines, Lucia Avarone, told me that the concentration on listening that music demands is the best vehicle to work up to listening to one's own body, breathing, heartbeat and blood flow. Lucia used the term 'echo' to define the response of the body to musical stimuli. We could call

---

[48]   Interview with Monica, physiotherapist and instructor of gentle and postural gymnastics, February 2012.

[49]   See Sherry B. Shapiro (ed.), *Dance in a World of Change: Reflections on Globalization and Cultural Difference* (Champaign, IL, 2008) and Susan Miyo Asai, *Nōmai Dance Drama: A Surviving Spirit of Medieval Japan* (Westport, CT, 1999).

it 'resonance'. But this time it is not a hectic resonance, powerful, able to move groups of hundreds of people, as in aerobics. Here, the relationship with sounds is essentially intimate. Fitness centre users are not all the same: depending on age, disposition and physical characteristics, they look for different answers to their need for well-being. Choosing music can be very individual, as Alessandra notes: 'We use new age music or something else. For example, I like Ludovico Einaudi a lot. … Classical music … no. You know, often people don't like it. And we need to put people at ease.' And yet a participant in a Pilates class declared that she uses Bach to achieve maximum concentration during exercises, isolating herself from all potential distractions – be they external, like noises, or internal, like other thoughts. Even more than in step, music must be part of the participant's listening habits

Let us also note how musical communication has different effects on concentration levels. Both in aerobic and holistic disciplines it is used to isolate from the outside by creating a special reality in which what counts is fitness. However, in the former it helps to divert attention from the intensity of physical work, while in the latter, less intense but requiring high motor control, it helps concentration on movements.

Conclusion

In this chapter, I have looked at how music is used in fitness centres in Italy to best direct physical work, and make it easier and more pleasant. The qualities of music at work in this process are several. Some have a direct effect on the efficiency of the movements (rhythm control, lateralization, reduction of muscular tension, increase of concentration on the movements themselves), others on the quality of the experience (improvement of socialization and of the relationship with the instructor and the other participants in the group, construction of pleasant moments, evocation of pleasant emotions and symbolic contexts).

'Being in synch', 'being in tune' and 'resonance' are keywords that explain the kind of relationship that instructors intend to establish between participants and the music that saturates the sonic environment of gyms. The phenomenon of entrainment seems, in all cases, significant in understanding the neurophysiological prerequisites that regulate the broad range of reactions our bodies have to music.

I also proposed another keyword that seemed interesting from the perspective of musical anthropology: 'musicalization' – that is, disguising the real aim (physical work) with motivations belonging more to music as an autonomous activity (the pleasure of listening, dancing and partying). Valentina says that '[i]n fact, for many coming to the gym is tiring and repeating the exercises is boring. Music helps to overcome all this.' Her statement leaves us to imagine that instructors intend music to have a predominantly functional role, and that we indeed find ourselves in front of an almost exemplary case of applied music. But then Tony says that:

> In sport it's different. In competitive activities there's a goal that unites all the participants and the audience: winning. In the gym the aim, that is fitness, is much less immediate and not very galvanizing. So we need to construct a situation that gives the activity cohesion and strength. Music is essential in doing this. (Tony)

Here, he describes the need to replace one horizon of motivation with another, a fictitious one. The instructor, through the various strategies that I have analysed, puts up a sort of representation, crossing into the territory of performing arts (from dance to theatre). Even more intriguing is Alessandra's statement – 'You know, in the end silence worries' – which touches upon deep psychological territory for the reasons behind music's ubiquity.

Finally, I have also highlighted aesthetic motivations: music makes physical work more pleasant and fun. This would perhaps require greater care in dedicated musical production. For musicians like Marco Manara, composing for fitness is seen as frustrating. Instructors like Gil, who have shown good musical competence and knowledge of repertoires, say that they have to come to terms with the participants' tastes. In short, as often happens in Italy, the issue of musical education and cultural politics also emerges in sports centres.

Chapter 9

Taboo Listening
(or, What Kind of Attention?)

Franco Fabbri

The status of background listening in music studies is low. Following the hierarchy in Adorno's *Introduction to the Sociology of Music*,[1] any kind of listening below the level of 'structural listening' is considered to be a symptom of an incorrect attitude towards music. Moreover, as gifted listeners – who can instantly decrypt all underlying structures in the perceived sounds – are *obviously* able to distinguish 'bad music' from 'good music', 'low-level' listening becomes synonymous with 'low-level' music. Music that is received inattentively, not just unwillingly, is considered to be 'music pollution'. Some say this is 'passive music', heard by inattentive listeners just like non-smokers inhale passive smoke. So many discourses about background listening are full of contempt against 'bad music you can listen to everywhere' (in bars, shops, on public transport or just the music teenagers listen to while studying – how can they do this?), that suspicions arise about the whole syllogistic machinery being set up to demonstrate – at last! – that art music is good and all other musics are bad. Serious professors, asked to comment on the matter, were heard saying: 'Once music was art, one would go to a concert and listen. Now we have all this bad music coming out of loudspeakers. See all those young people with their iPods.' It usually takes some time in the discussion to remind them about other functions of music in mankind's history; some appear to be amazed when facing the evidence that listening via earphones can be a way of focusing all possible attention on music, while some concertgoers often fall asleep. In other words, some musicologists need to be reminded that the interaction of technology, music's social and linguistic functions, genres and the semiotics and psychology of music perception is just a bit more complex than dividing the world of sounds in two: good on one side (generally a Brahms or Mozart concerto listened to attentively in a concert hall) and bad on the other (loud pop music broadcast from your neighbour's radio on the beach, which you hear with disgust).

---

[1]   Theodor W. Adorno, *Introduction to the Sociology of Music*, trans. E.B. Ashton (New York, 1976 [1962]). References to the German edition are to Theodor W. Adorno, *Einleitung in die Musiksoziologie: Zwölf theoretische Vorlesungen*, in *Gesammelte Schriften*, Volume 14, ed. Rolf Tiedemann (Frankfurt am Main, 1973 [1962]), pp. 169–420.

The challenge to people who want to understand how music 'works' in today's world – including musicologists, of course – implies that we should be attentive to all the ways music is listened to, or used. We should not have 'a priori' hierarchies or taboos. Unfortunately, such taboos do exist in music studies. What about listening to music while you are driving? Is it attentive? Is it background? How can people work and listen to music? What about claims that some jobs can be done while listening and others cannot? What about a practice so many people will comment on privately, but no musicologist seems to be willing to address: listening to music while making love? What does that 'say' about how music is perceived? Is there a (popular) aesthetics of such music? Are we not hiding from ourselves a real *Dark Side of the Moon* of music psychology, semiotics, aesthetics, sociology and practice?

To Listen or to Hear

Many widely used Western languages have at least two (or more) distinct verbs to indicate the action of receiving sounds passively or actively or, to put it in a more philosophically correct way, sensing or perceiving sounds. 'To hear' or 'to listen to', *udire, sentire* or *ascoltare* (Italian), *sentir* or *escoltar* (Catalan), *oír* or *escuchar* (Spanish), *ouvir* or *escutar* (Portuguese), *ouïr, entendre* or *écouter* (French), *hören, anhören, zuhören, horchen* (German). In fact, we can listen (or *ascoltare, escoltar, escuchar*, and so on) even if we are not sensing (or hearing) any sound: we are just concentrating our attention on our sense of hearing (as we shall see later, 'paying attention' is defined by cognitive scientists and neurologists as the act of concentrating on selected stimuli or neural 'channels'). And we can, of course, sense (hear) a sound without listening to it. I remember the manager of a Silicon Valley computer company, trying to persuade attendees at a commercial meeting about the advantages of a diskless and fanless workstation: she just switched off the fan of the overhead projector, which had been on for the whole meeting, and everyone said: 'Oh!', *listening* at last to the absence of a sound that had not been *heard* for hours. So we can switch from hearing to listening not only because a new sound captures our attention, but also because a sound disappears (electrical hums or other background noises are among the most common sources of such attention switches). The languages I mentioned (and probably others I do not know of) prove that, in the relevant cultures, semantic 'spaces' exist that relate to at least two different attitudes to sound reception: one involving our deliberate act of paying attention to that sensorial channel, another involving its actual functioning. One can notice that similar semantic 'spaces' exist for the sense of sight, represented in languages by verbs like 'to look at' or 'to see', *guardare* or *vedere, mirar* or *ver*, and so on. This distinction between paying attention to senses and 'pure' sensation seems to be a common trait in many cultures. This is obviously the case in so-called Western culture (where it was investigated by philosophers for nearly 30 centuries, articulating the perception/sensation dichotomy, and by experimental psychologists, semioticians and cognitive scientists for decades), although I would not dare to extend it to other cultures and call it 'human', at least in the form of a given culture's common-sense knowledge. If we go back to our linguistic examples, anomalies and asymmetries appear even within European languages. For example (an interesting example, I think), German verbs which mean 'to listen' (*anhören, zuhören* and the intransitive *horchen*) are based on the same root as *hören* ('to hear'), and all nouns referring to active perception of sounds and music ('listening', 'listener') are derived from *hören* (*Hören, Hörer, Zuhören, Zuhörer*). Apparently, in German there is a variety of compound verbs and phrasal expressions that can be used to describe different attitudes to sounds, but the basic terms that refer to the act of listening or to the person who listens are the same as those that refer to the act of hearing or to the person who hears: it is peculiar, even if we acknowledge the semantic role of particles like *an* or *zu* in that language. In English and Italian, however, 'hearer' and *uditore* are much more specific terms than 'listener' and *ascoltatore*, so the situation is reversed compared to German: nouns related to wider meanings and used in a more general sense are based on the root of attentive listening. But German is particularly interesting, because Germany is the *Vaterland* of *Musikwissenschaften*. It is a language – and a country – in which many important *Hörertypologien* (and *Hörtypologien*) were born, despite (or just because of) the fact that a basic-level distinction between those two attitudes to sounds seems to be fuzzier or almost non-existent compared to other languages. Does this mean that German musicology is less refined, less detailed about listening and listeners, just like all of us have a very rough and unsophisticated perception of snow compared to the Inuits (the good old example from all semantics textbooks)? Not really. But the suspicion arises that some misunderstandings or commonplaces of German-influenced musicology (that is, all musicology) might have originated at the level of the assumption that all hearing is listening or vice versa. In other words, a removal of inattentive listening or hearing (confined to the obscure universe of sensation) also implies the removal of any constructive interplay between different modes of reception.

Those who like metaphors and conceptual mappings as tools to shift meanings and construct theories, like those who claim that 'passive listening' is a way of absorbing 'music pollution', do not seem to be disturbed by Heinrich Besseler's definition of *passives Hören* as the typical *Hörstile* of Romantic music, as opposed to *aktives Hören* for music of the Classical period, *verknüpfendes* (linking, tying) for Baroque and *vernehmendes* (sensitive) for Renaissance.[2] Passive listening, as Besseler implies, is typical for music like Schumann's Piano Quintet in E flat major, not just for loud Italian dance music in a Foot Locker shop. But we are not allowed to extrapolate: Besseler's typology, of course, is rooted in the canon of Western art music, although the way listening types are related to general structural characteristics of the relevant music styles is possibly a foundation for

---

[2]   Heinrich Besseler, 'Grundfragen des musikalischen Hörens', *Jahrbuch der Musik-bibliothek Peters*, 32 (1926): pp. 35–52.

Adorno's better-known typology, where 'structural listening' is idealized. And Besseler's *Hören* is definitely attentive listening: if I understand what he meant, listeners have to put themselves in a condition of deliberate *passives Hören* if they want to listen correctly to Schumann's quintet, as opposed to, for example, one of Mozart's quartets.

Adorno's Hierarchy

Theodor Wiesengrund Adorno's well-known typology of listeners (and/or of listening behaviours) is by no means the first hierarchical one. Judgement is implied in older *Hörtypologien*, like Friedrich Rochlitz's (from 1799), where people *die mit ganzer Seele hören*, 'who listen with their whole soul', are, of course, the best listeners (compared to those who just 'hear with their ears'), or the audience classification in an issue of the *Allgemeine Musikalische Zeitung* of 28 October 1824, where the 'mother who takes her daughter to concerts to look for a husband' is described as the *Seelenverkäuferin* ('souls dealer').[3] And the history of musicology does not even lack a racially-oriented *Hörertypologie*, based on 'experimental' data collected by Albert Wellek in 1938–39, under the Third Reich.[4]

What is new and – one may add – *typical* in Adorno's typology, is the link between various listeners and listening attitudes on one side and musical genres on the other. Quite rightly – Adorno is always right, even when he is wrong, and he is always wrong, even when he is right (this is the privilege of dialectics). Different genres – I would say – imply different listening attitudes; to some degree, they are *defined* by different listening attitudes (and listeners). Moreover, different media imply different listening. Adorno is well aware of this, and his discussion of the musical use of radio (with symphonies losing in the little box their *gemeinschaftbildende Kraft*)[5] is more stimulating than his only moderately dialectic *Hörertypologie* (at least in the form that was inherited by musicology). I am not an expert (or a fan) of deconstructionist methods, but the first chapter of the *Introduction to the Sociology of Music*, where 'types of musical conduct' are introduced, would offer good examples of narrative rhetoric to such an analysis. The 'expert listener', the first one, is defined as someone who 'tends to miss nothing and at the same time, at each moment,[6] accounts to himself for what he

---

[3]   Quoted in Herbert Bruhn, Rolf Oerter and Helmut Rösing, *Musikpsychologie: Ein Handbuch* (Reinbeck bei Hamburg, 1993), pp. 130–35.

[4]   Ibid.

[5]   Theodor W. Adorno, *Der getreue Korrepetitor*, in *Gesammelte Schriften*, Volume 15, ed. Rolf Tiedemann (Frankfurt am Main, 1984 [1976]), pp. 157–368.

[6]   Another linguistic pitfall here, in the original text: 'at each moment', in German, is 'in jedem Augenblick'. There is no auditory equivalent for 'a glance'!

has heard'.[7] This is the first kind and the best ('entirely adequate'[8]). Adorno is not bothered to explain here the values according to which this kind of listening is the best and why it is a 'privilege' to belong to this type of listener: he has done it elsewhere. But one might argue that in the first chapter of an *Introduction* to music sociology, enouncing some basic categories, he could have *not* taken the reading of his *Philosophy of Modern Music*[9] for granted. In fact, he helps the reader with an example of this 'entirely adequate' behaviour, which should be defined as '*structural listening*': someone who 'has his first encounter with the second movement of Webern's Trio for Strings and can name the formal components of that dissolved, architectonically unsupported piece'.[10]

Of course, Adorno could have given many examples of 'difficult' music that might put an expert listener to the test: for example (the *Introduction* was first issued in 1962) Ornette Coleman's *Free Jazz* (released in 1960) or a song by Umm Kulthum or a piece of Indian *raga*. All good tests; all void (for a European 'expert listener') of clear architectural signposts. Although it is not a great discovery to notice that Adorno was not a cultural relativist, it may be useful to point out that his typology of musical behaviours, with all the underlying rhetoric and all its hierarchical assumptions, was adopted as a kind of Bible by 'official musicology' (a term which is quoted with contempt in the *Introduzione* of the Italian edition by Luigi Rognoni).[11] *Expert* (number one), *good listener* (number two), *culture consumer* (number three), *emotional listener* (number four), *resentment listener* (be it a fan of pre-Romantic music or a jazz fan, numbers five and six), *entertainment listener* (the one who listens to *Unterhaltung Musik* – that is, popular music, number seven) and finally the non-listener, the *anti-musical listener* (number eight), were incorporated in most musicologists' common sense, despite many caveats and warnings by Adorno himself.[12] He talked about contradictions among types, about the non-linearity of his classification, explicitly described as 'non one-dimensional':[13] he even stated that the association between listening behaviours and music types was not meant to be bi-univocal ('from different points of view, the type closest to the subject matter may be now this, now that'[14]), dialectically criticizing his own basic assumption that the criteria driving the typology's construction are 'the adequacy or inadequacy of the act of listening to that which

---

[7]   Adorno, *Introduction to the Sociology of Music*, p. 4.

[8]   Ibid.

[9]   Theodor W. Adorno, *Philosophy of Modern Music* (New York, 2003 [1949]).

[10]   Adorno, *Introduction to the Sociology of Music*, p. 4.

[11]   Theodor W. Adorno, *Introduzione alla sociologia della musica*, intro. Luigi Rognoni, trans. Giacomo Manzoni and Carlo Vitali (Turin, 1971 [1962]).

[12]   Adorno, *Introduction to the Sociology of Music*, pp. 4–18. In German: *Experte, guter Zuhörer, Bildungshörer, emotionaler Hörer, Ressentiment-Hörer, Unterhaltungshörer, gleichgültiger/unmusikalischer/antimusikalischer Hörer*; see Adorno, *Einleitung in die Musiksoziologie*, pp. 181–96.

[13]   Adorno, *Introduction to the Sociology of Music*, p. 3.

[14]   Ibid., pp. 3–4.

is heard'.[15] Useless warnings: with very few changes (mainly about jazz, recently promoted from resentful to good or structural listening), Adorno's typology – in a crystallized, undialectical form – is still among the founding categories of 'official musicology', with all its corollaries (which Adorno might have proven false), such as 'popular music does not demand (or deserve) structural listening', 'the least competent (or attentive) the listening, the worse the music' or (a slightly different form) 'music that people listen to while not paying attention to it is bad music'.

To some degree, the whole musicological discourse about music that is not meant to be in the foreground has been an articulation (with very little use of Adornian dialectics) of that typology, a self-indulgent syllogistic machinery (see how some musicologists smile when they speak of 'consumption music') and a set of theorems derived from Euclidean postulates that never encountered any Riemann (the mathematician, of course).

A Phenomenology of Background Listening: 'Baby You Can Drive my Car'

Music not meant to be listened to attentively, as a massive undifferentiated set, includes music performed live as well as music played through loudspeakers. As all students of Western music's history know, but many (even historical) musicologists too often forget, many pieces that were created as a sonic backdrop were later incorporated in the canon of concert music. Legend has it that even pieces like the *Goldberg Variations* could be added to this list, but to remain on more solid ground, one could say that genres like *Tafelmusik, serenata, cassazione* and *ouverture* (even Rossini's) were defined by their function of accompanying banquets, masquerades or other social gatherings, or to gently take the audience's attention to music from almost nil to a degree more suitable for subsequent musical attractions. In most Italian opera theatres, for a long time, food (or sex) used to be the foreground. As we have seen, such behaviours were already being criticized in the name of high art then: this does not mean that nothing has changed, but it is a warning against a possible loss of sense and value, if we just dismiss background music as such.

However, current discourses about background listening are mostly about music played through loudspeakers in private or public spaces, and not in a concert setting. Most of this music is recorded. Although every step in the chain that leads from the source of this music to the listener's ear and mind may be meaningful, discussion is usually focused on the listener's end – that is, from the loudspeaker to the mind. In describing some situations that I do not dare to define as typical but have experienced personally, I will also start from there. A brief methodological warning, however, is necessary. I am going to put together some empirical data with personal observations about my own experience; the latter, because of their

---

[15]   Ibid., p. 3.

hermeneutic nature, have no *proof*. I hope they can be of some use, at least for those who will try to prove they are not true.

According to a 1983 survey,[16] about 24 per cent of interviewees in two Italian cities declared that they would listen to music in their car every day. These people would listen for a daily average of a little less than an hour. Averages over the total of interviewees across different media and listening settings added up to about 2 hours and 50 minutes (4 hours and 10 minutes for teenagers) of daily listening to so-called 'reproduced music'. Similar data emerged at that time from other surveys carried out in various countries. It must be pointed out that the questionnaire referred in general to 'music' and specifically to 'listening to tapes in a car', so – in principle – answers to that question would not cover listening to radio programmes in a car, not even those including music. These should be included in the answers about 'radio' (about 70 per cent of interviewees, for about 70 minutes a day). A general caveat about this kind of research is, of course, that answers are about the subjective memory of having listened to music and can easily exceed reality. However, for that 24 per cent of interviewees, a little less than an hour a day is a fair estimate for the time they spent in cars driving to their workplace and back home if we do an average between people living in the two cities and commuters. Thirty years ago, cars in Italy were usually sold without a car stereo (one had to buy it and have it installed) and obviously there were no car CD players around. One can imagine that today's figures would be much higher not only in percentage terms (more people owning cars and car stereo equipment), but also in timings (traffic has increased a lot).

Working at Radio Tre (Italy's 'cultural' radio station, part of the state-owned Rai), I was informed years ago that many of the listeners actually listened to that channel in their cars. This was no surprise for me not only because I was a long-time car listener myself, but also because many people I know told me they listened to my programme while driving. It was a surprise, however, for the radio's director who until then – when I suggested specifically addressing the 'car audience' – used to answer: 'You know, so few people listen to Radio Tre in their cars.' This was not a lack of experience or imagination on the director's part, however. It was a problem with radio audience surveys. When the research team finally decided to address the question properly, the car audience was discovered, even for Radio Tre. Quite recently, in some countries, new research methods were introduced that bypass interviews and related systematic errors. The Swiss Radiocontrol (www.radiocontrol.ch) system is based on a small digital recorder, the size of a wristwatch, which records short samples of the sonic environment at regular intervals. The 'watch' is distributed to a sample of the population and collected after one week; recorded data are compared to an audio database including all radio programmes in the week, and the software is able to detect whether recorded samples correspond to what was broadcast by some station at exactly that time of

---

[16] Nemesio Ala, Franco Fabbri, Umberto Fiori and Emilio Ghezzi, *La musica che si consuma* (Milan, 1985), p. 77.

the day. So, Radiocontrol offers audience data that cover all possible radio sources (at home, in the car, in public spaces), provided they were audible, and eliminates some of the most common sources of error (like a radio switched on in another room, which would be included in the listening time during an interview, but not 'heard' by the 'watch').

If I was a carrier of the Radiocontrol 'watch', research figures would show that I switch on my car stereo whenever I start my car, even for a very short ride, and usually switch it off just before parking. I listen to the radio or CDs. On long trips, I connect my iPod to the car stereo and listen to it in shuffle mode. Quite often I listen to more music in my car – each day – than at home. Of course, what the Radiocontrol cannot tell is *what happens* when I listen to music in my car. I wrote about the subject many years ago,[17] and I am still trying to understand. First, I drive. Quite trivial, but not exactly so. I discovered what many other people know, that the audio level that suits me when I am driving is usually too high for my passengers. The same happens when someone else drives; they like the volume to be louder than I do. Why? The only explanation that occurs to me is that my mind is partly absorbed by activities related to driving – maybe not so much the almost automatic actions involved as paying attention to the road. So the psychoacoustic gate for listening could be at a higher level. But whenever I get to this point in my effort to explain this apparently simple and quite common situation, I have to face the vagueness of the very concept I am trying to base it on. What does 'paying attention' mean? What is 'attention'? Well, from my experience as a driver – which is almost as long and varied as my experience as a listener – and from what people usually know, suggest and teach about driving, I know what 'paying attention to the road' does *not* mean: it does not mean that we should scrutinize at every moment all details in our field of vision, watching for possible sources of danger. If we do this, we cannot drive. To become safe drivers, we are taught: (1) to focus on a certain point ahead of our car – not too close, not too far; (2) to be open to any kind of signal that might come from elsewhere; (3) to filter out all details related to common situations. A good driver is someone who has learnt how to balance these (and probably other) sensorial and mental processes; we may call 'attention' each of the processes, or the resulting balance, but still know very little about all of them. Research was carried out about the use of mobile telephones while driving: it was proved that holding a mobile is dangerous (who could doubt it?), but also that talking over the phone using a hands-free headset (and even the car stereo's audio) can prolong reaction times in case of unforeseen events. How? At what level? Why should a normal conversation (with other people in the car) not produce the same effect? And music?

---

[17]   Franco Fabbri, 'Il mezzo elettroacustico, lo spazio musicale, la popular music', in Raffaele Pozzi (ed.), *La musica e il suo spazio* (Milan, 1987), reprinted in part as 'Le "bolle musicali": musica e automobile', in Franco Fabbri, *Il suono in cui viviamo* (Milan, 2008 [1996]), pp. 310–13.

Conversely, I wonder if what we call attention to music works in the same way or differently. Is Adorno's expert (or structural) listener a 'good driver'? Or rather, according to Adorno's description as 'the fully conscious listener who tends to miss nothing and at the same time, at each moment, accounts to himself for what he has heard',[18] is the expert listener that kind of goofy learner driver overwhelmed by stimuli, incapable of filtering out unnecessary details, incapable of doing two things at the same time – look at the road and drive? I bet not.

But then there must be something wrong, maybe not in Adorno's description but in the related idea that attention to music (which differentiates listening from hearing) is something like exploring, constantly probing the acoustic field, like the eye does on the page when reading a score. It does not work like that. But then attention is something else. And there must be different modes of listening and attention that we learn to use and balance in our loudspeaker-saturated environment.

Going back to car listening, there are common experiences that are most probably related to multidimensional attentions and to our (learned) ability to combine mental activities. There are 'road songs', where the use of reverb, chorusing, flanging, Leslie and other effects, and tempo and performing intentions suggest and relate to wide spaces, so that those songs – while often referring to 'the road' in their lyrical content – suggest the car and car listening (quite Adornian, in a way) as the most adequate place and attitude. I think of songs like Springsteen's 'Tougher than the Rest'[19] ('The road is dark, and it's a thin, thin line…' and at exactly that point the organ becomes louder and switches to vibrato, suggesting the distant shimmering of heated asphalt), Joni Mitchell's 'Night Ride Home',[20] with a sampled cricket sound that passes by, together with trees or wayside posts, or Ivano Fossati's 'Una notte in Italia',[21] where the 'road song' sound cliché suggests a car as the place, although we learn from the lyrics that it is just parked 'on top of the world', and characters in the song are just making love in it. But I also think about music that resembles the flowing intermittent continuum of white stripes on the road, trees, posts and buildings, like a Baroque allegro, or music that contradicts that flow, like a huge late-Romantic adagio; they are both among my favourite car music. A matter of taste, of course. But there are reasons for it.

A Phenomenology of Background Listening: Taboo Listenings

Another piece of evidence from my radio job is the number of people listening to the radio (and to music) while working. I do that myself. Not while writing a paper, or an article. Maybe while writing a letter. Quite often while consulting a

---

[18] Adorno, *Introduction to the Sociology of Music*, p. 4.
[19] Bruce Springsteen, 'Tougher Than The Rest', *Tunnel of Love* (Columbia, 1987).
[20] Joni Mitchell, 'Night Ride Home', *Night Ride Home* (Geffen, 1991).
[21] Ivano Fossati, 'Una notte in Italia', *Dal vivo Volume 1 – Buontempo* (Epic, 1993).

database or inputting data, preparing the layout of documents, doing any kind of work with numbers or formulae. I used to write computer programs while listening to music, but could not listen to spoken programmes on the radio. When I had a programme that was broadcast during working hours at Radio Tre, I realized that whenever I spoke about matters that might interest architects, designers, scientists, painters or craftsmen I had many more calls or letters. Maybe I am too boring for writers, poets, teachers, philosophers and sales people. Maybe also, people doing some jobs cannot listen to the radio while they work, whereas others can – and not just manual labourers. So, in Italy there are intellectual labourers (hundreds of thousands of them) who listen to Radio Tre in the morning and afternoon, while working; they listen to news, comments and discussions, and music: classical music (from Gregorian to avant-garde to post-minimalism), jazz, world music, singer/songwriter genre (*canzone d'autore*), rock and pop. This is seen as normal practice by virtually everybody. However, whenever I have the opportunity to discuss how music is used by young people, especially at academic conferences where the subject is popular music or soundscape (or 'music pollution'), the first arguments raised by other participants (whom I could not distinguish from the above-mentioned crowd of 'intellectual working radio listeners') run along the following lines: 'They listen to music while they're studying or doing their homework!' 'Have you ever been in those shops they go to? With that loud music?' 'They go out and put their earphones on, and they walk and take the bus while listening to music!' Oh shame! Poor wasted teenagers! What fascinates me most, however, is how 'attention' sooner or later becomes the theoretical focus of such arguments, maybe because it is so difficult for many adults (or for such adults) to get attention from teenagers. Then, attention is the problem – in general as well as with music. Music is (or used to be) art inasmuch as you pay attention to it, and the canon of such adequate behaviour is a concert hall. Adorno is looming.

So any kind of listening behaviour different from that is not even worth discussing, except for placing it in the dustbin of bad music and music pollution. It is a taboo. On such occasions, I often wished I could discuss another taboo that, believe it or not, never emerged or was not even suspected by these 'musicological parents', so to speak. I am talking about the fact that apparently so many people, during their life from teenage to late adulthood (including those parents' children and, who knows, perhaps even the parents themselves), listen to music while making love – not unlike those 'listeners' used to do during shows in Italian opera theatres. Well, here we are. I do not know if there are any theories or pieces of research available (like the one that recently showed how people usually tilt their heads to the right when they kiss), but I am sure there are 'folk theories'. I occasionally heard judgements about albums deemed particularly adequate to the function (Pink Floyd's *The Dark Side of the Moon* apparently being one of the favourites[22]) and I wonder about the interrelated musicological and sexological implications of LP duration. Were psychedelic and progressive rock (with their

---

22   Pink Floyd, *The Dark Side of the Moon* (EMI, 1973).

side-long pieces or suites) favoured because of this? What does 'long play' actually mean? Were cassettes (and autoreverse) successful for the same reason? Is it true that Norio Ohga (Sony's vice-president) asked the total playing time of a CD to be enough to contain the whole of Beethoven's Ninth Symphony or did he have 'other' requirements? Humour, as usual, helps to hide embarrassment. Hermeneutical efforts, whether to complement or surrogate invisible evidence, need to enter very private regions. Anyway, let's do it. Personally, I do not particularly like to have music on while making love: that is, I would not suggest it unless I knew my partner wanted it. But it did happen to me quite a few times. If someone asked me, then, if I *listened* to the music, I would answer 'yes'. Some were quite thrilling listening experiences (I am not kidding now): the memories I have of some pieces of music listened to in those situations are the only memories I have of that music, and I never listened to it again. From what I have heard, people quite commonly remember and remain emotionally linked to music for the same reason, the 'our song' cliché being the romanticized version of this widespread phenomenon. Again, the question about attention emerges, from the background of our thoughts.

As a matter of fact, although attention has been widely used as a foundation for most discourses on listening (and on 'proper' listening), we know almost nothing about it in relation to music. Research on attention in neurosciences is basically focused on vision, and auditory stimuli used in experiments are generally limited to speech or non-organized sound. Of course, as James said, 'Everyone knows what attention is. It is the taking possession of the mind, in clear and vivid form, of one out of what seem several simultaneously possible objects or trains of thought. Focalization, concentration of consciousness are of its essence.'[23]

However, even if researchers were able to demonstrate that attention is an independent brain function and observed significant neural firing and localized brain activity associated with attentional processes related to visual stimuli, even the best available sources on the subject[24] provide no evidence of similar results with regard to musical attention. So, discourses about the function of attention in listening (in musicology as well as in music psychology) seem to be based on James's commonplace and on the same metaphorical assumptions (basically visual) that seem to be guiding the cognitive psychology of attention.[25] To put it perhaps too simply (hopefully provoking a wave of counterexamples), musicology does not know more about attention than is known about 'inspiration', but while a

[23]   William James, *Principles of Psychology* (New York, 1890), pp. 403–4.

[24]   See Risto Näätänen, *Attention and Brain Function* (Hillsdale, NJ, 1992); and Michael I. Posner and Gregory Digirolamo, 'Attention in Cognitive Neuroscience: An Overview', in Michael S. Gazzaniga (ed), *The New Cognitive Neurosciences* (Cambridge, MA, 2000), pp. 623–31.

[25]   See Diego Fernandez-Duque and Mark L. Johnson, 'Attention Metaphors: How Metaphors Guide the Cognitive Psychology of Attention', *Cognitive Science*, 23/1 (1999): pp. 83–116.

statement like 'good listening is based on attention' seems completely acceptable and 'scientific', a similar statement like 'a good composition is based on inspiration' would engender embarrassment in highbrow circles and be ascribed to a Romantic and surpassed mythology of creative processes. But to paraphrase James, everyone knows what inspiration is or, at least, everyone who is involved in creative processes knows what it means to be in those certain mental states that are experienced when writing, drawing, composing, improvising and so on. And, I repeat, we do not know more about attention than about those 'inspired' mental states.

What kind of attention is it, in the case of 'bedroom' music? I heard of musicians (or, anyway, 'musical' people) who could 'do it' with many kinds of music, but definitely not with others. I found it fascinating that amongst the latter, along with examples I could also suspect (like Webern's Trio for Strings, just to mention it again), someone included 'anything by Johann Sebastian Bach', commenting that their mind was so captured by the logic of contrapuntal development that they could not care about anything else. This seems to be a piece of evidence that music demands adequate listening, confirming Adorno's theory, and advising that you should not have a structural listener either as a driver or as a sexual partner. Or maybe it is a confirmation of Besseler's typology, hinting that, in such circumstances, passive listening (for Romantic music) is more suitable than *verknüpfendes Hören*. Or, who knows, perhaps a suggestion that for such background music the Western listener refers to a semantic encyclopaedia based on film-music clichés – and one wonders if a love scene accompanied by Webern's Trio or by a canon from the *Goldberg Variations* in a successful movie might bring a sudden change in preferences. One also wonders if any of the above considerations might apply to other cultures and when the time will come that such questions can be asked everywhere. There are many taboos around; one can at least lend an ear to them.

Conclusion

Attention is a widely accepted cultural construct ('everyone knows what attention is'). However, it is easy to find examples in everyday life suggesting that the concept covers different phenomena and that the concentration model (based substantially on visual metaphors) cannot be applied generally. Unfortunately, the visually-oriented idea of attention as focusing on a selected sensorial channel not only is crucial in some musicological definitions of 'good' listening, but also seems to have influenced neurological/cognitive research. Probably due to practical difficulties in experiments, it seems that rather than testing neural activity in 'critical' conditions (those where different modes of attention or multichannel attention apply), scientists start from a rather uncritical and common-sense definition of attention and therefore end up testing neural activity related to heterogeneous – and visually biased – phenomena.

Future research should involve musicologists willing to examine new theories on listening, music anthropologists willing to make ethnographic research on some hidden but widely accepted musical practices and neurologists/cognitive scientists willing to design experiments on the basis of a deeper analysis of listening and attentional processes. Listening to music while driving, doing intellectual work or making love may offer good test conditions. Any volunteers for participant observation?

Bibliography

Adorno, Theodor W. (with the assistance of George Simpson), 'On Popular Music' (1941), in *Essays on Music*, ed. Richard Leppert (Berkeley: University of California Press, 2002), pp. 437–69.

Adorno, Theodor W., 'The Radio Symphony' (1941), in *Essays on Music*, ed. Richard Leppert (Berkeley: University of California Press, 2002), pp. 251–70.

Adorno, Theodor W., *Philosophy of Modern Music* (New York: Continuum, 2003 [1949]).

Adorno, Theodor W., *Einleitung in die Musiksoziologie: Zwölf theoretische Vorlesungen*, in *Gesammelte Schriften*, Volume 14, ed. Rolf Tiedemann (Frankfurt am Main: Suhrkamp Verlag, 1973 [1962]), pp. 169–420.

Adorno, Theodor W., *Introduction to the Sociology of Music*, trans. E.B. Ashton (New York: The Seabury Press, 1976 [1962]).

Adorno, Theodor W., *Introduzione alla sociologia della musica*, intro. Luigi Rognoni, trans. Giacomo Manzoni and Carlo Vitali (Turin: Einaudi, 1971 [1962]).

Adorno, Theodor W., *Der getreue Korrepetitor*, in *Gesammelte Schriften*, Volume 15, ed. Rolf Tiedemann (Frankfurt am Main: Suhrkamp Verlag, 1984 [1976]), pp. 157–368.

Adorno, Theodor W., 'Culture and Administration', *Telos*, 37 (1978): pp. 93–111.

Agee, James and Walker Evans, *Let Us Now Praise Famous Men* (Boston, MA: Houghton Mifflin, 1969).

Ala, Nemesio, Franco Fabbri, Umberto Fiori and Emilio Ghezzi, *La musica che si consuma* (Milan: Unicopli, 1985).

Althusser, Louis, *Lenin and Philosophy*, trans. Ben Brewster (New York: Monthly Review Press, 1971).

Anderson, Tim, 'As if History was Merely a Record: The Pathology of Nostalgia and the Figure of the Recording in Contemporary Popular Cinema', *Music, Sound, and the Moving Image*, 2/1 (2008): pp. 51–76.

Apter, Emily, 'Technics of the Subject: The Avatar-Drive', *Postmodern Culture*, 18/2 (2008) <http://pmc.iath.virginia.edu/text-only/issue.108/18.2apter.txt> (accessed 10 June 2012).

Archer, W. John, 'Ideology and Aspiration: Individualism, the Middle Class, and the Genesis of the Anglo-American Suburb', *Journal of Urban History*, 14/2 (1988): pp. 214–53.

Arnold, Doris, 'These You Have Loved', *Radio Times*, 10 May 1940, p. 10.

Asai, Susan Miyo, *Nōmai Dance Drama: A Surviving Spirit of Medieval Japan* (Westport, CT: Greenwood, 1999).

Attali, Jacques, *Noise: The Political Economy of Music*, trans. Brian Massumi (Minneapolis: University of Minnesota Press, 1985).

Auden, W.H., *Collected Poems*, ed. Edward Mendelssohn (New York: Random House, 1991).

Auslander, Philip, *Liveness: Performance in a Mediatized Culture* (New York: Routledge, 1999).

Baade, Christina L., *Victory Through Harmony: The BBC and Popular Music in World War II* (New York: Oxford University Press, 2012).

Baldwin, Neil, *Edison: Inventing the Century* (New York: Hyperion, 1995).

Banta, Martha, *Taylored Lives: Narrative Productions in the Age of Taylor, Veblen, and Ford* (Chicago and London: University of Chicago Press, 1993).

Barthes, Roland, *The Responsibility of Forms: Critical Essays on Music, Art, and Representation*, trans. Richard Howard (Berkeley: University of California Press, 1991), pp. 245–60.

Bateman, Anthony and John Bale (eds), *Sporting Sounds: Relationships between Sport and Music* (London: Routledge, 2009).

Baudrillard, Jean, *For a Critique of the Political Economy of the Sign*, trans. Charles Levin (St Louis, MO: Telos Press, 1981).

BBC Written Archives Centre, R9/1/1: Audience Research/Bulletins, Sound/1–68 (1941).

BBC Written Archives Centre, R9/1/2: Audience Research/Bulletins, Sound/69–121 (1942).

BBC Written Archives Centre, R9/15/1: Audience Research/Head of Audience Research Department/Wartime Listener.

BBC Written Archives Centre, R27/73/1: Music General/Dance Music Policy, file 1 (1941–1942).

BBC Written Archives Centre, R27/74/1: Music General/Dance Music Policy Committee, file 1 (1942–1946).

BBC Written Archives Centre, R27/172/1: Music General/Light Music, file 1 (1939–1943).

BBC Written Archives Centre, R27/228: Music General/Music for the Forces (1941–1944).

BBC Written Archives Centre, R27/245/1: Music General/Music Policy, file 1A (1930–1943).

BBC Written Archives Centre, R27/416/1: Music General/Overseas Service, file 1 (1936–1942).

BBC Written Archives Centre, Research Policy (1939–49).

Benjamin, Walter, 'The Work of Art in the Age of its Technological Reproducibility', in *Illuminations*, ed. and intro. Hannah Arendt, trans. Harry Zohn (New York: Schocken Books, 1969), pp. 217–51.

Benzel, Jan and Alessandra Stanley Benzel, '1990: The Agony and the Ecstasy', *The New York Times*, 30 December 1990, p. 1.

Berland, Jody, 'Contradicting Media: Toward a Political Phenomenology of Listening', in Neil Strauss (ed.), *Radiotext(E)* (New York: Semiotext(e), 1993), pp. 209–17.

Besseler, Heinrich, 'Grundfragen des musikalischen Hörens', *Jahrbuch der Musikbibliothek Peters*, 32 (1926): pp. 35–52.

Bigand, Emmanuel, 'Ethnomusicology, Evolutionary Musicology and the Neurosciences', paper presented at the 17th International Seminar in Ethnomusicology, Fondazione Cini, Venice, January 2012.

Blacking, John, *How Musical is Man?* (Seattle and London: University of Washington Press, 1974).

Blacking, John (ed.), *The Anthropology of the Body* (London: Academic Press, 1977).

Blake, Gary, 'Running Music – Rhythm and Beat', in *Run2Rhythm* <http://www.run2r.com/rhythm-n-beat.aspx> (accessed 31 May 2012).

Bliss, Arthur, *As I Remember* (London: Faber, 1970).

Boschi, Elena, '"Playing" Cultural Identities in and out of the Cinematic Nation: Popular Songs in British, Spanish, and Italian Cinema of the Late 1990s' (PhD thesis, University of Liverpool, 2010).

Boschi, Elena, '"Canción prohibida": Simulacros musicales y otros mundos en *Barrio* de Fernando León de Aranoa', in Eduardo Viñuela Suárez and Teresa Fraile Prieto (eds), *La música en el lenguaje audiovisual* (Seville: Arcibel, 2012), pp. 399–406.

Boykin, E.C., 'Putting Over the Mood Change Parties: Sophisticated New York City Finds Them Unique and Refreshing – Educational Institutions Co-Operate on This Big Psychological Experiment', *Edison Diamond Points*, 4/5 (April 1921): pp. 6–7.

'The Broadcasters', 'Both Sides of the Microphone', *Radio Times*, 19 April 1940, p. 8.

'Broadcasting and Music', *The Times*, 19 November 1943, p. 6c.

Browning, Robert, *The Shorter Poems of Robert Browning*, ed. William Clyde Devane (New York: Appleton-Century-Crofts, 1934).

Bruhn, Herbert, Rolf Oerter and Helmut Rösing, *Musikpsychologie: Ein Handbuch* (Reinbeck bei Hamburg: Rowohlt, 1993).

Bull, Michael, *Sounding Out the City: Personal Stereos and the Management of Everyday Life* (Oxford: Berg, 2000).

Bull, Michael, 'No Dead Air! The iPod and the Culture of Mobile Listening', *Leisure Studies*, 24/4 (October 2005): pp. 343–55.

Bull, Michael, 'Investigating the Culture of Mobile Listening: from Walkman to iPod', in Kenton O'Hara (ed.), *Consuming Music Together: Social and Collaborative Aspects of Music Consumption Technologies* (New York: Peter Lang, 2006), pp. 131–49.

Bull, Michael, *Sound Moves: iPod Culture and Urban Experience* (London and New York: Routledge, 2006).

Bull, Michael and Les Back (eds), *The Auditory Culture Reader* (Oxford: Berg, 2003).

Burnham, John, 'The New Psychology', in Adele Heller and Lois Rudnick (eds), *1915, the Cultural Moment* (New Brunswick, NJ: Rutgers University Press, 1991), pp. 117–27.

Butler, Judith, *Excitable Speech: A Politics of the Performative* (New York: Routledge, 1997).

Butler, Mark J., *Unlocking the Groove. Rhythm, Meter, and Musical Design in Electronic Dance Music* (Bloomington: Indiana University Press, 2006).

Cannadine, David, 'The "Last Night of the Proms" in Historical Perspective', *Historical Research*, 81/212 (2008): pp. 315–49.

Chanan, Michael, *Repeated Takes: A Short History of Recording and its Effects on Music* (London and New York: Verso, 1995).

Clark, Ronald W., *Edison: The Man Who Made the Future* (New York: G.P. Putnam's Sons, 1977).

Clarke, Eric, 'Music and Psychology', in Martin Clayton, Trevor Herbert and Richard Middleton (eds), *The Cultural Study of Music: A Critical Introduction* (New York and London: Routledge, 2003), pp. 113–23.

Clarke, Eric, Nicola Dibben and Stephanie Pitts, *Music and Mind in Everyday Life* (Oxford: Oxford University Press, 2009).

Clausen, Wendell, *A Commentary on Virgil: Eclogues* (Oxford: Oxford University Press, 1994).

Clayton, Martin, Rebecca Sager and Udo Will, 'In Time with the Music: The Concept of Entrainment and its Significance for Ethnomusicology', *European Meetings in Ethnomusicology*, 11 (ESEM-CounterPoint, 1) (2005): pp. 1–82.

Clough, Patricia Tiniceto (ed.), with Jean Halley, *The Affective Turn* (Durham, NC: Duke University Press, 2007).

Cohen, Debra Rae, 'Intermediality and the Problem of the Listener', *Modernism/Modernity*, 19/3 (2012): pp. 569–92.

Cook, Nicholas, 'Perception: A Perspective from Music Theory', in Rita Aiello and John A. Sloboda (eds), *Musical Perceptions* (Oxford: Oxford University Press, 1994), pp. 64–95.

Cover, *Radio Times*, 22 August 1941, p. 1.

Crafts, Susan D., Daniel Cavicchi, Charles Keil and the Music in Daily Life Project, *My Music: Explorations of Music in Daily Life* (Middletown, CT: Wesleyan University Press, 1993).

Crary, Jonathan, *Techniques of the Observer: On Vision and Modernity in the Nineteenth Century* (Cambridge, MA: MIT Press, 1990).

Cross, Ian, 'Listening as Covert Performance', *Journal of the Royal Musical Association*, 135/sup. 1 (2010): pp. 67–77.

Damasio, Antonio, *The Feeling of What Happens: Body, Emotion and the Making of Consciousness* (London: Vintage Books, 2000).

Davenport, T.H. and J.C. Beck, *The Attention Economy: Understanding the New Currency of Business* (Watertown, MA: Harvard Business School Press, 2001).

Davis, Mike, *City of Quartz: Excavating the Future in Los Angeles* (New York: Vintage Books, 1992).

de Certeau, Michel, *The Practice of Everyday Life*, trans. Steven Rendall (Berkeley: University of California Press, 1984).

Delanda, Manuel, *Intensive Science and Virtual Philosophy* (New York: Continuum, 2002).

Delanda, Manuel, *Deleuze: History and Science*, ed. Wolfgang Schirmacher (New York: Atropos Press, 2010).

Deleuze, Gilles, *Foucault*, trans. Sean Hand (Minneapolis: University of Minnesota Press, 1988 [1986]).

Deleuze, Gilles, *Spinoza: Practical Philosophy*, trans. Robert Hurley (San Francisco, CA: City Lights Books, 1988 [1970]).

Deleuze, Gilles, 'Desire and Pleasure', in *Two Regimes of Madness: Texts and Interviews 1975–1995*, ed. David Lapoujade, trans. Ames Hodges and Mike Taormina (New York: Semiotext(e), 2006).

Deleuze, Gilles and Félix Guattari, *A Thousand Plateaus*, trans. Brian Massumi (Minneapolis: University of Minnesota Press, 1987 [1980]).

Deleuze, Gilles and Félix Guattari, *What is Philosophy?*, trans. Hugh Tomlinson and Graham Burchell (New York: Columbia University Press, 1994 [1991]).

DeNora, Tia, *Music in Everyday Life* (Cambridge: Cambridge University Press, 2000).

Dimanno, Rosie, 'Headsets Drown out the Maestros', *Toronto Star*, 25 March 1998, p. 1b.

Doctor, Jenny, *The BBC and Ultra-modern Music, 1922–1936: Shaping a Nation's Tastes* (Cambridge: Cambridge University Press, 1999).

Doctor, Jenny, '"Virtual Concerts" – The BBC's Transmutation of Public Performances', paper presented at the conference 'Britannia (Re-) Sounding: Music in the Arts, Politics, and Culture of Great Britain', organized by the North American British Music Studies Association, Oberlin, OH (June 2004), unpublished.

Douglas, Susan J., *Listening In: Radio and the American Imagination* (New York: Times Books, 1999).

Du Gay, Paul, Stuart Hall, Linda Janes, Hugh Mackay and Keith Negus, *Doing Cultural Studies. The Story of the Sony Walkman* (London: Sage, 1997).

'Easy Listening', *Washington Post*, 27 August 1990, p. A10.

Edison, Thomas A., 'The Perfected Phonograph', *The North American Review* 146/379 (June 1888): pp. 641–50.

'Edison's Phonographic Doll', *Scientific American*, 62/17 (26 April 1890): p. 263.

Etherington, Darrell, 'Apple Hardware Sales in FY 2012: 125.04M iPhones, 58.23M iPads, 18.1M Macs and 35.2M iPods', *TechCrunch*, 25 October 2012 <http://techcrunch.com/2012/10/25/apple-hardware-sales-in-fy-2012-125-04m-

iphones-58-23m-ipads-18-1m-macs-and-35-2m-ipods/> (accessed 11 February 2013).

Evens, Aden, *Sound Ideas: Music, Machines, and Experience* (Minneapolis: University of Minnesota Press, 2005).

Ewen, Stuart, *Captains of Consciousness: Advertising and the Social Roots of the Consumer Culture* (New York: McGraw-Hill, 1976).

Fabbri, Franco, 'Il mezzo elettroacustico, lo spazio musicale, la popular music', in Raffaele Pozzi (ed.), *La musica e il suo spazio* (Milan: Unicopli, 1987).

Fabbri, Franco, *Il suono in cui viviamo. Saggi sulla popular music* (Milan: Il Saggiatore, 2008 [1996]).

Fabbri, Franco, *L'ascolto tabù: Le musiche nello scontro globale* (Milan: Il Saggiatore, 2005).

Fabbri, Franco, 'La musica nell'era digitale', in T. Gregory (ed.), *XXI secolo. Comunicare e rappresentare* (Rome: Istituto della Enciclopedia Italiana Fondata da Giovanni Treccani SPA, 2009), pp. 625–34.

Fabbri, Franco, 'What is Popular Music? And What isn't? An Assessment, after 30 Years of Popular Music Studies', *Musiikki*, 2 (2010): pp. 72–92.

Facci, Serena, 'Akazehe del Burundi: Saluti a incastro polifonico e cerimonialità femminili', in Maurizio Agamennone (ed.), *Polifonie. Procedimenti, tassonomie e forme: Una riflessione 'a più voci'* (Venice: Il Cardo, 1996), pp. 123–61.

Facci, Serena, 'Musicalizzazioni: le suonerie', *AAA TAC: Acoustical, Art and Artifacts. Technology, Aesthetics, Communication*, 2 (2005): pp. 179–94.

Facci, Serena, '"Funziona?" Valori e usi della musica nella contemporaneità', in Serena Facci and Francesco Giannattasio (eds), *Etnomusicologia e musiche contemporanee*, (Venice: Fondazione Cini, 2007) <http://www. cini.it/publications/letnomusicologia-e-le-musiche-contemporanee-it> (accessed 20 January 2013).

Feld, Steven, *Sound and Sentiment: Birds, Weeping, Poetics, and Song in Kaluli Expression* (Philadelphia: University of Pennsylvania Press, 1990 [1982]).

Fernandez-Duque, Diego and Mark L. Johnson, 'Attention Metaphors: How Metaphors Guide the Cognitive Psychology of Attention', *Cognitive Science*, 23/1 (1999): pp. 83–116.

Fishmann, Robert, *Bourgeois Utopias: The Rise and Fall of Suburbia* (New York: Basic Books, 1989).

Flinn, John, 'Stores Turn on Classics to Turn Away Teens', *Houston Chronicle*, 27 June 1993, p. 4a.

'The Fortress of the Spirit', *The Listener*, 28 September 1939, p. 606.

Foucault, Michel, 'Governmentality', in Graham Burchell, Colin Gordon and Peter Miller (eds), *The Foucault Effect: Studies in Governmentality* (Chicago: University of Chicago Press, 1991), pp. 87–104.

Franck, Georg, *Ökonomie der Aufmerksamkeit* (Munich: Carl Hanser, 1998).

Frank, Thomas, *The Conquest of Cool: Business Culture, Counterculture, and the Rise of Hip Consumerism* (Chicago: University of Chicago Press, 1998).

Frith, Simon, 'Music and Everyday Life', *Critical Quarterly*, 44/1 (2002): pp. 35–48.

Frow, George L., *The Edison Disc Phonographs and the Diamond Discs: A History with Illustrations* (Sevenoaks: George L. Frow, 1982).

'Full-Time Programmes for the Forces', *Radio Times*, 16 February 1940, p. 3.

García Quiñones, Marta, 'Listening in Shuffle Mode', *Lied und populäre Kultur/ Song and Popular Culture. Jahrbuch des Deutschen Volksliedarchivs*, 52 (2007): pp. 11–22.

García Quiñones, Marta (ed.), *La música que no se escucha: aproximaciones a la escucha ambiental* (Barcelona: Orquestra del Caos, 2008).

Gay, Peter, *The Naked Heart: The Bourgeois Experience Victoria to Freud, Volume IV* (New York and London: W.W. Norton & Co., 1995).

'Geraldo's Super Albert Hall Concert', *Melody Maker*, 13 December 1941, p. 1.

Giannattasio, Francesco, *Il concetto di musica* (Rome: La Nuova Italia Scientifica, 1992).

Gitlin, Todd, *Inside Prime Time* (New York: Pantheon, 1985).

Gitlin, Todd, *Media Unlimited: How the Torrent of Images and Sounds Overwhelms Our Lives* (New York: Metropolitan Books, 2001).

Giuriati, Giovanni and Laura Tedeschini Lalli (eds), *Spazi sonori della musica* (Palermo: L'Epos, 2010).

Glover, C. Gordon, 'This Week's Miscellany', *Radio Times*, 29 August 1941. p. 5.

Glover, C. Gordon, 'This Week's Miscellany', *Radio Times*, 19 September 1941, p. 5.

Glover, C. Gordon, letter to *Radio Times*, 17 October 1941, p. 4.

Goddard, Scott, 'Broadcasting and the Teaching of Music', *The Listener*, 20 July 1939, p. 153.

Goddard, Scott, 'Broadcast Music during 1939', *The Listener*, 28 December 1939, p. 1296.

Goehr, Lydia, *The Imaginary Museum of Musical Works: An Essay in the Philosophy of Music* (Oxford: Clarendon Press, 1992).

Good, Kelsey and Steven Moulton, 'Consequences of Camera Phones in Today's Society', in Kay R. Larsen and Zoya A. Voronovich (eds), *Convenient or Invasive: The Information Age* (Boulder, CO: Ethica Publishing, 2007), pp. 200–209. Available at: <http://www.ethicapublishing.com/Convenientor Invasive.pdf> (accessed 10 June 2012).

Goodman, Steve, *Sonic Warfare: Sound, Affect, and the Ecology of Fear* (Cambridge, MA: MIT Press, 2009).

Gorbman, Claudia, *Unheard Melodies: Narrative Film Music* (Bloomington: Indiana University Press, 1987).

Gracyk, Theodore, *Listening to Popular Music: Or, How I Learned to Stop Worrying and Love Led Zeppelin* (Ann Arbor: University of Michigan Press, 2007).

Grajeda, Tony, 'The Sound of Disaffection', in Henry Jenkins, Tara McPherson and Jane Shattuc (eds), *Hop on Pop: The Politics and Pleasures of Popular Culture* (Durham, NC, and London: Duke University Press, 2002), pp. 357–75.

Green, Stanley, 'Music to Hear but Not to Listen To', *Saturday Review*, 28 September 1957, pp. 55–6.

Greene, Alex, 'The Tyranny of Melody', *Etc.*, 43/3 (1986): pp. 285–90.

Greene, Paul D., 'Sound Engineering in a Tamil Village: Playing Audio Cassettes as Devotional Performance', *Ethnomusicology*, 43/3 (1999): pp. 459–89.

Greenway, Rob, 'A Balance of Music on the Forces Programme' (BA thesis, University of York, 2007).

Groom, Nick, 'The Condition of Muzak', *Popular Music and Society*, 20/3 (1996): pp. 1–17.

Grosz, Elizabeth A., *Chaos, Territory, Art: Deleuze and the Framing of the Earth* (New York: Columbia University Press, 2008).

Grow, Doug, 'City Turns to Classical Tunes to Keep Tunes off Block E', *Minneapolis Star Tribune*, 3 March 1995, p. 3b.

Gunn, Joshua and Mirko M. Hall, 'Stick it in Your Ear: The Psychodynamics of iPod Enjoyment', *Communication and Critical/Cultural Studies*, 5/2 (2008): pp. 135–57.

Gunning, Tom, 'Doing for the Eye What the Phonograph Does for the Ear', in Richard Abel and Rick Altman (eds), *The Sounds of Early Cinema* (Bloomington and Indianapolis: Indiana University Press, 2001), pp. 13–31.

Habermas, Jürgen, *The Structural Transformation of the Public Sphere: An Inquiry into a Category of Bourgeois Society*, trans. Thomas Burger with the assistance of Frederick Lawrence (Cambridge, MA: MIT Press, 1989).

Hall, Stuart, 'Encoding/Decoding', in Stuart Hall, Dorothy Hobson, Andrew Lowe and Paul Willis (eds), *Culture, Media, Language: Working Papers in Cultural Studies 1972–9* (London: Hutchinson, 1980), pp. 128–38.

Hallam, Susan, Ian Cross and Michael Thaut (eds), *The Oxford Handbook of Music Psychology* (Oxford: Oxford University Press, 2009).

Hamm, Charles, 'Privileging the Moment of Reception: Music and Radio in South Africa', in S. Paul Scher (ed.), *Music and Text: Critical Inquiries* (Cambridge: Cambridge University Press, 1992), pp. 21–37.

Hardy, Thomas, *Far from the Madding Crowd* (New York: New American Library, 1971).

Harvith, John and Susan Edwards Harvith (eds), *Edison, Musicians, and the Phonograph: A Century in Retrospect* (Westport, CT: Greenwood Press, 1987).

Hassan, Nedim, '"He'll Have To Go": Popular Music and the Social Performing of Memory', *Journal of the International Association for the Study of Popular Music*, 1/1 (2010) <http://www.iaspmjournal.net> (accessed 31 May 2012).

Hawkes, Ralph, 'Music in the Open Air', *Tempo*, June 1944, p. 10.

Hay, Bryan, 'The 90s Has Muzak Customers Whistling to a Different Tune', *The Morning Call*, 12 May 1996, p. 3b.

Hay, James, 'Unaided Virtues: The (Neo)Liberalization of the Domestic Sphere and the New Architecture of Community', in Jack Z. Bratich, Jeremy Packer and Cameron McCarthy (eds), *Foucault, Cultural Studies, and Governmentality* (Albany: State University of New York Press, 2003), pp. 165–206.

Helmholtz, Hermann, *On the Sensations of Tone as the Physiological Basis for the Theory of Music*, trans. Alexander J. Ellis (London: Longmann, Green and Co., 1912).

Herbert, Trevor, *The British Brass Band: A Musical and Social History* (New York: Oxford University Press, 2000).

Herron, Jerry, 'Muzak: A Personal View; or, a Superstructural Mystery in Five Pieces', *Journal of American Culture*, 4/4 (1981): pp. 116–31.

Higgins, Will, 'Ohio Merchants Aim Muzak at Skateboarders', *Indianapolis News*, 19 July 1995, p. 2a.

Hill, Ralph, 'Radio Music in 1940', *Radio Times*, 29 December 1939, pp. 6–7.

Hill, Ralph, 'This Week's Radio Music', *Radio Times*, 26 September 1941, p. 5.

Hill, Ralph, 'This Week's Radio Music', *Radio Times*, 10 October 1941, p. 4.

Hill, Ralph, letter to *Radio Times*, 24 October 1941, p. 4.

Hill, Ralph, 'Some Music – and Letters', *Radio Times*, 27 August 1943, p. 4.

Hirschkind, Charles, *The Ethical Soundscape: Cassette Sermons and Islamic Counterpublics* (New York: Columbia University Press, 2006).

Hosokawa, Shuhei, 'The Walkman Effect', *Popular Music*, 4 (1984): pp. 171–3.

Hull, Robin, letter to *Radio Times*, September 1941, p. 345.

Hulting, Jane, 'Muzak: A Study in Sonic Ideology' (MA thesis, University of Pennsylvania, 1988).

Husch, Jerri, 'Music of the Workplace: A Study of Muzak Culture' (PhD dissertation, University of Massachusetts, 1984).

Huyssen, Andreas, 'Mass Culture as Woman: Modernism's Other', in *After the Great Divide: Modernism, Mass Culture, Postmodernism* (Bloomington: Indiana University Press, 1986), pp. 44–62.

'Hylton Saves the Phil. Orch.', *Melody Maker*, 3 August 1940, p. 1.

IMAI (Internet and Mobile Association of India), *Report on Mobile VAS in India: 2010* <http://www.iamai.in/rsh_pay.aspx?rid=TyuYXL2OyFA=> (accessed 10 June 2012).

'iPod Advertising', *iPod History – The Complete History of the iPod* (n.d.) <http://www.ipodhistory.com/ipod-advertising/> (accessed 30 May 2012).

Ito, Mizuko, Daisuke Okabe and Misa Matsuda (eds), *Personal, Portable, Pedestrian: Mobile Phones in Japanese Life* (Cambridge, MA: MIT Press, 2005).

Jackaway, Gwenyth, 'Selling Mozart to the Masses: Crossover Marketing as Cultural Diplomacy', *Journal of Popular Music Studies*, 11/12 (1999/2000): pp. 125–50.

Jacobs, Jane, *The Death and Life of Great American Cities* (New York: Vintage, 1961).

James, William, *Principles of Psychology* (New York: Holt, 1890).

Jha, Nilabh, 'Reliance 3G in 140 Cities by March', *The Mobile Indian*, 25 February 2011 <http://www.themobileindian.com/news/709_Reliance-3G-in-140-cities-by-March> (accessed 10 June 2012).

Jha, Nilabh, 'Upcoming Phones Worth Waiting for', *The Mobile Indian*, 26 April 2012 <http://www.themobileindian.com/news/6275_Upcoming-phones-worth-waiting-for_full> (accessed 10 June 2012).

Johnson, James H., *Listening in Paris: A Cultural History* (Berkeley: University of California Press, 1995).

Jones, Carys Wyn, *The Rock Canon: Canonical Values in the Reception of Rock Albums* (Aldershot: Ashgate, 2008).

Jones, Simon and Thomas Schumacher, 'Muzak: On Functional Music and Power', *Critical Studies in Mass Communication*, 9 (1992): pp. 156–69.

Kahney, Leander, *The Cult of iPod* (San Francisco, CA: No Starch Press, 2005).

Kalinak, Kathryn, *Settling the Score: Music and the Classical Hollywood Film* (Madison: University of Wisconsin Press, 1992).

Karageorghis, Costas I., *Inside Sport Psychology* (Champaign, IL: Human Kinetics, 2010).

Karageorghis, Costas I. and Peter C. Terry, 'The Psychological, Psychophysical, and Ergogenic Effects of Music in Sport: A Review and Synthesis', in Anthony Bateman and John Bale (eds), *Sporting Sounds: Relationships between Sport and Music* (London: Routledge, 2009), pp. 13–36.

Karel, Ernst K.L., 'Kerala Sound Electricals: Amplified Sound and Cultural Meaning in South India' (PhD dissertation, University of Chicago, 2003).

Kassabian, Anahid, 'Popular', in Bruce Horner and Thomas Swiss (eds), *Key Terms in Popular Music and Culture* (Oxford: Blackwell, 1999), pp. 113–23.

Kassabian, Anahid, *Hearing Film: Tracking Identifications in Contemporary Hollywood Film Music* (New York and London: Routledge, 2001).

Kassabian, Anahid, 'Ubiquitous Listening', in David Hesmondhalgh and Keith Negus (eds), *Popular Music Studies* (London: Arnold, 2002), pp. 131–42.

Kassabian, Anahid, 'Would You Like Some World Music with your Latte? Starbucks, Putumayo, and Distributed Tourism', *Twentieth-Century Music*, 1/2 (2004): pp. 209–23.

Kassabian, Anahid, *Ubiquitous Listening: Affect, Attention, and Distributed Subjectivity* (Berkeley: University of California Press, 2013).

Katz, Mark, 'Making America More Musical through the Phonograph', *American Music*, 16/4 (1998): pp. 448–75.

Katz, Mark, *Capturing Sound: How Technology Has Changed Music* (Berkeley: University of California Press, 2004).

Kearney, Mary Celeste, 'Girlfriends and Girl Power: Female Adolescence in Contemporary U.S. Cinema', in Frances Gateward and Murray Pomerance (eds), *Sugar, Spice, and Everything Nice: Cinemas of Girlhood* (Detroit, MI: Wayne State University Press, 2002), pp. 125–42.

Kennett, Chris, 'Is Anybody Listening?', in Allan F. Moore (ed.), *Analyzing Popular Music* (Cambridge: Cambridge University Press, 2003), pp. 196–217.

Kenney, William Howland, *Recorded Music in American Life: The Phonograph and Popular Memory, 1890–1945* (New York: Oxford University Press, 1999).

Kenyon, Nicholas, *The BBC Symphony Orchestra: The First Fifty Years, 1930–1980* (London: British Broadcasting Corporation, 1981).

Klein, Naomi, *No Logo* (New York: Picador, 2009).

Korosec, Thomas, 'Mcfugue, No Cheese: Beethoven and the Dead European Males Clean up a Notorious Street Corner', *Dallas Observer*, 24 April 1997, p. 1b.

Kramer, Lawrence, *Classical Music and Postmodern Knowledge* (Berkeley: University of California Press, 1995).

Kramer, Lawrence, *Musical Meaning: Toward a Critical History* (Berkeley: University of California Press, 2001).

Kramer, Lawrence, 'The Mysteries of Animation: History, Analysis, and Musical Subjectivity', *Music Analysis*, 20 (2001): pp. 151–76.

Kramer, Lawrence, 'The Talking Wound and the Foolish Question: Symbolization in *Parsifal*', *Opera Quarterly*, 22 (2006): pp. 208–29.

Kramer, Lawrence, *Why Classical Music Still Matters* (Berkeley: University of California Press, 2007).

Kramer, Lawrence, *Interpreting Music* (Berkeley: University of California Press, 2010).

Kristeva, Julia, *Powers of Horror: An Essay on Abjection*, trans. Leon S. Roudiez (New York: Columbia University Press, 1982).

Lanza, Joseph, *Elevator Music: A Surreal History of Muzak, Easy-Listening and other Moodsong* (New York: St Martin's Press, 1994).

Lee, Dong-Hoo, 'Mobile Snapshots and Private/Public Boundaries', *Knowledge, Technology & Policy*, 22/3 (2009): pp. 161–71.

LeMahieu, D.L., *A Culture for Democracy: Mass Communication and the Cultivated Mind in Britain between the Wars* (Oxford: Clarendon Press, 1988).

Leong, Tuck, Frank Vetere and Steve Howard, 'Abdicating Choice: The Rewards of Letting Go', *Digital Creativity*, 19/4 (2008): pp. 233–43.

Leppert, Richard, 'Commentary', in Theodor W. Adorno, *Essays on Music*, ed. Richard Leppert (Berkeley: University of California Press, 2002), pp. 213–50.

Letter to *The Musical Times*, March 1943, p. 91.

Levine, Lawrence W., *Highbrow/Lowbrow: The Emergence of Cultural Hierarchy in America* (Cambridge, MA: Harvard University Press, 1988).

Levitin, Daniel J., *This is Your Brain on Music: The Science of a Human Obsession* (London: Plume/Penguin, 2007).

Levitin, Daniel J., *The World in Six Songs: How the Musical Brain Created Human Nature* (Boston, MA: Dutton, 2008).

Levy, Steven, *The Perfect Thing: How the iPod Shuffles Commerce, Culture, and Coolness* (New York: Simon & Schuster, 2006).

Lewin, David, 'Amfortas's Prayer to Titurel and the Role of D in *Parsifal*: The Tonal Spaces of the Drama and the Enharmonic C-flat/B', *19th-Century Music*, 7 (1984): pp. 336–49.

Macale, Sherilynn, 'Apple Has Sold 300M ipods, Currently Holds 78% of the Music Player Market', *TNW: The Next Web – Apple Channel*, 4 October 2011 <http://thenextweb.com/apple/2011/10/04/apple-has-sold-300m-ipods-currently-holds-78-of-the-music-player-market7> (accessed 30 May 2012).

McChesney, Robert, *Rich Media, Poor Democracy: Communication Politics in Dubious Times* (Urbana: University of Illinois Press, 1993).

Mack, P.H., letter to *Radio Times*, 10 November 1939, p. 5.

Mackenzie, Compton, 'Editorial: The BBC', *Gramophone*, February 1940, p. 307.

McLuhan, Marshall, *Understanding Media: The Extensions of Man* (New York: McGraw-Hill, 1964).

McN., W., 'The BBC Comes of Age', *The Musical Times*, December 1943, p. 367.

McNelis, Timothy, 'Popular Music, Identity, and Musical Agency in U.S. Youth Films' (PhD thesis, University of Liverpool, 2010).

Macpherson, Sandy, letter to *Radio Times*, 10 October 1941, p. 8.

Manuel, Peter, *Cassette Culture: Popular Music and Technology in North India* (Chicago and London: University of Chicago Press, 1993).

Martí, Josep, 'When Music Becomes Noise: Sound and Music Which People in Barcelona Hear but Don't Want to Listen to', *The World of Music*, 39/2 (1997): pp. 9–17.

Mass-Observation Archive, File Report 1138, 'Music: Effect of the War on the Musical Tastes of Panel', 6 March 1942.

Matanhelia, Priyanka, 'Mobile Phone Use by Young Adults in India: A Case Study' (PhD dissertation, University of Maryland, 2010).

Mazey, Steven, 'Messiah Beats Muzak for Sounds of the Season', *Ottawa Citizen*, 28 November 1998, p. 5e.

Meehan, Eileen, 'Why We Don't Count: The Commodity Audience', in Patricia Mellencamp (ed.), *Logics of Television* (Bloomington: Indiana University Press, 1990), pp. 117–37.

Meintjes, Louise, *Sound of Africa! Making Music Zulu in a South African Studio* (Durham, NC: Duke University Press, 2003).

Merker, Björn H., Guy S. Madison and Patricia Ekerdal, 'On the Role and the Origin of Isochrony in Human Rhythmic Entrainment', *Cortex – Elsevier*, 45 (2009): pp. 4–17.

Merriam, Alan, *The Anthropology of Music* (Evanston, IL: Northwestern University Press, 1964).

Middleton, Richard, *Voicing the Popular: On the Subjects of Popular Music* (New York: Routledge, 2006).

'Mike' [Spike Hughes], 'Stop the Jazzing-Up Pop-Song Process!', *Melody Maker*, 7 February 1942, p. 5.

Millard, Andre, *Edison and the Business of Innovation* (Baltimore, MD: Johns Hopkins University Press, 1990).

Molnar-Szakacs, Istvan and Katie Overy, 'Music and Mirror Neurons: From Motion to "E"motion', *SCAN*, 1 (2006): pp. 235–41.

'Mood Change Parties a New Sensation', *Edison Diamond Points*, 4/4 (March 1921): pp. 14, 18.

Mood Music (Orange, NJ: Thomas A. Edison, Inc., 1921).

Morley, David, *Television, Audiences, and Cultural Studies* (New York: Routledge, 1993).

Mosco, Vincent, *The Political Economy of Communication: Rethinking and Renewal* (Thousand Oaks, CA: Sage, 1996).

Munster, Anna, *Materializing New Media: Embodiment in Information* (London: Dartmouth University Press, 2006).

Murphy, Catherine, '"On an Equal Footing with Men?" Women and Work at the BBC, 1923–1939' (PhD thesis, Goldsmiths College, University of London, 2011).

'Music Tonic for Workers', *Edison Diamond Points*, 3/5 (April 1918): pp. 10–11.

'The Musical Table d'Hôte', *The Listener*, 28 December 1939, p. 1264.

Näätänen, Risto, *Attention and Brain Function* (Hillsdale, NJ: Lawrence Erlbaum Associates, 1992).

Negus, Keith, *Popular Music in Theory: An Introduction* (Cambridge: Polity Press, 1996).

Negus, Keith, *Music Genres and Corporate Cultures* (New York: Routledge, 1998).

Noble, Peter, *Kings of Rhythm: A Review of Dance-Music and British Dance-Band Personalities* (London: Dunlop Publications, n.d. [1944]).

'Notes and News', *The Musical Times*, December 1942, p. 378.

'Notes and News', *The Musical Times*, January 1943, p. 27.

Nott, James J., *Music for the People: Popular Music and Dance in Interwar Britain* (Oxford: Oxford University Press, 2002).

Nye, Sean, 'Headphone-Headset-Jetset. DJ Culture, Mobility and Science Fictions of Listening', *Dancecult: Journal of Electronic Dance Music Culture*, 3/1 (2011): pp. 64–96. Available at: <http://dj.dancecult.net/index.php/journal/article/view/90> (accessed 30 May 2012).

'Over 55,000,000 Readers Will See This Ad in the February Issues of Leading Magazines', *Edison Diamond Points*, 4/2 (January 1921): p. 11.

Parisi, Luciana, *Abstract Sex* (New York: Continuum, 2004).

Parr, Adrian (ed.), *The Deleuze Dictionary* (Edinburgh: Edinburgh University Press, 2005).

Pascual, Psyche, 'This 7-Eleven is Alive with the Sound of Muzak', *Los Angeles Times*, 17 November 1991, p. 1b.

Pasquinelli, Matteo, *Animal Spirits* (Rotterdam: NAi Publishers, 2008).

Payne, W. E., letter to *Radio Times*, 2 October 1941, p. 8.

Peretz, Isabelle, 'La musica e il cervello', in Jean Jacques Nattiez with Margaret Bent, Mario Baroni and Rossana Dalmonte (eds), *Enciclopedia della musica*: *Il sapere musicale*, Volume 2 (Turin: Einaudi, 2002), pp. 241–70.

Peretz, Isabelle, 'Musical Emotions: Brain Organization', in Patrik N. Juslin and John Sloboda (eds), *Handbook of Music and Emotion: Theory, Research, Applications* (Oxford: Oxford University Press, 2010), pp. 104–26.

Peters, John Durham, *Speaking into the Air: A History of the Idea of Communication* (Chicago: University of Chicago Press, 1999).

'Playfellow', '"Swinging" of the Classics', *Huddersfield Daily Examiner*, 22 January 1942, BBC Press Cuttings.

Posner, Michael I. and Gregory Digirolamo, 'Attention in Cognitive Neuroscience: An Overview', in Michael S. Gazzaniga (ed.), *The New Cognitive Neurosciences* (Cambridge, MA: MIT Press, 2000), pp. 623–31.

Programme Listings, *Radio Times*, 24 November 1939.

Puar, Jasbir K., *Terrorist Assemblages: Homonationalism in Queer Times* (Durham, NC: Duke University Press, 2007).

Rabinbach, Anson, *The Human Motor: Energy, Fatigue, and the Origins of Modernity* (Berkeley and Los Angeles: University of California Press, 1992).

Radano, Ronald H., 'Interpreting Muzak: Speculations on Musical Experience in Everyday Life', *American Music*, 7 (1989): pp. 448–60.

'Radio: For the Princes', *News Review*, 16 April 1942, BBC Written Archive Centre Press Cuttings.

Rai, Amit S., *Untimely Bollywood: Globalization and India's New Media Assemblage* (Durham, NC: Duke University Press, 2009).

Raykoff, Ivan, 'Concerto con Amore', *Echo*, 2/1 (2000) <http://www.echo.ucla. edu/volume2-issue1/raykoff/raykoff-article.html> (accessed 25 April 2012).

'Real Music and Hard Work', *Edison Diamond Points*, 4/9 (September 1921): pp. 9, 12.

Reitman, Valerie, 'Muzak Once Again Calls the Tune in Retailers' War on the Unwanted', *Wall Street Journal*, 14 December 1992, p. B1.

Rentschler, Carrie, 'Designing Fear: Environmental Security and Violence against Women', *Cultural Studies: A Research Annual*, 5 (2000): pp. 281–310.

Rizzolatti, Giacomo and Laila Craighero, 'The Mirror-Neuron System', *Annual Review of Neuroscience*, 27 (2004): pp. 169–92.

Rose, Sonya O., *Which People's War? National Identity and Citizenship in Britain 1939–1945* (Oxford: Oxford University Press, 2003).

Rosen, David, 'The Sounds of Music and War: Humphrey Jennings's and Stewart McAllister's *Listen to Britain* (1942)', in Cliff Eisen (ed.), *'Coll'astuzia, col giudizio': Essays in Honor of Neal Zaslaw* (Ann Arbor, MI: Steglein Publishing, Inc., 2009), pp. 389–427.

Ross, Andrew, *The Celebration Chronicles: Life, Liberty and the Pursuit of Property in Disney's New Town* (New York: Ballantine, 1999).

Rowe, Peter, *Making a Middle Landscape* (Cambridge, MA: MIT Press, 1991).

Sachs, Curt, *Eine Weltgeschichte des Tanzes* (Berlin: Dietrich Reimer-Ernst Voshen AG, 1933).

Sassatelli, Roberta, *Anatomia della palestra: Cultura commerciale e disciplina del corpo* (Bologna: Il Mulino, 2000).

Scannell, Paddy and David Cardiff, *A Social History of British Broadcasting, Volume 1: 1922–1939: Serving the Nation* (Oxford: Basil Blackwell, 1991).

Schafer, R. Murray, *The Soundscape: Our Sonic Environment and the Tuning of the World* (Rochester, VT: Destiny Books, 1994).

Schiller, Dan, *Digital Capitalism: Networking the Global Market System* (Cambridge, MA: MIT Press, 1999).

Schiller, Herbert, *Culture, Inc.: The Corporate Takeover of Public Expression* (New York: Oxford University Press, 1989).

Scholes, Percy, *Music Appreciation: Its History and Techniques* (New York: M. Witmark and Sons, 1935).

Schwarz, David, *Listening Subjects: Music, Psychoanalysis, Culture* (New York: Routledge, 1997).

Selfridge-Field, Eleanor, 'Experiments with Melody and Meter, or the Effects of Music: The Edison-Bingham Music Research', *The Musical Quarterly*, 81/2 (Summer 1997): pp. 291–310.

Sennett, Richard, *The Fall of Public Man* (New York: Knopf, 1977).

Shakespeare, William, *The Complete Works*, ed. Alfred Harbage *et al.* (Baltimore, MD: Pelican, 1969).

Shapiro, Sherry B. (ed.), *Dance in a World of Change: Reflections on Globalization and Cultural Difference* (Champaign, IL: Human Kinetics, 2008).

Shelley, Percy Bysshe, *Shelley's Poetry and Prose*, ed. Donald H. Reiman and Sharon Powers (New York: W.W. Norton, 1977).

Sinfield, Alan, *Out on Stage: Lesbian and Gay Theatre in the Twentieth Century* (New Haven, CT: Yale University Press, 1999).

Skogan, Wesley, *Disorder and Decline: Crime and the Spiral of Decay in American Neighborhoods* (New York: The Free Press, 1990).

Small, Christopher, *Musicking. The Meanings of Performing and Listening* (Hanover, NH: Wesleyan University Press/University Press of New England, 1998).

Smith, Jeff, *The Sounds of Commerce: Marketing Popular Film Music* (New York: Columbia University Press, 1998).

Smith, Neil, *The New Urban Frontier: Gentrification and the Revanchist City* (New York: Routledge, 1996).

Smith, Susan J., 'Beyond Geography's Visible Worlds: A Cultural Politics of Music', *Progress in Human Geography*, 21/4 (1997): pp. 502–29.

Smolowitz, Peter, 'Muzak's Offbeat Approach Appeals to York County, S.C., Businessmen', *Charlotte Observer*, 31 January 2001, p. 1b.

Smythe, Dallas, *Counterclockwise: Perspectives on Communication* (Boulder, CO: Westview Press, 1994).

Soja, Edward, *Postmodern Geographies: The Reassertion of Space in Critical Social Theory* (New York: Verso, 1989).

Soja, Edward, *Thirdspace: Journeys to Los Angeles and Other Real-and-Imagined Places* (Oxford: Basil Blackwell, 1996).

Sorkin, Michael (ed.), *Variations on a Theme Park: The New American City and the End of Public Space* (New York: Hill and Wang, 1992).

'Special Programmes for the Forces beginning this Week', *Radio Times*, 5 January 1940, p. 5.

Sperb, Jason, '*Ghost* without a Machine: Enid's Anxiety of Depth(lessness) in Terry Zwigoff's *Ghost World*', *Quarterly Review of Film and Video*, 21/3 (2004): pp. 209–17.

Stengers, Isabelle, *Thinking with Whitehead: A Free and Wild Creation of Concepts* (Cambridge, MA: Harvard University Press, 2011).

Sterne, Jonathan, 'Sounds Like the Mall of America: Programmed Music and the Architectonics of Commercial Space', *Ethnomusicology*, 41/1 (1997): pp. 22–50.

Sterne, Jonathan, *The Audible Past: Cultural Origins of Sound Reproduction* (Durham, NC, and London: Duke University Press, 2003).

Sterne, Jonathan, 'The Death and Life of Digital Audio', *Interdisciplinary Science Reviews*, 31/4 (2006): pp. 338–48.

Sterne, Jonathan, 'The mp3 as Cultural Artifact', *New Media & Society*, 8 (2006): pp. 825–42.

Sterne, Jonathan, *MP3: The Meaning of a Format* (Durham, NC: Duke University Press, 2012).

Stilwell, Robynn J., 'Vinyl Communication: The Record as Ritual Object in Girls' Rites-of-Passage Films', in Phil Powrie and Robynn Stilwell (eds), *Changing Tunes: The Use of Pre-existing Music in Film* (Aldershot: Ashgate, 2006), pp. 152–66.

Stockfelt, Ola, 'Adequate Modes of Listening', in David Schwarz and Anahid Kassabian (eds), *Keeping Score: Music, Disciplinarity, Culture* (Charlottesville: University Press of Virginia, 1997), pp. 129–46.

Stowe, David W., *Swing Changes: Big-Band Jazz in New Deal America* (Cambridge, MA: Harvard University Press, 1994).

Straw, Will, 'Sizing Up Record Collections: Gender and Connoisseurship in Rock Music Culture', in Sheila Whiteley (ed.), *Sexing the Groove: Popular Music and Gender* (London, 1997), pp. 3–16.

'The Stuff to Give the Troops', *The Listener*, 15 February 1940, p. 308.

Tagg, Philip, 'From Refrain to Rave. The Decline of Figure and the Rise of Ground', *Popular Music*, 13/2 (1994): pp. 209–22.

Tagg, Philip and Bob Clarida, *Ten Little Title Tunes: Towards a Musicology of Mass Media* (New York and Montreal: The Mass Media Musicologists' Press, 2003).

Taylor, (Mrs) B., letter to *Radio Times*, 17 November 1939, p. 14.

Taylor, Clyde, 'The Master Text and the Jeddi Doctrine', *Screen*, 29/4 (1988): pp. 96–105.

Taylor, Timothy D., 'Music and the Rise of Radio in Twenties America: Technological Imperialism, Socialization, and the Transformation of Intimacy', in Paul D. Greene and Thomas Porcello (eds), *Wired for Sound: Engineering and Technologies in Sonic Cultures* (Middletown, CT: Wesleyan University Press, 2005), pp. 245–68.

Taylor, Timothy D., Mark Katz and Tony Grajeda (eds), *Music, Sound, and Technology in America: A Documentary History of Early Phonograph, Cinema, and Radio* (Durham, NC: Duke University Press, 2012).

Thibaud, Jean-Paul, 'The Sonic Composition of the City', in Michael Bull and Les Back (eds), *The Auditory Culture Reader* (Oxford: Berg, 2003), pp. 329–42.

Thomas Edison National Historical Park, Phonograph Division, Box 19, letter of William Maxwell to Thomas A. Edison, dated 14 March 1921.

Thomas Edison National Historical Park, Phonograph Division, Box 19, letter of W.V. Bingham to William Maxwell, dated 17 March 1921.

Thomas Edison National Historical Park, Phonograph Division, Box 19, letter of William Maxwell to Thomas A. Edison, dated 19 March 1921.

Thomas Edison National Historical Park, Phonograph Division, Box 20, clipping file folder, 'Note Changes in Mood Caused By Hearing Music', *New Haven Sunday Register*, 22 May 1921.

Thomas Edison National Historical Park, Phonograph Division, Box 24, Esther L. Gatewood, 'An Experimental Study of the Use of Music in an Architectural Drafting Room', unpublished ms, n.d.

Thompson, E.P., *The Making of the English Working Class* (New York: Vintage Books, 1966).

Thompson, Emily, *The Soundscape of Modernity: Architectural Acoustics and the Culture of Listening in America, 1900–1933* (Cambridge, MA and London: MIT Press, 2002).

Toop, David, *Ocean of Sound: Aether Talk, Ambient Sound and Imaginary Worlds* (London: Serpent's Tail, 1995).

Truax, Barry, *Acoustic Communication* (Norwood, NJ: Ablex, 1984).

'Two Hopeful Schoolgirls', letter to *Radio Times*, 10 October 1941, p. 8.

Tyler, Linda L., '"Commerce and Poetry Hand in Hand": Music in American Department Stores, 1880–1930', *Journal of the American Musicological Society*, 45 (1992): pp. 75–120.

Untitled article, *The Star*, 22 December 1942, BBC Written Archive Centre Press Clippings.

Vanel, Herve, 'John Cage's Muzak-Plus: The Fu(rni)ture of Music', *Representations*, 103 (2008): pp. 94–128.

Vickers, Earl, 'The Loudness War: Background, Speculation and Recommendations', paper presented at the AES 129th Convention, San Francisco, CA, USA, 4–7 November 2010 <http://www.sfxmachine.com/docs/loudnesswar/> (accessed 30 May 2012).

Weber, Heike, 'Taking Your Favorite Sound Along: Portable Audio Technologies for Mobile Music Listening', in Karen Bijsterveld and José van Dijck (eds), *Sound Souvenirs. Audio Technologies, Memory and Cultural Practices* (Amsterdam: Amsterdam University Press, 2009), pp. 69–82.

'What Music Does For Labor', *Edison Diamond Points*, 4/11 (November 1921): pp. 16–17.

White, Diane, 'Mantovani Clears the Mall', *Boston Globe*, 1 September 1990, p. 9.

White, M.N., letter to *Radio Times*, 26 September 1941, p. 8.

Whitehead, Alfred North, *Science and the Modern World* (New York: Free Press, 1967 [1925]).

Whitehead, Alfred North, *Process and Reality: An Essay in Cosmology,* corrected ed. by David Ray Griffin and Donald W. Sherburne (New York: Free Press, 1978).

Williams, Andrew, *Portable Music and its Functions* (New York: Peter Lang, 2007).

Williams, Raymond, *Problems in Materialism and Culture* (London: Verso, 1980).

Williamson, Victoria, 'Earworm Project', Music, Mind and Brain Research Group at Goldsmiths, University of London <http://www.gold.ac.uk/music-mind-brain/earworm-project/> (accessed 15 June 2012).

'Wireless in War', *The Listener*, 7 September 1939, p. 464.

Wojcik, Pamela Robertson, 'The Girl and the Phonograph; or the Vamp and the Machine Revisited', in Pamela Robertson Wojcik and Arthur Knight (eds), *Soundtrack Available: Essays on Film and Popular Music* (Durham, NC: Duke University Press, 2001), pp. 433–54.

Wurtzler, Steve J., *Electric Sounds: Technological Change and the Rise of Corporate Mass Media* (New York: Columbia University Press, 2007).

Zatorre, Robert J., Joyce L. Chen and Virginia B. Penhune, 'When the Brain Plays Music: Auditory-Motor Interactions in Music Perception and Production', *Nature Reviews/Neuroscience*, 8 July 2007: pp. 547–58.

Zemen, Ned and Lucy Howard Zemen, 'Let's Split', *Newsweek*, 20 August 1990, p. 2.

Zimmer, Carl, 'Neuron Network Goes Awry, and Brain Becomes an IPod', *The New York Times: Science Times*, 12 July 2005, pp. 1, 6.

Zukin, Sharon, *Loft Living: Culture and Capital in Urban Change* (Baltimore, MD: The Johns Hopkins University Press, 1982).

Zukin, Sharon, *Landscapes of Power: From Detroit to Disney World* (Berkeley: University of California Press, 1991).

Zuniga, Janine, 'McDonald's in Dallas Gives Thugs the Bach', *Austin American Statesman*, 25 April 1996, p. 1c.

Discography

Fossati, Ivano, 'Una notte in Italia', *Dal vivo Volume 1 – Buontempo* (Epic, 1993), EPC 473901 2.

Gibbons, Carroll and the Savoy Hotel Orpheans, *Time Was ...* (Empress Music, 1996), RAJCD 823.

Mitchell, Joni, 'Night Ride Home', *Night Ride Home* (Geffen, 1991), GEFD-24302.

Pink Floyd, *The Dark Side of the Moon* (EMI, 1973), SHVL 804.

Richard, Cliff, 'Devil Woman', *I'm Nearly Famous* (EMI, 1976), EMI 2448.

Shaggy, featuring Brian and Tony Gold, 'Hey Sexy Lady', *Lucky Day* (MCA Records, 2002), 113 119–2.

Springsteen, Bruce, 'Tougher Than The Rest', *Tunnel of Love* (Columbia, 1987), CK 40999.

Films and Audiovisuals

All Over Me (1997, USA), dir. Alex Sichel, music Miki Navazio, music supervision Bill Coleman, Alliance.

'Apple – iPod touch – TV Ad – Share The Fun', uploaded by Apple, 23 November 2011 <http://www.youtube.com/watch?v=gGrDMVk2isc> (accessed 30 May 2012).

Barrio (1998, Spain), dir. Fernando Léon de Aranoa, music Hechos contra el decoro, music supervision Lucía Cárdenes, Warner Sogefilms SA.

Breakfast at Tiffany's (1961, USA), dir. Blake Edwards, music Henry Mancini, Paramount Home Entertainment.

'Dancing with an iPod in Public – Christmas Edition', uploaded by Preston Leatherman, 28 November 2011 <http://www.youtube.com/watch?v=VlZ8 DXRnM-0> (accessed 30 May 2012).

Do the Right Thing (1989, USA), dir. Spike Lee, music Bill Lee, Universal Studios Home Entertainment.

Dostana (2008, India) dir. Tarun Mansukhani, lyrics Anvita Dutt Guptan, Kumaar Vishal Dadlani, vocals Shankar Mahadevan and Sunidhi Chauhan, Dharma Productions.

The Full Monty (1997, UK), dir. Peter Cattaneo, music Anne Dudley, music supervision Liz Gallacher, 20th Century Fox.

Ghost World (2001, USA), dir. Terry Zwigoff, music David Kitay, music supervision Melissa Axelrod and Christine Bergren, Icon Home Entertainment.

Guide (1965, India), dir. Vijay Anand, lyrics Shailendra, music S.D. Burman, Navketan International Films.

Gumnaam (1965, India), dir. Raja Nawathe, music Jaikishan Dayabhai Pankal and Shankarsingh Raghuwanshi, Eros Entertainment.

Ishqiya (2010, India), dir. Abhishek Chaubey, music Vishal Bhardwaj, Shemaroo Entertainment and Vishal Bhardwaj Pictures.

Listen to Britain (UK, 1942), dir. Humphrey Jennings and Stewart McAllister, reissued by Image Entertainment (2002). Also available online: 'LISTEN TO BRITAIN, 1942?', uploaded by PublicResourceOrg, 2 December 2009 <http://www.youtube.com/watch?v=6h8pHumy7NE> (accessed 25 April 2012).

'OFFICIAL Apple iPod Nano-chromatic Commercial', uploaded by AppleInc, 8 October 2008 <http://www.youtube.com/watch?v=lEwYjF2Igjg&feature=re lated> [accessed 30 May 2012].

Rab Ne Bana Di Jodi (2008, India), dir. Aditya Chopra, lyrics Jaideep Sahni, vocals Roopkumar Rathod, Yash Raj Films.

'Samsung MP3 Player K5 Commercial "Bubble"', uploaded by princetongolfer, 5 September 2006 <http://www.youtube.com/watch?v=BKSmW6TI5kU&feat ure=related> (accessed 30 May 2012).

'Samsung MP3 Player Dance to the Music Cool Ads', uploaded by amyloer, 2 June 2008 <http://www.youtube.com/watch?v=8LgfnQmi7VQ> (accessed 30 May 2012).

Save the Last Dance (2001, USA), dir. Thomas Carter, music Mark Isham, music supervision Michael McQuarn, Paramount Home Video.

Sholay (1976, India), dir. Ramesh Sippy, lyrics Anand Bakshi, vocals Kishore Kumar, Eros Entertainment.

Index